Being the People of God

Being the People of God

Missional Ecclesiology in Uncertain Times

Edited by

Paul Bradbury, Isabelle Hamley
and Andy Smith

scm press

© Editors and Contributors 2025

Published in 2025 by SCM Press

Editorial office
3rd Floor, Invicta House,
110 Golden Lane,
London EC1Y 0TG, UK
www.scmpress.co.uk

SCM Press is an imprint of Hymns Ancient & Modern Ltd
(a registered charity)

Hymns Ancient & Modern® is a registered trademark of
Hymns Ancient & Modern Ltd
13A Hellesdon Park Road, Norwich,
Norfolk NR6 5DR, UK

All rights reserved. No part of this publication may be reproduced,
stored in a retrieval system, or transmitted,
in any form or by any means, electronic, mechanical,
photocopying or otherwise, without the prior permission of
the publisher, SCM Press.

The Authors have asserted their right under the Copyright, Designs and
Patents Act 1988 to be identified as the Authors of this Work.

British Library Cataloguing in Publication data

A catalogue record for this book is available
from the British Library

ISBN: 978-0-334-06642-2

EU GPSR Authorized Representative
LOGOS EUROPE, 9 rue Nicolas Poussin, 17000, LA ROCHELLE, France
E-mail: Contact@logoseurope.eu

No part of this book may be used or reproduced in any manner for the
purpose of training artificial intelligence technologies or systems.

Typeset by Regent Typesetting

Contents

List of Contributors ix

Introduction 1
Paul Bradbury, Isabelle Hamley, Andy Smith

Part I Being Worship

1 Being Worship in the Making of Disciples 9
   Hannah Steele

2 Being Worship in a Neighbourhood Ecology 22
   Al Barrett

3 Being Worship, Being Eucharist 38
   Alison Milbank

4 Being Worship: The Tender-hearted community –
   Why Inclusion Means Interdependence 51
   Sharon Prentis

5 On the Ground: Being Worship in the Parish 64
   Andy Smith

6 On the Ground: Life, Death and Resurrection in
   Church Planting 70
   Sarah McDonald Haden

7 Being Worship: To Proclaim Afresh in each Generation 75
   Isabelle Hamley

Part II Being Witness

8   Being Witness in a Global City   83
    Ana França-Ferreira and Angus Ritchie

9   Being Witness to the Edges   98
    Jonny Baker

10 Being Witness at the End of Modernity: Paradigm Shifts
    in Mission for the English Parish Church   112
    Nigel Rooms

11 On the Ground: Pioneering a Fresh Expression of Church
    on an Outer Estate in Southampton   125
    Jon Oliver

12 On the Ground: Ecological Conversion and the Awakening
    from Earth Amnesia   134
    John White

13 Being Witness: Mission in a Changing Landscape   140
    Andy Smith

Part III Being Pilgrim

14 Being Pilgrim, Being Parish   149
    Chris Hodder

15 Being Pilgrim in the Cathedral   166
    David Monteith

16 Being Pilgrim in the Shadow of Empire   181
    James Butler and Cathy Ross

17 Being Pilgrim into the Unknown   196
    Tina Hodgett

18 On the Ground: Garden Church, Norfolk   210
    David Lloyd

19 On the Ground: Being Pilgrim on the Margins 217
   Fiona Gibson

20 On the Ground: Navigating Faith and Identity –
   The Journey of Iranian Christian Converts in the UK 223
   Omid Moludy

21 Being Pilgrim: The Church in the Movement of the Spirit 233
   Paul Bradbury

In Place of a Conclusion 239
Mike Harrison

Index of Names and Subjects 245

List of Contributors

Jonny Baker is the director at the Church Mission Society (CMS) of mission in post-Christian Britain. He is an advocate for pioneers, has set up a pioneer training pathway at CMS, helped set up hubs around the country and sought to encourage pioneers in their practice. He has published several books – *Alternative Worship, Curating Worship, Pioneer Gift, Pioneer Practice, Pioneer Spirituality, Future Present* – and contributed to others, as well as blogging consistently for over 20 years. He is a lay pioneer in the Church of England and on the leadership of Grace, a Church of England congregation in London.

Al Barrett has been Rector of Hodge Hill Church (a CofE–URC local ecumenical partnership) in east Birmingham since 2010. He has been involved in long-term journeys of intergenerational community building with neighbours and pursuing racial and environmental justice within and beyond the local church community. Al is engaged in ongoing theological explorations (in writing and elsewhere) in the intersecting fields of gender, class, race and ecology, including (with Ruth Harley) *Being Interrupted: Reimagining the Church's Mission from the Outside, In* and (co-edited with Anthony Reddie and Jill Marsh) *Towards a Critical White Theology*.

Paul Bradbury is an ordained pioneer minister and the founder of Poole Missional Communities, which plays host to a number of fresh expressions of church and pioneer mission initiatives. He is an associate tutor with Sarum College, Church Mission Society and RCC Cuddesdon. He is currently studying for a DTh with the University of Roehampton, exploring the connections between emergence and the ecclesiology of pioneers. He writes in the field of missional ecclesiology, spirituality and leadership. His publications include *Stepping Into Grace, Home By Another Route* and *In the Fullness of Time*.

James Butler is pioneer MA lecturer at the Church Mission Society, Oxford and a postdoctoral researcher at the University of Roehampton. His teaching and research interests are around mission, ecclesiology and practical theology. He has worked on a number of theological action research projects, including looking at faith and learning, ecumenical social action and faith in 'edgy' places. He has published a number of articles exploring themes of discipleship and mission and is part of the steering group of the Theology and Action Research Network (TARN).

Ana França-Ferreira is an Assistant Director at the Centre for Theology and Community. She oversees the research arm of the charity, where she is developing a participatory research centre to encourage the voices, experiences and insights of communities and their members to contribute to the development of theological understanding and faith-filled community organizing. Ana is also a trained community organizer and researcher with experience in designing and implementing research projects that have appetite for working with and learning from communities. She is currently writing her PhD thesis.

Fiona Gibson is Archdeacon of Ludlow in the Diocese of Hereford and chairs the Hereford Diocesan Board of Education. Prior to becoming Archdeacon she was vicar of three rural parishes in the Diocese of St Albans, having served her curacy in a large church in Bedford. She is a member of General Synod. Fiona has recently completed a Doctorate through Trinity College Bristol and the University of Aberdeen. Her research examined acedia (sloth), doctrinally and pastorally. Before ordination Fiona was a primary school teacher and then a lay children's worker. She is married to Dave, with two adult children.

Sarah McDonald Haden serves as vicar and Pioneer Minister in Gloucester Diocese, where she leads a Parish and Bishop's Mission Order partnership. Previously she was associate vicar in Islington, London, where she established a church dedicated to supporting individuals facing mental health challenges. Sarah trained at St Mellitus College and holds a Doctorate in Ministry in Organizational Leadership from Asbury Seminary. She is interested in holistic, trauma-informed approaches to church planting and pioneering.

Isabelle Hamley is a theologian, writer and broadcaster with a specialism in the Old Testament and in questions of justice, personhood and mental health. She is currently serving as Principal of Ridley Hall, Cambridge, after posts as university chaplain, parish priest, chaplain to the Archbishop of Canterbury and theological adviser to the House of Bishops. Her publications include *God of Justice and Mercy: A Theological Commentary on the Book of Judges*, *Embracing Justice*, and together with John Swinton and Chris Cook, *Struggling with God*.

Mike Harrison took up his present role as Bishop of Exeter in November 2024. Mike has a national responsibility for Pioneer Ministry, represents the Church of England on the national Fresh Expressions Board and is one of the Bishops' champions for the mixed ecology. Before this he was suffragan Bishop of Dunwich in the diocese of St Edmundsbury and Ipswich from 2016 to 2024. He was Director of Mission and Ministry in Leicester diocese for a decade before this, having previously been a parish priest in a variety of settings. His academic training includes a Masters in Psychotherapy and Theology and a Doctorate in Christian Doctrine.

Chris Hodder was ordained in 2001 and has a PhD in Practical Theology. He was curate at Emmanuel and St Mary's, Loughborough. He then became Pastoral Services Co-ordinator at the University of Derby and Chaplain to Derby Cathedral, a time that included providing support to the leadership team of St Alkmund's, Derby. He became vicar of St Paul's, Wilford Hill, and was a member of the General Synod of the Church of England. In 2018 Chris joined the RAF to serve as a military chaplain, and continues to serve locally in the Lincolnshire rural parish where he lives.

Tina Hodgett is a priest, pioneer, teacher, writer and speaker. She is leader of the Church Mission Society Southwest Hub, which innovates in the field of mission education and prepares lay people for pioneering mission. She is co-founder of Pioneering Parishes, a small training organization that aims to make pioneering integral to parish life. She works at the Church Mission Society and loves to lead people into exploring opportunities for mission 'with a twinkle in its eye'. She lives in Yeovil.

David Lloyd has a Doctorate in Church Planting in Post Christendom Europe from Asbury Theological Seminary. He studied theology at Oxford University as an undergraduate in 1998 and trained as a lawyer in London. He enjoys the entrepreneurial edge of ministry and by the grace of God has helped to plant a Church of England free school on an estate in London, a resource church in Norwich and helped revitalize a number of satellite churches and a pub. Since 2019 he has been involved in developing lay-led missional communities in rural Norfolk. He is married to Anna and has two teenage children, loves the sea and is a jazz/gospel/salsa/folk trumpet player.

Alison Milbank is Professor Emeritus of Theology and Literature at the University of Nottingham and Canon Theologian of Southwell Minster. Her publications in the field of religion and the arts include *Dante and the Victorians*, *Chesterton and Tolkien as Theologians* and *God and the Gothic: Religion, Romance and Reality in the English Literary Tradition*. She also writes on the role of imagination in Christian apologetics and on ecclesiology, in *On the Parish: A Critique of Fresh Expressions* (with Andrew Davison) and *The Once and Future Parish*.

Omid Moludy was born in Iran. He founded St Aphrahat the Persian Church in Manchester in 2004, where he continues to serve as minister. In 2014 he joined the Church of England as a Priest for Cultural Diversity, contributing significantly to inclusivity and diversity initiatives. He was appointed to the Archbishops' College of Evangelists in 2017 and received the Alphege Award for Evangelism and Witness from the Archbishop of Canterbury in 2021. He has an interest in medieval philosophy, especially the works of Thomas Aquinas and Shihab al-Din Suhrawardi.

David Monteith was installed as Dean of Canterbury in 2022. He previously served as Dean of Leicester, having responsibility for the reburial of King Richard III as well as chairing the interfaith work in one of Britain's diverse cities. He was previously associate vicar of St Martin-in-the-Fields and a Team Rector and Area Dean in Wimbledon. David chairs the College of Deans of the Church of England. He grew up during the Troubles in Northern Ireland and is interested how faith plays out in society and public life. He sees art and culture, heritage and history as crucial missional tools.

Jon Oliver is an ordained pioneer minister. He's also been a youth worker, nightclub chaplain and charity CEO. Jon is passionate about finding creative ways to help people explore faith and the possibilities of God. A few years ago he published *Night Vision*, a collection of inspiring stories about mission in club culture and the nightlife. He lives on the south coast with Tammy (also an ordained pioneer minister) and their two young children. Jon loves reading, writing, running, going on adventures and making up silly games with his family.

Sharon Prentis serves as the Deputy Director of the Racial Justice Unit for the Church of England, bringing a wealth of experience in education, community development and intercultural mission. Formerly the Intercultural Mission Enabler for Black, Asian and Minority Ethnic Affairs in Birmingham, she is also an Honorary Canon Theologian at Lichfield Cathedral. A Mary Seacole Scholar, she has been recognized for her commitment to enhancing health awareness in diverse communities. Sharon passionately advocates for social justice through faith-based initiatives, teaches on inclusion, and edited the book *Every Tribe*, celebrating diverse saints.

Angus Ritchie is the founding Director of the Centre for Theology and Community (www.ctcuk.org), which helps churches to harness the potential of community organizing for both congregational renewal and social action. Ordained in 1998, he has served in parishes in east London throughout his ministry, currently assisting at St George-in-the-East in Tower Hamlets. His most recent book, *Inclusive Populism: Creating Citizens in the Global Age*, was cited by Pope Francis as expressing his vision of 'a politics of fraternity, rooted in the life of the people'.

Nigel Rooms is an Anglican priest, missiologist and practical theologian based in Leicester. He holds a professional Doctorate in missiology from Birmingham University and is an honorary research fellow at UNISA, South Africa and the Queens Foundation in Birmingham. He works freelance and as a consultant with the Church Mission Society in cultural change towards the *missio Dei* in local churches, and also as a facilitator, researcher, author, editor and spiritual director. He is the founder and co-editor of the journal *Ecclesial Futures* and, when not elsewhere, leads worship on Sundays at St Margaret's, Leicester.

Cathy Ross is head of Pioneer Leadership Training at the Church Mission Society in Oxford and Lecturer in Mission at Regent's College, Oxford. She has published in the areas of mission, hospitality and contextual theology, and her work includes *Women with a Mission*, *Mission in the 21st Century* (with Andrew Walls), *Mission on the Road* to *Emmaus* (with Steve Bevans) and *Reimagining Mission with John V. Taylor* (with Jonny Baker).

Andy Smith is the Team Rector in Ambleside, overseeing a network of churches in the central Lake District's fells and valleys. With a passion for missional church and church planting, he is pioneering sustainable church planting in a rural context. Prior to this role, Andy was the diocesan lead for youth, young adults and children's ministry across Cumbria within the Diocese of Carlisle. His experience also includes leading a large international church in Southeast Asia and revitalizing a parish church in Southampton. Andy is married to Nicky and is dad to three teenage children.

Hannah Steele is Director of St Mellitus College, London, where she is also a lecturer in missiology and evangelism. Hannah has published a number of books on missional ecclesiology and evangelism, including *New World, New Church* and *Living His Story: Revealing the Extraordinary Love of God in Ordinary Ways*, which was the Archbishop's Lent book in 2021 and a *Sunday Times* bestseller.

John White is the founder and leader of Hazelnut Community, an innovative eco-community in Bristol. Hazelnut Community Bristol provides space for growing food, worship, community development and reimagining church land use. The Hazelnut Community Network also supports churches across the UK and beyond in developing eco-communities on their land. John lives in Bristol with his wife Pippa and their two children.

Introduction

PAUL BRADBURY, ISABELLE HAMLEY,
ANDY SMITH

This collection developed initially from the work of a Faith and Order Commission group on missional ecclesiology. The group met in the context of ongoing debates in the Church of England that have reflected on the church–mission relationship, and which it seems have become more entrenched. We explored many of the themes explored in this book, before convening a conversation at Bishopthorpe in York in early 2023. The day in York brought academics, practitioners and policy makers together for a facilitated conversation around three themes: mission, Kingdom and church. Those attending were drawn from the breadth of the Anglican theological tradition, and from across the spectrum of perspectives within the ongoing debate on missional ecclesiology, which one might broadly characterize in terms of a dynamic between tradition and innovation.

As mentioned in some of the editorial reflections later in the book, the conversation in York yielded a high degree of common ground amid a diversity of perspectives, particularly in the areas of missiology and Kingdom theology. It was in our conversation focused on ecclesiology, however, that the lines of division showed most clearly. Despite a tangible commitment to exploring together some central tenets of the church around which we might gather, this proved remarkably difficult. This provided an enduring insight in itself however, and it was decided following the symposium that the best way to reflect the conversation that had taken place was to produce an accessible multivoiced publication. We have therefore sought to offer here a reflection of the unity that we can celebrate across our differences, while also inviting the articulation of particular perspectives in a spirit of open, learning conversation.

It was clear from the group's discussions beforehand that trying to offer *a* missional ecclesiology *for* the Church of England was going to be an impossible and possibly fruitless task. A cursory glance at recent literature, and on the range of groups and organizations broadly representing different 'positions', makes it evident that the Church of England contains a complex mix of theologies, often very strongly held, on this issue. Furthermore, any attempt to provide a theology *for* the church would seem to suggest a more formal and definitive approach to theology. That is, one that places greater emphasis on formal theology over practical experience and that presents theology as something finished rather than something always developing. However, what York affirmed, despite the friction in some areas of our discussion, was the importance of conversation on these themes.

It is sadly rare within our rich and diverse church to find such spaces of generative discussion where it is not just common ground or differences that are revealed, but new insights developed from the dynamic of conversation. Therefore we took the practice of conversation into the development of this book, not simply as a way of presenting different theologies, or of holding different theologies in tension in the hope of resolution, but as a way of *doing* theology. Clare Watkins has argued that the church might understand itself as 'a community of discerning conversation, open to the necessary incomplete and flawed contributions of all who seek what is most true' (Watkins, p. 246). Rather than seeing the cracks that seemed to open up in our discussion as problems to be solved, might they offer clues to some of the essential dynamics within the contemporary church where our theology is being most stretched and where there is the greatest potential for insight, creativity and learning? For example, we might place our differences around one of the fault lines that will emerge throughout this book, that between what we might call respectively tradition and innovation (language as a contested medium being another theme of the conversation in York), in the light of Alasdair MacIntyre's statement that any living tradition 'is an historically extended, socially embodied argument, and an argument precisely about the goods that constitute that tradition' (MacIntyre, p. 257). This book offers a flavour of the quality and diversity of the conversation in York, but further, an invitation to a deeper and ongoing discussion on these critical themes as a way of doing theology and living our tradition as the Church of England in this nation and at this time.

Our title *Being the People of God* invites us to hold the essence of the church primarily as a set of relationships. This relational view of the church is often obscured by the complexity, and sometimes predominance, of institutions and structures in our thinking and discourse.

However, in view of an emphasis on conversation as a way of doing theology, we wanted to affirm a relational metaphor for the church, and to recognize therefore that the work of theology sits within that complex sociality that we call the church.[1] This understanding of the church therefore affirms the value and ongoing importance of conversation as a way of continuing to be the people of God. What it means to be the people of God is never finished, and central to the ongoing development of that meaning is conversation across difference.

The book's subtitle also recognizes the context of that conversation: that we are seeking to do *Missional ecclesiology in uncertain times*. Any ecclesiology that engages seriously with context is going to have to grapple with the disruption and interrogation that time and change bring. In that sense time always brings uncertainty. If we live in time we live, to some extent at least, in uncertainty. However, there is a profound sense that we live in a time of unprecedented change. Pope Francis argued that 'we do not live in an era of change, but a change of era' (San Martin, 2015). That may or may not be the case, though it does point to the deep sense that the period of change we are experiencing is disrupting, even unravelling, many of the normative assumptions that have held society, certainly Western society, in some form of stability for a significant period of time.

The context of uncertainty and profound change can be keenly felt in the background to many of the contributions here, and in some cases is addressed directly (for example, Nigel Rooms' chapter 'Being Witness at the End of Modernity'). However, the dynamic of time, often a dynamic given less emphasis in the church in modernity in particular, is given deliberate attention here. Missional ecclesiology as a field of enquiry holds within its title a dynamic between our gathered life as a worshipping community and our life of witness and active mission in the world. We wanted, however, to give attention to a third dynamic, the dynamic of time, exploring how we as a church are reflecting, adapting and discovering ourselves anew in the extraordinary times we are living through.

The book is therefore divided into three parts ('Being Worship', 'Being Witness', 'Being Pilgrim'). In each part the dynamic conversation between worship, mission and time is explored by the various authors. However, the individual parts provide an emphasis, a particular priority of lens perhaps, on that conversation. Each part has a number of chapters offering longer theological reflections, plus a number of shorter 'On the Ground' reflections from practice. Not that more formal theological reflection and practical theology are completely separate in these different contributions. Many of those writing longer chapters are immersed in practice of one sort or another, and as is evident, those offering stories of practice are offering rich theological insights through their reflections on these stories. However, the shorter practical reflections invite a closer attention to the lived reality of the issues we are exploring from those engaged in it on a daily basis.

In the first part, 'Being Worship', each contributor was invited to reflect on how the nature of gathered worship is coming into conversation with mission in the time that we are in. Hannah Steele argues for a greater integration of worship and mission through the lens of Christian community. This theme of integration is developed by Al Barrett, who offers an ecological metaphor of 'entanglement' to argue for greater fluidity between the gathered church and its witness in the neighbourhood. Sharon Prentice looks to the gathered worshipping community to be the generator of diverse inclusion through a practice of 'tender-heartedness'. Alison Milbank challenges the tendency towards binary conceptions of worship and mission by arguing for integrating practice of the Eucharist. Two On the Ground chapters then root this part in stories of local ministry: Sarah Haden reflects honestly and insightfully from her experiences of church planting, while Andy Smith reflects on his experience of leading a parish in Southampton where mission and worship, the new and the old, the pioneering and the established developed interdependently.

In Part II, 'Being Witness', the lead partner in the conversation switches to mission. Angus Ritchie and Ana França-Ferreira bring a perspective from the practice of community organizing, arguing that this process generates an important shift in our missional posture towards the 'unrecognized'. Jonny Baker, drawing on the examples of Jesus in the Gospels, likewise invites us to a renewed posture and imagination as the church, through intentional engagement with 'the edges'. This theme of a shift in the church's paradigmatic disposition is then explored by Nigel Rooms as he reflects on his experience with Partnership for Missional Church (PMC). PMC, used by many dioceses across the Church of England in recent years, invites churches to adopt a number of spiritual practices that help to reshape a congregation's relationship with its community.

Two very different practical stories then bring a more particular and local perspective to these themes. Jon Oliver tells the story of the emergence of a new worshipping community on a social housing estate in Southampton, while John White tells the story of the Hazelnut Community, a fresh expression of church that focuses its life in response to the fifth mark of mission, our care for creation.

Finally, Part III, 'Being Pilgrim', attempts to bring our wrestling with the dynamic of time into the forefront of the conversation. In the first two chapters both authors reflect on the challenge of cultural change for a part of the Church of England's traditional ministry: Chris Hodder explores the dynamic between tradition and innovation in a traditional parish, while David Monteith draws on both the practice and metaphor of pilgrimage in his reflection on the changing nature of worship and mission in our nation's cathedrals. James Butler and Cathy Ross draw our attention to the particular historical legacies of empire. They argue for an attentiveness to those at the edges of our institution, rather than a reassertion of the centre, as a means of inhabiting what it means to be a pilgrim church. The pilgrim theme is then taken up by Tina Hodgett, who offers a pilgrim ecclesiology that draws on key transitions in the salvation story and which leads to a vision of a church led playfully by the Holy Spirit into the future. Three On the Ground theological reflections draw this part and the book to a close. David Lloyd tells the story of Garden Church, a network of small communities in Norfolk that have emerged quite spontaneously and are creating a new ecology of church in their context. Fiona Gibson offers a rural parish perspective that asserts the patient, vulnerable witness of the church through time. Finally, Omid Moludy tells the story of Iranian Christianity, moving from Iran to Manchester. He offers a long history of the agency of the Spirit in the lives of Iranian people, which is now enriching the story of Christian worship and witness here in England.

There is not the space here to reflect at length on the themes emerging from the many contributions to this book. However, each part ends with an editorial reflection that offers some insights into the common themes and issues raised by the various authors and what we might be learning from the conversation between them. A final reflection on the whole collection of essays is then offered by Mike Harrison, who facilitated our conversation at York.

We invite you to engage with this book in a spirit of conversation. Conversation, while constrained by the irreversibility of time, nevertheless has a non-linear, emergent quality. Connections are made, themes circle back on one another, earlier points are returned to and amplified as the conversation develops. Sometimes new voices appear on the scene and take the conversation in an unexpected direction. Invariably something emerges from such a process, a new insight, a new idea, a new project – but not always in the way we might have expected. You may therefore not want to read this book in a standard linear fashion but in noticing different threads that connect the book together, follow paths of your own making, while at the same time inviting voices into those paths that might be unfamiliar, disruptive and creative.

Our thanks go to all those who have provided contributions to this book. Editing a multivoiced collection has been a new experience for most of the editorial team so we are grateful for the commitment and grace shown by all our authors as the project developed. Our thanks too to all those who attended the day in York that did so much to shape this book. Finally, our thanks also to David Shervington and his team at SCM Press for their enthusiasm for the book, and for navigating its passage into print.

Note

1 See in particular the work of Dan Hardy, who described the church as a 'redeemed sociality' (Hardy, p. 205).

References

Hardy, D., 1996, *God's Ways with the World: Thinking and Practising Christian Faith*, Edinburgh: T&T Clark.
MacIntyre, A., 1981, *After Virtue: A Study in Moral Theory*, London: Bloomsbury.
San Martín, I., 2015, 'Pope Francis says Catholics must be open to Change', *Crux*, 10 Nov., https://cruxnow.com/church/2015/11/pope-francis-says-catholics-must-be-open-to-change (accessed 25.11.24).
Watkins, C., 2020, *Disclosing Church: Generating Ecclesiology through Conversations in Practice*, London: Routledge.

PART I

Being Worship

I

Being Worship in the Making of Disciples

HANNAH STEELE

Pope Francis popularized the phrase 'missionary disciple' in his publication *The Joy of the Gospel*, and he returned repeatedly to this phrase, encouraging a vast crowd gathered in Lima at the climax of his 2018 visit to Latin America. Similarly, in a 2019 celebration of 150 years of mission in Africa, he declared: 'I encourage you to keep your gaze fixed on Jesus Christ, so as never to forget that the true missionary is a disciple above all.'

When the Church of England revealed its vision and strategy for the 2020s, along with the priority of becoming a church where mixed ecology is the norm and growing younger and more diverse, it named 'becoming a church of missionary disciples' as one of its core priorities, echoing Pope Francis's phrase. Pope Francis (2019) stated: 'In virtue of their baptism, all the members of the people of God have become missionary disciples.' This descriptor naming all Christians missionary disciples by means of baptism challenges three misconceptions that have often plagued dialogue about missiology and ecclesiology.

First, mission is not regarded as the vocation of the few to far-flung places, but the business of the local and everyday. Second, discipleship is no longer viewed through the narrow confines of post-Second World War evangelicalism's emphasis on conversion-orientated Bible study programmes, but as something quintessential to all expressions of Christian spirituality. Third, calling all God's people missionary disciples challenges the false narrative that the priority of ecclesiology and its sacramental life (of which baptism is a central part) has a centripetal tendency, a drawing inwards and upwards, whereas missiology by contrast has a centrifugal emphasis, a pulling outwards and away. The phrase 'missionary disciples' demands a correlation between ecclesiology and missiology, as this chapter will explore.

Missionary disciples in a Post-Christendom world

Matthew 28.18–20 ('the Great Commission') has often been regarded as the great rallying cry of overseas mission. Since William Carey's famous 'Expect Great Things, Attempt Great Things' speech at the Baptist Association Gathering in Northampton in May 1792, and his subsequent publication of *An Enquiry*, the Great Commission has been deployed as the mandate for missionary obedience:

> Our Lord Jesus Christ, a little before his departure, commissioned his apostles to *Go*, and *teach all nations*; or, as another evangelist expresses it, *Go into all the world, and preach the gospel to every creature*. This commission was as extensive as possible, and laid them under obligation to disperse themselves into every country of the habitable globe, and preach to all the inhabitants, without exception, or limitation. (Carey, p. 7; italics original)

For Carey, this was not just a command given to the first apostles but to all Christians, something he responded to by his own missionary journey to India and thus galvanizing a century of Western Missionary activity.

Now, in our post-Christian, post-colonial West, the mandate to make disciples is one that is being re-evaluated. Humbled by the experiences of those who testified to the atrocities associated with Christian mission and recognizing that 'The astonishing religious changes of the twentieth century have produced a post-Christian West and a post-Western Christianity', the church in the West is now rethinking what it means to make disciples (Walls).

The Western church now finds itself in the minority, compelled to face the question of what mission now means for an institution facing decline. Many believe that this provides a new and crucial opportunity to re-evaluate what we mean by disciple-making:

> Official and unofficial Christendom arrangements have powerfully shaped our understanding of evangelism and missions, over many centuries. The worldview of Christendom also assumes that every important question has already been canvassed and answered. Christendom eventually lost the capacity to listen to new questions. With the collapse of Christendom the structures built on its paradigms are no longer viable. (Tennent, p. 20)

Until its use within the era of missions, this Matthean text was not known by the title 'The Great Commission' nor used in that way. It was deployed, rather, 'as the trinitarian foundation of ecclesiology, not as fanfare for missiology' (Castleman, p. 68). This is significant because its narrow application within the context of overseas mission potentially downplays the ecclesial and Christological significance of these words. Often used as a rallying cry to individual missiological obedience, the Great Commission is a profoundly ecclesiological statement with its three-fold priority of making disciples, obedience to the teachings of Christ and baptism. It is in drawing missiology and ecclesiology together that we can begin to explore what it is to be a community of missionary disciples.

Mission and worship

For God's people, synthesis between its worshipping life and its outward orientation has always been crucial to its identity, as God's call to Abraham in Genesis 12 demonstrates. Abraham is called to be the progenitor of God's people, courageously leaving behind the familiar and comfortable, and 'he stayed for a time in the land he had been promised, as in a foreign land, living in tents' (Heb. 11.9). Abraham and Sarah, despite their maturity in years, become parents to a son, the fulfilment of God's promise that Abraham would be the Father of a great nation. God's promise to Abraham is one of fruitfulness and blessing, the founding of a new people whom God would later call 'my treasured possession out of all the peoples' (Exod. 19.5). However, despite what seems a narrowing exclusivity of focus, God's mandate to Abraham is one of blessing beyond: 'in you all the families of the earth shall be blessed' (Gen. 12.3). This blessing in Genesis echoes the creation story, where God blesses the world he has made, humanity within it and the sabbath rest. 'Blessing then, at the very beginning of our Bible, is constituted by fruitfulness, abundance and fullness on the one hand, and by enjoying rest within creation in holy and harmonious relationship with our Creator God on the other' (Wright, p. 67). Put simply, God's blessing has both vertical and horizontal dimensions: it is concerned with our relationship both to God and to one another.

Abraham's story reveals a further synthesis between particularity and universality, which is also at the heart of a missiological interpretation of God's people. Abraham and his family in particular are called to be a source of universal blessing. Johannes Blauw expresses it like this: no doubt the Old Testament is 'particularistic', in the sense that salvation and the service of God are confined to one special people; but this 'particularism' is the instrument for the universal ends of God with the world (p. 25). This pattern of particularity and universality, of gathering inwards in order to be a blessing outwards, is core to the identity of God's people.

These two tensions between, on the one hand, horizontal and vertical dimensions of God's blessing and, on the other, particularity and universality, are formative in shaping an understanding of being God's missionary disciples.

When we look forward to mission in the New Testament the notion of blessing shapes an understanding of God's mission as incorporating both horizontal and vertical dimensions. The Anglican Five Marks of Mission carry this dual emphasis on relationship with God through proclamation of the gospel and nurturing believers, and relationships with one another through responding to human need, pursuing justice and the harmony of all creation. Acts shows the earliest gathering of Christian community: 'They devoted themselves to the apostles' teaching and fellowship, to the breaking of bread and the prayers' (Acts 2.42). Their community prioritized the vertical dimension of their relationship to God. However, they also performed signs and wonders and 'had all things in common; they would sell their possessions and goods and distribute the proceeds to all, as any had need' (2.44–45), attending to the horizontal dimension of their mission by serving those in need. And they grew steadily each day.

In addition, the themes of universality and particularity are important when thinking about missional ecclesiology. As Jesus' disciples wait in Jerusalem for the promised gift of the Spirit, they are a particular few whom Christ has called, but the gift of the Spirit is given to them to be poured out to others. They find themselves speaking the good news of the Kingdom in unfamiliar languages, and the Abrahamic promise that all nations will be blessed takes on new significance as the gospel is proclaimed 'in Jerusalem, in all Judea and Samaria, and to the ends of the earth' (Acts 1.8). It is the presence of God with his people, now by the indwelling of his Spirit, that is distinctive in Christian mission through community. Mission is not primarily about the busyness or activity of the church, but the indwelling of the Spirit in the life of God's people who are a witness to the gospel. Mission and worship are not polar opposites pulling the church in different directions. It is through being the people within whom God dwells by his Spirit that the church declares and embodies the gospel to the world:

> Mission ... is entirely dependent on the hidden activity of God within His Church, and is the fruit of a life really rooted in God. The evangelisation of the world is not primarily a matter of words or deeds: it is a matter of presence – the presence of the People of God in the midst of mankind and the presence of God in the midst of His People. (Martin-Achard, p. 79)

God's people look forward to the day when every nation, tribe and tongue will worship before the throne of Jesus. Until that day the church is to be the people with whom God dwells by his Spirit who are making disciples of all nations.

> The business of the church is to tell and embody a story, the story of God's mighty acts in creation and redemption and of God's promises concerning what will be in the end. The church affirms the truth of this story by celebrating it, interpreting it, and enacting it in the life of the contemporary world. (Newbigin, 1998, p. 76)

The story of the gospel is that which the church enacts in its Eucharistic worship, its teaching and prayers, and it is also that which it embodies and proclaims in its corporate witness to the world. Mission and worship, then, are eternally connected and central to ecclesiology. This challenges the oft-cited adage that 'missions exist because worship doesn't'. Such a sentiment suggests that the eternal goal is worship and that mission is merely the temporary means to that end. However, this reading of mission disregards any understanding of mission as rooted in the being and nature of God in the concept of *missio Dei*, which has shaped missiological thinking since the mid-twentieth century. As David Bosch summarizes it: 'To participate in mission is to participate in the movement of God's love towards people, since God is a fountain of sending love' (p. 391). This posits mission in the realm of participation within God's activity in the world, dependent upon divine initiative and action. Prayer and worship are, in part, the place in which such dependence upon divine initiative is born and the means by which we are shaped and equipped for participation in God's missionary task.

Fundamental to the concept of *missio Dei* is the recognition that mission is part of who God is for all eternity: 'If mission is an attribute of God then it bespeaks something of God's nature and of reconciled human existence with God' (Flett, p. 75). Mission, then, is not a temporary activity like planting churches or overseas missions trips, a means to the end of worship, but is rather to participate within the sending and receiving of Trinitarian love, that which will endure for all eternity, surrounded by worship. We must be careful not to overlook the ministry of the Spirit within missional ecclesiology and, by logical consequence, its mandate for growth and its inherent need for flexibility of form:

> It is not the church that has a mission of salvation to fulfil to the world; it is the mission of the Son and the Spirit through the Father that includes the church, creating a church as it goes on its way ... The church participates in Christ's messianic mission and in the creative mission of the Spirit. We cannot therefore say what the church is in all circumstances and what it comprises in itself. But we can tell where the church happens. (Moltmann, p. 64)

This prevents us from regarding mission as something that is done that is external to the core life of the church, by the specialized few (the keen or the called!). Such an approach, which sees mission as outsourced to the professional missionaries, can assume a somewhat deistic perspective, as though God has set his mission running but stepped back from the action to let humanity do the rest. *Missio Dei* reminds us that the church at worship is the church in mission, and participation in the reconciling work of God in all creation is the privilege of all. It is sometimes the case that in our praxis there can be a 'kind of missionary zeal which is forever seeking to win more proselytes but which does not spring from or lead back into a quality of life which seems intrinsically worth having in itself' (Newbigin, 1987, p. 148). The missionary nature of the church is not somehow secondary to its worshipping life, but these inward and outward movements of love shape its place in the world today: 'The worship and mission of the church are the gift of participating through the Holy Spirit in the incarnate Son's communion with the Father and the Son's mission from the Father to the world' (Torrance, p. ix).

Let us then return to our opening question and the re-evaluation of the missionary mandate to make disciples in the post-Christendom world. We have established that the call to make disciples is intrinsic to the identity of God's people who participate in God's mission in the world, but let us now consider three principles from Matthew 28.18–20 to guide our current practice.

1 Going and staying in the making of disciples

One of the most pressing questions with which the church in the West is faced is how to live as disciples of Jesus in light of the collapse of Christendom. There is a posture of humility that accompanies this question as the church in the West reflects upon its complicity in colonialism while also reimagining what it is to be a missional church at home in the changing contours of its local identity. That the church in the West faces a crisis is evidenced by the 2021 Census, which saw the number of those identifying as 'Christian' in the UK fall from 59.3% (in 2011) to 46.2%, and those identifying as 'none' with regard to religious belief tripling during that time.

When it comes to the making of disciples, the mission field is no longer overseas but on the doorstep. The question asked by Lesslie Newbigin upon returning to the UK after decades of missionary work in India seems equally poignant and even more urgent than in 1984: 'Can there be an effective missionary encounter with this culture – this so powerful, persuasive and confident culture which (until very recently) simply regarded itself as "the coming world civilization". Can the West be converted?' (Newbigin, 1987, p. 25). Newbigin's answer was that what the West needed was not a new strategy or apologetic approach, but an embodied witness of the church, a living exegesis of the gospel within community. In challenging times of institutional decline, it is tempting to look outside for resources to be plundered and utilized, new technologies and media to be harnessed for the gospel. While these things can certainly have their place and there is an urgency about the church's need to read the times and understand its surrounding cultures more fully, we must not lose sight of the simple call to be the people of God in the world; no longer a powerful institution at the centre of societal life, but learning how to live prophetically, courageously and compassionately on the edges. This is the particular challenge that faces a declining church where the temptation to keep its head down and focus on self-preservation is all too real.

The themes of particularity and universality mentioned earlier are especially pertinent here. The central question of discipleship is: How do we live as followers of Christ in this time and place? The church is always the church *in situ*, and Pete Ward insists that we can only truly understand the church by viewing it as both theological and social/cultural (p. 3). Abstract notions of ecclesial identity can inspire us but unless they are rooted in the reality of human life and society they cannot guide the church in her witness or worship. The witness of the church is through the living out of the gospel in the everyday, the ordinary and the unspectacular. The call to make disciples is not to the individual but to the whole body, and through its life together, centred around the death and resurrection of Christ, a new way of being in the world is demonstrated and opened up. This is the most powerful missional apologetic in the post-Christendom world: 'It is surely a fact of inexhaustible significance but what our Lord left behind him was not a book, nor a creed nor a system of thought, nor a rule of life, but a visible community' (Newbigin, 1998, p. 27). In reflecting on the ways in which the early church grew so substantially in its early centuries, Michael Green observes that while the Apostles' itinerant and public proclamation of the gospel was integral, it was the informal missionaries, the unknown and ordinary people who lived a life of Christ-inspired word and action, whose witness lead to such phenomenal growth as the first disciples were scattered (p. 208). All our expressions of church, be they a parish in a thriving market town, a multicultural worshipping community that grows out of a food bank, a messy church or a church plant among a younger generation, carry within them the potential to witness to the universal gospel in their particular context. John Taylor suggests that 'We must expect the "little congregations" to take different forms and fulfil different functions precisely because they are meant to match the different circumstances in which human life and need presents itself' (p. 148). It is through the embodied witness to the gospel, through the everyday living out of faith in varying local contexts and networks, that the church fulfils her call to go and make disciples.

2 Making disciples of all nations

Carey's 1792 *Enquiry* contained extensive research into the spiritual and religious identity of the non-Western world to accompany his impassioned plea for the conversion of 'the Heathen'. The rise of global Christianity in the twentieth century means the world is no longer viewed in such terms and that we are on the cusp of what Philip Jenkins foretells as a non-white, non-European Christianity (p. 20). As is often cited, the average Anglican now is a Sub-Saharan African woman in her 30s. In addition, globalization means that the call to make disciples of all nations no longer necessarily means stepping on a plane but is about our local communities where different ethnicities, religious and social groups live cheek by jowl with one another. Where Wesley once famously cried 'the world is my parish' we must now recognize the world is *in* my parish (Tennent, p. 45).

On the day of Pentecost the world was on the doorstep of Jerusalem. The promised gift of the Spirit is received not just as an internal manifestation to the gathered believers in the rushing wind and fire, but in a propulsion outwards towards the world. The gift of the Holy Spirit is demonstrated in the translation of the gospel message into dialects and tongues unfamiliar to Galilean fishermen, such that the gathered crowd cry, 'And how is it that we hear, each of us, in our own native language?' (Acts 2.8). In the making of disciples today we need to be just as dependent upon the gift of the Spirit to us in the church to enable us to translate the gospel into the languages, be that linguistic or cultural, of our surrounding environment:

> Mission is to be a continuing process of translation and witness, whereby the evangelist and the mission community will discover again and again that they will be confronted by the gospel as it is translated, heard and responded to, and will thus experience ongoing conversion while serving as witness. (Guder, p. 73)

However, it is also the case that in the making of disciples of all nations the church strengthens her own witness. In Ephesians, Paul addresses the way in which Jew and Gentile are united in the gospel and brought together in community. What is striking is the image Paul uses to describe this coming together: 'abolishing the law with its commandments and ordinances, that he might create in himself one new humanity in place of the two, thus making peace' (Eph. 2.15, NRSVUE). God has created a new humanity through the bringing together of Jew and Gentile, those who were previously divided and distant. A new way of being human and being community together is opened up by the redemptive work of Christ and sustained by the reception of the same Spirit (Eph. 2.18). Paul later goes on to describe this miraculous unity in cosmic terms as making known the wisdom of God in the heavenly realms (Eph. 3.10). A multiethnic community of missionary disciples gathered together as one church is a remarkable sight in which one can glimpse the goal of all creation (Rev. 7.9), and serves as a powerful witness in a society marred by division, injustice, prejudice and fear:

The church made up of Jews and Gentiles is a mobile home, whose cornerstone is the incarnate Son of God. It is a community in pursuit of Christ and will not find what it is looking for until Christ – their cloud and pillar of fire – establishes his people in the Promised Land. The church goes out into the world and reaches out to all people so that people from every nation might become members of God's household and royal nation. (Harper and Metzger, p. 137)

Making disciples of *all nations* is not only the urgent priority of the church but also the means by which it lives out its embodied witness in the world today. Those who are different from us can be a source of significant blessing: 'Our diversity is a gift from God – a precious gift that is too valuable to waste. It is to be sought after, not shunned. It is what makes us the body' (Kwiyani, p. 107). Embracing its identity as God's new humanity transcending societal divisions is the task of the missionary church, and in so doing it witnesses to a God who is making all things new in Christ.

3 Making disciples in a secular world

As stated earlier, Matthew 28.18–20 is a profoundly ecclesial statement. Often understood as a rallying cry to make converts, a closer look suggests that it is more community orientated than that: teaching and baptism are arguably marks of an ecclesial community. This broadens our perspective from a concern of how to get people to 'pray the prayer' or become a Christian, to one of incorporation within a community of disciples, be that new or existing:

> personal conversion is not a goal in itself ... Conversion does not pertain merely to an individual's act of conviction and commitment; it moves the individual believer into the community of believers and involves a real – even a radical – change in the life of the believer, which carries with it moral responsibilities that distinguish Christians from 'outsiders' while at the same time stressing their obligation to those 'outsiders'. (Bosch, p. 117)

However, the question of discipleship in a post-Christendom context where there is little to no prior understanding of the Christian narrative, especially among emerging generations, is challenging. Evangelicals have often led the way with programmes of discipleship and courses to introduce people to the Christian faith, but concepts such as 'radical change' and obligation to others do not sit easily in a consumeristic individualistic culture. Ajith Fernando draws attention to the costly and sacrificial nature of discipling others and suggests that such a journey might take years rather than weeks (p. 31). It is worth noting that significant periods of revival in the history of the church have often been accompanied by a renewed commitment to discipleship. Celtic Christianity grew through the establishment of ecclesial communities embodying faith, which George Hunter argues addressed everyday issues of Christian discipleship not just ultimate realties: 'Celtic Christians prayed while weaving, hunting, fishing, cooking, or traveling' (p. 23). Wesley's itinerant preaching ministry was accompanied by extensive programmes of discipleship in his three-fold model of societies, classes and bands.

In *Ancient Future Evangelism* (2003), Robert Webber recalls the Four Stage Process of discipleship in the early church associated with Hippolytus, a structure developed in response to the vast number of 'pagans' converting to Christianity with little or no understanding of what Christian discipleship was all about. The four stages of Seeker, Hearer, Kneeler and Faithful were part of a progressive journey towards full discipleship, each stage marked by a period of intensive catechesis and culminating in a rite of passage in which baptism and eucharist played a part. While the contemporary application of such an approach now might be feared too rigid or inaccessible, our current preference for short-term gain might not sit adequately alongside discipleship and formation:

> the church in the West has largely forgotten the art of disciple-making and has largely reduced it to an intellectual assimilation of theological ideas. As a result, we have a rather anemic cultural Christianity highly susceptible to the lures of consumerism. This in turn works directly against a true following of Jesus. In our desire to be seeker-friendly and attractional, we have largely abandoned the vigorous kind of discipleship that characterized early Christianity and every significant Jesus movement since. (Hirsch, p. 64)

The making of disciples is an ecclesial matter that involves immersion and formation within the life of a community that is willing to be sacrificial, flexible and understanding. If the church wants to take seriously the call to make disciples of Jesus in the twenty-first century, then we need to give thought and attention to how we can create spaces where people can feel able to bring themselves with no prior understanding of Christian discipleship, with complex relationships and lifestyles but willing to journey together to become a living exegesis of the gospel of Christ.

And yet in all this we must not forget the promise that surrounds the call to make disciples of all nations: 'And remember, I am with you always, to the end of the age' (Matt. 28.20). The making of disciples will not be engineered ultimately by renewed strategy and vision, funding bids or shiny new initiatives, although they can play their part, but by prayer and deeper reliance on the Spirit of mission to breathe new life into our often comfortable and settled forms of church and to inspire and equip us for the task of being a community of missionary disciples.

References

Blauw, Johannes, 1962, *The Missionary Nature of the Church: A Survey of the Biblical Theology of Mission*, Cambridge: Lutterworth Press.
Bosch, David, 1991, *Transforming Mission: Paradigm Shifts in Theology of Mission*, Maryknoll, NY: Orbis Books.
Carey, William, 1792, *An Enquiry into the Obligations of Christians to Use Means for the Conversion of the Heathen*, London.
Castleman, 2007, 'The Last Word: The Great Commission: Ecclesiology', *Themelios* 32(3), pp. 68–70.
Fernando, Ajith, 2019, *Discipling in a Multicultural World*, Wheaton, IL: Crossway Books.
Flett, John, 2010, *The Witness of God: Trinity, Missio Dei, Karl Barth, and the Nature of Christian Community*, Grand Rapids, MI: Eerdmans.
Francis (Pope), 2013, *Evangelii Gaudium: The Joy of the Gospel*, London: Catholic Truth Society.
Francis (Pope), 2019, *Go Forth: Toward a Community of Missionary Disciples*, Maryknoll, NY: Orbis Books.
Green, Michael, 1970, *Evangelism in the Early Church*, Grand Rapids, MI: Eerdmans.
Guder, Darrell L., 2000, *The Continuing Conversion of the Church*, Grand Rapids, MI: Eerdmans.
Harper, Brad and Paul Louis Metzger, 2009, *Exploring Ecclesiology: An Evangelical and Ecumenical Introduction*, Grand Rapids, MI: Baker Books.
Hirsch, Alan, 2009, *The Forgotten Ways Handbook: A Practical Guide for Developing Missional Churches*, Grand Rapids, MI: Baker Books.
Hunter, George G. III, 2010, *The Celtic Way of Evangelism: How Christianity can Reach the West Again*, Nashville, TN: Abingdon Press.

Jenkins, Philip, 2002, *The Next Christendom: The Coming of Global Christianity*, Oxford: Oxford University Press.
Kwiyani, Harvey, 2020, *Multicultural Kingdom: Ethnic Diversity, Mission and the Church*, London: SCM Press.
Martin-Achard, Robert, 1962, *A Light to the Nations: A Study of the Old Testament Conception of Israel's Mission to the World*, Edinburgh and London: Oliver & Boyd.
Moltmann, J., 1977, *The Church in the Power of the Spirit: A Contribution to Messianic Ecclesiology*, London: SCM Press.
Newbigin, Lesslie, 1987, 'Can the West Be Converted?', *Princeton Seminary Review* 6(1), pp. 25–37.
Newbigin, Lesslie, 1995, *Proper Confidence: Faith, Doubt, and Certainty in Christian Discipleship*, Grand Rapids, MI: Eerdmans.
Newbigin, Lesslie, 1998, *The Household of God*, London: Paternoster.
Office for National Statistics, 'Religion, England and Wales: Census 2021' , 29 November 2022, https://www.ons.gov.uk/peoplepopulationandcommunity/culturalidentity/religion/bulletins/religionenglandandwales/census2021 (accessed 10.06.2024).
Taylor, John, 1972, *The Go-Between God: The Holy Spirit and Christian Mission*, London: SCM Press.
Tennent, Timothy, 2010, *Invitation to World Missions: A Trinitarian Missiology for the Twenty-first Century*, Grand Rapids, MI: Kregel Academics.
Torrance, J., 1996, *Worship, Community and the Triune God of Grace*, London: Paternoster.
Walls, Andrew, 2003, 'Endorsement', in Lamin Sanneh, *Whose Religion is Christianity? The Gospel beyond the West*, Grand Rapids, MI: Eerdmans.
Ward, Pete (ed.), 2012, *Perspectives on Ecclesiology and Ethnography*, Grand Rapids, MI: Eerdmans.
Watkins, Devin, 2019, 'Pope Francis: "A true Missionary is a Disciple First"', *Vatican News*, 8 February, https://www.vaticannews.va/en/pope/news/2019-02/pope-francis-missionaries-of-africa-150-anniversary.html (accessed 07.06.2024)
Webber, Robert, 2003, *Ancient Future Evangelism: Making your Church a Faith-forming Community*, Grand Rapids, MI: Baker Books.
Wright, Chris, 2010, *The Mission of God's People: A Biblical Theology of the Church's Mission*, Grand Rapids, MI: Zondervan.

2

Being Worship in a Neighbourhood Ecology

AL BARRETT

A gathering of slugs

A handful of us are praying Morning Prayer, walking the gravel path that runs parallel to the M6 motorway (above) and the River Tame (below), newly laid as part of the development of local flood defences. It's a damp, grey morning, thick clouds preventing any glimmers of sunlight from reaching us, and for a moment our attention is drawn downwards. To our surprise, and involuntary disgust, we notice a gathering of slugs: in their shimmering browns and greys, blacks and oranges, they cluster around a common focus, which, belatedly, we realize is a small pile of dog poo – a frequent and unwelcome feature of the local landscape for neighbourhood-walkers – on which the slugs are feasting.

Later, around the breakfast table at one of our community houses, a little online research reveals that slugs consume the faeces of other animals and, after digestion, produce excrement that enriches the surrounding soil. They are super-decomposers, undervalued contributors to our neighbourhood ecology. We take a moment in wonder, and gratitude, for this new discovery, this strange gift.

'Neighbourhood ecology': a lexicon

neighbourhood: a place where people live alongside each other – and more-than-human life too; neighbours are those who are *nearby*, whether they are conscious of their proximity to each other or not.

gifts: the treasure of a place and its inhabitants; a God-given abundance much deeper and richer than the 'skills' or 'assets' valued by a neoliberal economy; includes all the wonderful things that people *know* or can *do* (for the benefit of themselves, others or the wider world), but also the gifts of presence, attention, care, experience and story, often hard-won, intimately entangled in needs and longings, losses and struggles, passions and wounds,[1] and the complex beauty of the activity, and the 'just being there', of our more-than-human neighbours (even the slugs!).

connecting: the art of bringing neighbourhood interconnections to visibility; drawing into encounter those who have been feeling isolated or on the edges; discovering common ground between those who have been strangers to each other; unearthing gifts and nurturing relationships of gift-exchange and sharing between neighbours.

community: what emerges, however fleetingly or fragmented, in the work of connecting, as neighbours begin to notice, appreciate, enjoy and deepen our interconnectedness; we sometimes talk of 'community building', as if it is constructing a solid edifice, but in reality it is often more like nurturing plant life, with its fragilities and life cycles.

spaces and *places* are entangled but subtly different: a neighbourhood is a *space* turned into a *place* by its inhabitants; but it is an encompassing *place* full of smaller-scale *spaces* waiting to be lived in, moved through, interacted with, made home, made *places* themselves.[2]

bumping-places: spaces that have become – whether by accident or by intentional inhabiting and/or creating – places of encounter, where we bump into each other.

places of welcome: places (indoors or outdoors) that are intentionally inhabited, at regular times each week, in ways that offer a warm and inclusive welcome, a listening ear, something to eat and drink, and opportunities for people to connect, belong and contribute their gifts. (www.placesofwelcome.org.uk)

entanglements: the ways our lives are inescapably bound up with each other in relationships of interaction and interdependence: interpersonally between human beings and between human and more-than-human life; from the microscopic scale, through the local, to the planetary; and including structural forces and systems, both creative and destructive.

neighbourhood ecology: the web of geographically proximate entanglements and connections, activities and interactions between neighbours (human and more-than-human), spaces and places, that make up the living system of a neighbourhood.

root system: the deep values, stories and longings that inspire and shape the 'how' of our inhabiting, interacting, connecting, creating and nurturing within the neighbourhood ecology.

Neighbourhood as 'parish': place-formation between nostalgia and apocalypse

Place still matters. There is a complexity, a fluidity to our (human) relationships to place, but place still matters – more than ever before. If most modern and postmodern trajectories of 'the human' (usually centring a very particular kind of 'human') have been 'dis-placing' us – persuading us to imagine ourselves as disembodied, hypermobile individuals, independent of earthed places, and to see patches of ground as no more than commodities to be possessed, resources to be extracted – our twenty-first-century world of societal and ecological breakdown makes a (re)discovery of place, of neighbourhood, nothing less than a matter of life and death.

The enduring role of the *parish* within the Church of England is, as Andrew Rumsey puts it, a commitment to both *place* and *time*: to 'localities small enough for people to know and be known', and to a rooted faithfulness over time (a 'local monogamy') that recognizes that places are not fixed, but always 'characterized by flow and interrelation' (pp. 181–2). Rumsey acknowledges the dangers of a 'dysfunctional type of nostalgia' – linked precisely with a static, territorial (and ultimately idolatrous) possessiveness – that 'conscript[s] and thereby fossilize[s]' the parochial in defence of xenophobias on both local and national levels. By contrast, he discerns in the best moments of nostalgia a *future*-orientated aspiration, a longing for *home* and *belonging*, manifested in what he names 'an ecology of care' that embraces the local entanglements of human society and more-than-human ecosystems.

Where nostalgia implies a *dislocation* from home, the ecophilosopher Glenn Albrecht developed the term 'solastalgia' to describe that desolating 'homesickness' felt *while still in the place*, but when that home environment is being damaged, degraded or destroyed. While solastalgia is primarily a response to *local* change, it is of course entangled with terrors, anxieties and griefs at cataclysmic ecological change on a *global* level, which Albrecht collects together under the heading of 'global dread'. To diagnose such negative 'earth emotions' is also, however, to begin to identify the necessary response: what we often call the 'environmental' crisis, Albrecht argues, is better understood as 'a loss of *love*' for the Earth to which we belong. What is needed is a (re)discovery, and embodied practices, of *love* within our entanglements with the earth: 'the simultaneous restoration and rehabilitation of mental, cultural, and biophysical landscapes', a 'sumbiophilia' that acknowledges that such loving repair can only ever be 'a *cooperative* enterprise between many different types of organisms' (Albrecht, pp. 38–9, 80–81, 119, 148–9; emphases added).

Between nostalgia and apocalypticism, then, it critically matters how we *see* – and therefore respond to – the places of which we are a part. 'We make things holy by the kind of attention we give them', the mythologist Martin Shaw reminds us (p. 5); and conversely, how we perceive a place is deeply entangled with how the place presents itself *to us*. Beginning with the biblical ancestor Jacob's discovery, through a dream, that 'YHWH is in this place', Rumsey proposes a cyclical process of 'place-formation' where the 'is-ness' of a place (*'location'*) is encountered by human perception (*'revelation'*), which is then 'storified' (*'tradition'*) in ways that call for practical response (*'vocation'*), which then, to come full circle, has a transformative impact on the 'is-ness' of the place itself. If we discern the presence of God in that local reality, Rumsey suggests, 'we cannot but act on this belief, so that our behaviour becomes, to some degree, a response to God in that place.' This is an *eschatological* response, moreover, because it involves believing not just that God is *present* here, but that in Christ 'this place has [already] been reconciled to God' – and reorientating ourselves towards that reconciled reality. It is the vocation of the *parish* – not solely the church, we should note – 'to give spatio-temporal expression to the "new place" [coming] in the midst of the old' (Rumsey, pp. 30, 113, 171).

For the church *within* that parochial ecology, we can discern in Rumsey's proposals a three-fold calling that we might describe as *prophetic* (to 'articulate' that nostalgic '"longing for home" of which the world is tacitly aware', and 'relocate' it within an eschatological story); *priestly* (to liturgically offer 'the whole life of [the] place' to God and vice versa, as a witness to God's reconciliation of all things); and *place-forming* (to 'foster in each locality the conditions that enable loving encounter with God and neighbour') (Rumsey, pp. 113, 84, 59). I would suggest that this three-fold calling needs a three-fold qualification:

- First, that the church is also the *recipient* of prophetic challenge by its neighbours, particularly those who have been marginalized by the church's temptations to colonial and hetero-patriarchal forms of power-as-mastery (Barrett, 2020, p. 202);
- Second, that eschatological tendencies towards *hope* are put in tension with a realist-and-apocalyptic sense of *doom* for the Earth as we know it, and so the 'priestly' offering of the church must include deep lament, grief, rage and confession;
- Third, that if the church is indeed a (Spirit-empowered) 'transforming agent' in forming, loving and reconciling places (Rumsey, p. 14), then it knows itself as but *one among many* such entangled, interconnected and Spirit-empowered transforming agents, both human and more-than-human (which might, incidentally, be a cause for tentative hope, as Albrecht suggests).[3]

Placing worship in a (radically receptive) neighbourhood ecology

In our book *Being Interrupted: Reimagining the Church's Mission from the Outside, In*, Ruth Harley and I described in some detail the 'missional economy' we were discovering through our local church's participation in the wider work of place-formation in Hodge Hill, on the eastern edge of the city of Birmingham. It was (and still is) a missional economy shaped primarily not by the church *counting in* or *giving out*, but by opening our eyes and ears, hearts and hands to *treasure-seeking* in our neighbourhood and being *radically receptive* to (*being interrupted* and transformed *by*) the gifts and challenges of our neighbours (Barrett and Harley, pp. 63ff. and 128ff.).

Here, drawing on the lexicon I offered at the start, we might further describe this missional economy as *a way of seeing and responding* that pays a particular kind of attention to God's presence and activity in and among: the gifts, spaces and places; the agency of both human and more-than-human life; and the web of entanglements and connections within the neighbourhood ecology.[4] The particularities of this way of seeing and responding have a profound impact on the shape of our worship – and indeed on what even *counts* as worship.

First, it emphasizes a counter-flow to that which tends to dominate Christian worship. Rather than focusing on gathering together to *receive* from God in worship, with the purpose of being sent (filled, equipped and energized) to *give out* to the world, we need to pay more attention to *what we bring to the gathering*, what from our neighbourhoods flows in with us as we gather.

Second, we can see worship as a place where the entangled stories of place and stories of God are given space to interact with each other, in a process of mutual (not just one-way) rooting and transformation, orientated towards the reconciliation and restoration of place 'in Christ'. These storied interactions thus deepen, sharpen and broaden our capacities to see and respond: *What* do we attend to, and *how*?

Third, however, there is the possibility of a profound *de-centring* in our understanding of worship:

> Relocating our collective attention, so that the places we have thought of as 'edges' become the holy ground on which, together, we discover the glory of God, and therefore become the new 'centres' – but multiple, interdependent, disruptive, transformative 'centres' – of our listening, learning, discerning, gathering, sharing, worshipping, deciding and world-changing – through the power of the Spirit in our midst. (Barrett and Harley, p. 165)

Paying careful attention to our particular neighbourhood ecology, we can begin to see the various aspects of liturgical worship woven through other places, activities and gatherings that would never identify themselves as *church*. In some places these appear as a coherent liturgical thread (from 'gathering' to 'sending'); in others they show up as 'liturgy deconstructed': one element here, another there. It is only when we look at the neighbourhood ecology *as a whole*, therefore, that we are able to discern something what we might call an *ecology of worship*, spreading deep and wide through the root systems of this place.

Gathering and attending

The parish of Hodge Hill, on the eastern edge of the city of Birmingham, is overlooked by the M6 motorway, stretching out on its concrete pillars eastwards from Spaghetti Junction. Housing is a mix of middle-class suburbia (now mostly Pakistani-heritage Muslim households) and outer estate (maisonettes, tower blocks and terraces housing a mix of increasing ethnic diversity). Two rivers make parish boundaries: the Tame (to the north) and the Cole (to the south); with a large triangle of scrubland,

Hodge Hill Common, somewhere near the centre. The Bromford neighbourhood is named after an ancient ford across the River Tame, and the broom bushes that thrive on the nearby Common. A wooded corridor runs through Bromford, with a carpet of bluebells in the spring, and at the parish's eastern edge is a mix of marsh and woodland, a public space once owned by Lord and Lady Bradford.

During the Covid-19 pandemic, walking became for many people here (as in so many other places) a daily lifeline, with its combination of opportunities to move the body, get out into the open air, connect with other people (even from a distance) and connect with the natural world around us. And church moved outdoors too: all-age Muddy Church celebrated Christmas Eve in 'Lady Brad's' woods; the fading wooden decorations on one of the fir trees there can still be seen, if you know where to look. A more enduring legacy, though, is Morning Prayer: a small group of us continue to gather, twice-weekly, at one of our two Community Houses, go for a walk and say our prayers together, on the Common, in the woods, in the community orchard, under a tree (especially if it's raining!). In the seasonal, creation-centred liturgies we use,[5] there is always space for 'attending': prayerfully looking around us, listening for the songs of our more-than-human world, feeling the sun (or rain) on our faces, knowing the grounding of the earth beneath our feet. Sometimes we are interrupted by a curious dog (and more occasionally by its human companion), other times we are surprised by slugs. Praying in our green spaces has offered a schooling in slowing down, paying closer attention, knowing our place within a mysterious and complex ecology, and falling in love with a more-than-human world, which first loved us (see Kimmerer).

Glenn Albrecht retrieves an old root word in Indo-European languages, *ghehd*, which has 'meanings linked to Old English and Germanic words such as "together", "to gather", and "good"'. With it he wants to draw us to a fresh awareness:

> of the spirit ... that holds things together, a ... feeling of interconnectedness in life between the self and other beings (human and non-human) and their gathering together to live within shared Earth places and spaces, including our own bodies. (pp. 150–1)

As Christians walking and praying in our neighbourhood, we are *gatherers* of all that we see and hear, smell and touch; gatherers of the activities, connections and discoveries of our community; gatherers of its places and loves, its gifts and its goods.

But we Christian prayer-walkers are not the neighbourhood's only gatherers. Our neighbourhood's Street Connectors also walk the streets every week, knocking on doors and engaging people in conversation, just as our Green Connectors bring people together in some of our local green spaces, to engage with each other and the more-than-human world around us. The quality of attention in these encounters is just as profound as in our prayer walks: our Connectors seek to unearth people's gifts and passions, as well as listen to their angers, fears and frustrations. The 'gathering' happens as people are drawn into Places of Welcome and other local groups, as their gifts are unleashed and shared, their passions engaged in collective projects, and as they find support and solidarity in their frustrations. Some gatherings are convened specifically to enable local people to be heard by those in positions of decision-making power, giving voice to personal and collective hurts and seeking to find ways, together, of addressing and redressing them.

What is gathered into church on a Sunday, then, includes gratitude and praise but also shock, grief, pain, anger, weariness and wounds that are both deeply personal and often effects of structural injustice, both 'outside' and 'inside' the church. This 'gathering' is informed by our connections and entanglements with other gatherings in our neighbourhood, where deep emotions are often more readily expressed than in church settings still at least partly in the grip of deeply ingrained pressures towards politeness and positivity. The groaning of creation, and the cries of the oppressed and the weary, are 'heard to speech' within the web of relationships of the neighbourhood ecology, as are the songs of creation's life and joy and love.

Confessing and decomposing

The patient nurturing of neighbourhood spaces as Places of Welcome, encounter and connection has stirred a collective desire to 'go deeper': to let down our defences with one another, to acknowledge where we've been shaken by our experiences, brought to our limits, challenged by our encounters and our learning from each other. We have discovered the need for spaces where, in the company of others, we can look more honestly at ourselves – flaws, fears, fragilities and all – and at our entanglements in those structures and systems of domination and injustice that are destroying our world and dividing, disabling and wounding our communities.

This is, of course, at least partly what the Christian church means when it talks about *confession*, individual and corporate. But a liturgical moment of silence and a collective 'we have sinned' does not sufficiently *do justice* – literally – to what we have discovered that we need here. In our community work in the neighbourhood we have discovered the power of nurturing 'thinking environments': learning spaces that offer each of us hospitable place and generous time to 'do our best thinking', internally and with each other, rooted in a quality and *equality* of attention, an ease (rather than urgency), an appreciation (as well as challenge) and encouragement of each other, and an embrace of emotion (as well as information), difference and dissent, and 'incisive questions' that seek to free us from untrue assumptions and invite us into new discoveries, together.[6]

Within the life of our church community we have (re)discovered that those evening gatherings around fire pits, with enough time for plenty of silence, gazing at the flames or the sunset as we sink together into the darkness, have sometimes enabled us to share with each other, with God and with ourselves, things that we might not dare speak in the bright glare of day: some of those 'harder things' that we are ashamed of, fearful of, frustrated by, or which just refuse to go away. Sometimes we have intentionally gathered close to one of our neighbourhood compost heaps, inviting us to notice what has been decomposing *in us* and in the world around us, what might *need* to decompose, and how we might open ourselves to that decomposition.

For some of us locally (usually a mix of people that blurs and spans the boundaries of church and neighbourhood communities), one of the highlights in the cycle of the year is Easter Eve/Holy Saturday. In a different location each year around the parish (often in neglected or abandoned spaces), we practise 'hanging on in there', together, in the liminal, 'in-between' space, of grief, of trauma, of waiting. As in a more conventional Easter Vigil, we tell stories together, but not of triumphant victory: more of loss and absence and the silence of God, the 'we had hoped' of the Emmaus disciples, the cold of winter and the longing for springtime. Interweaving the ancient vigil with insights from eco-feminist philosophy, and Carmelite and Black spiritualities (among other rich traditions), Holy Saturday gives depth and shape to our more regular practices of 'staying with the trouble' (see Haraway), supporting each other to 'tarry awhile' in the 'dark night of the soul', both individual and collective, local and global (see Stone; Cassidy and Copeland). As the flood waters of solastalgia and climate dread rise ever higher, these are moments of *rooting* our spiritual lives as 'a *descent* into [our] earthly neighbourhoods' in all their complexity, in our exposure, vulnerability to and dependence on each other (human, more-than-human and divine): what Norman Wirzba names the 'dark night of the *soil*' (pp. 111–12; emphases added).

Tabling and commoning

Of the four stages of worship as I have outlined them in this chapter, it is probably the third – what we do around the *table* – that has the greatest 'gravitational pull' towards an explicitly *ecclesial* centre, particularly within the Church of England: canon law insists Holy Communion must be celebrated *in church*, presided over by an ordained priest (Canon B40).

In stark contrast, Romand Coles describes radical democratic practices of 'tabling' as: attending to the tension between those who already have 'a seat at the table' and those who do *not*; *continually moving* from one location to another; and where it is not 'those who typically preside' but those usually excluded who decide who will be 'included' and how the 'common space' will be shaped (2005, pp. 232–4).

In Hodge Hill parish, the human circle around the Table widens to the more-than-human ecology of the Common at the parish's geographical heart. The verb 'commoning' is, like tabling, a profoundly collaborative *making-place-together* – 'to engage with other beings in a manner that is ecological, caring for and attending to the relations between them' (Locke, p. 27) – and erodes further the distinction between *guest* and *host* (see Barrett, 2019). With significant eschatological resonances for us here, commoning has also been described as an exploratory, *prefigurative politics* that can 'help to open up the space of possibilities from which better futures may emerge' (see Smith), and which often emerges *within the ruins* of existing structures (literal and metaphorical) (Locke, pp. 123ff.).

In our neighbourhood ecology, then (marked by the crumbling buildings and derelict sites of Birmingham City Council's once-robust local infrastructure, within the wider, global crumblings of neoliberal capitalism), both 'tabling' and 'commoning' can often be seen in action in our grassroots community gatherings: from the weekly pantry to the monthly interfaith Community Kitchen, from our regular Places of Welcome to the summer street events, from the community orchard and regular gardening groups to the activities organized by Friends of Hodge Hill Common. Neighbours move from place to place – sometimes host or enabler, often guest or contributor – throwing doors open wide, levelling power differences and bridging divides, deepening connections through conversation, shared activity and care, and sharing all kinds of gifts: knowledge of gardening or of navigating the benefits systems; newly grown seedlings and harvested produce; hot cooked meals and end-of-day Greggs pastries; DIY expertise or a song on the guitar. Tabling and commoning are prefigurative, place-making activities that deepen kinships and forge solidarities-across-difference: a profound kind of *communion*. The 'priestly' *offering* of the whole life of the place to God (and vice versa, as Rumsey puts it) is of course a profoundly *eucharistic* activity, but one that we see embedded, *enfleshed*, in the life of our neighbourhood.

Sending and witnessing

One of the most consistent critiques of the kind of missiology I have described here is that it seems to lack *proclamation*. Where is the emphasis on 'telling people about Jesus' or 'proclaiming the Kingdom of God'? The witness of Scripture and of our personal and collective encounters with God are, of course, some of the gifts we Christians *bring* to the gatherings, the compost heaps and the tables of our neighbourhood ecology. But those places are also themselves sites of God's kin-dom coming in our midst, 'close at hand'. The places where we journey with strangers, share with one another stories of loss and longing and break bread together (with or without the church's liturgy) *are* the places where we Christians are continually surprised by the presence of the risen Christ – just as those disciples were on the Emmaus Road. Our vocation, like theirs, is to witness: to go and tell what we have just seen or heard, touched or sensed. Significantly, it is to *their fellow-disciples* that they go first. Like Jacob at the place he named Bethel, we find ourselves saying, again and again, 'YHWH is in this place!'

In Hodge Hill on Easter morning, before dawn, a smallish group of us return to the place where, the night before, we shared stories around the fire. From a new fire we light the Paschal candle, and we carry it through the streets and green spaces of our neighbourhood to its resting place in the church building. Along the way we find stopping-places to pause and proclaim 'Alleluia! Christ is risen!' as we see those places afresh through Easter eyes, illuminated by the rising sun. Our pilgrimage culminates with the *Exsultet*, as we enter the church, but it is not the first song that has been sung that morning. Before the Easter Gospel is read, before any words are uttered over fire or candle, the birds are always already singing.

A 'village of God'?

Some of us wonder if we are seeing the emergence here of what Ray Simpson names a 'village of God' – a place of interconnected, interdependent 'common' spaces serving many and diverse functions within a rich and holistic vision of fullness of life (including eating together, growing things, learning, creativity, healing, prayer in diverse faith traditions, and – yes – hospitality, to the many guests who find their way to visit us here) (Simpson, pp. 98ff.).

The idea that we might reimagine an urban council estate as a *village* has enduring appeal among some of our neighbours. Simpson's village *of God* adds theological depth – 'YHWH is in this place!' – as well as experiential resonances, to our more technical language of 'neighbourhood ecology'. But does it risk being *parochial* in some of its worst senses? Does it play into a dysfunctional *nostalgia* for a romanticized English village, gathered around the church, pub and village green? Does it revive the spectre of a colonizing *territorialism*: suspicious of outsiders, and subtly blurring the distinction between 'parish' and 'church'? Is it too *idealistic* – as indeed I may risk being in my 'ecological' explorations here – imagining a level of harmonious connection and kinship that just isn't borne out by the lived reality?

For Rumsey, resistance to parochial territorialism has etymological and historical roots: 'parish' comes from the Greek *paroikeis* – 'stranger' – the word used for the risen Christ on the Emmaus Road. The Greco-Roman *paroikia* was the community of non-citizens, the fellowship of those who did not belong; and thus a theologically shaped parochial vision sees 'neighbourhood as something offered especially *by and to the outsider*' (Rumsey, p. 188; emphasis added). In practice, of course, even the most 'inclusive' and 'receptive' communities are continually negotiating the tension between the desire to *belong* and an openness to the *strange* (both within and beyond their edges). As Coles puts it, co-creating *roots* in a place must be done by learning to *move with others*, with whom we must *relearn how to see*, imagine, act and tend (2016, p. 106).

As a church community in Hodge Hill, in our long-term commitment to learning to *move with* our neighbours, in messy entanglements of place-formation and worship, we have found ourselves learning to pay more careful attention particularly to the small, the fragile, the contradictory and the fleeting. And we have been learning too how to be more honest about our disappointments and failures. We still long to be more connected than we presently are.

We acknowledge the ongoing presence of divisions and disconnections, of fallings-out, stubborn territoriality, and places and incidents of *un*welcome. We recognize something of our efforts at community in The Old Oak pub in Ken Loach's film of the same name: a place entangled in nostalgia, resentment and contest for space; a crumbling structure within the ruins of neoliberal capitalism; but also a finite and fragile place for connecting strangers together and collectively 're-storying' the neighbourhood, with threads of grief, solidarity, resistance and hope.

The return of the slugs

A small group of us are outside the Hub (our shop-front community centre), potting up seedlings to give out to those visiting today's Place of Welcome. Rowan, in the midst of grieving the husband who is still slipping away from her, is telling us about the hundreds of seedlings she is propagating at home: in her greenhouse, her kitchen, on a shoe-rack in her bedroom, wherever she has space to accommodate the new life she is insistently nurturing. She shares with us her top tips for battling the slugs that are equally insistent on eating her precious plants.

In any healthy ecosystem, creatures eat each other – it's essential for their survival and for the thriving of the ecology as a whole. So too are death, decay and decomposition. New life, just as inevitable, rarely springs up in exactly the same place and the same form as that which has died. Rather, nutrients and chemical elements *move, circulate* within the ecosystem, just as leaves falling from a tree create *humus* that nourishes other forms of life on the ground.

We have discovered within our neighbourhood ecology that the same is true of people, places, groups and activities. Things come to an end. People die. The fragilities of us human creatures, our relationships and our capacities – as well as the fragilities exacerbated by systemic pressures on neighbourhoods like ours – mean that even the most committed and passionate neighbours often have to pull back from activities they were critical to sustaining. Groups have life cycles, not just of 'forming', 'storming', 'norming' and 'performing' – but also 'adjourning', 'mourning'[7] or just disintegrating. And yet in an entangled, interconnected neighbourhood ecology, *nothing is ever wasted*. There is always something *passed on*, a legacy that filters through complex root systems. Sometimes, in fact, the gifts are only released, made visible and available, in the dying and decomposition. Think of the funeral of the unsung hero who had quietly spent a lifetime loving their neighbours. Or the ending of a dysfunctional group that finally frees its members' energies for what they'd always been longing to do.

Writing at the turn of the eighteenth century, the Anglican bishop Edward Stillingfleet noted that the power of the parochial system was its capacity for making 'a broken, divided people' become 'one body within certain bounds' (Rumsey, p. 188). His description sounds to me very much like the work of a *compost heap*: a bounded container where necessarily diverse organic matter is *thrown together* in intimate proximity, where often-rigid structures and separations are slowly broken down to create something new and nourishing of new life. If it's us, or the things we depend on, that are being decomposed, then it can often be painful. But there is a *detoxifying* that often goes on in parallel to decomposition within a healthy ecosystem: even our shit is digested, metabolized and regurgitated in potentially nourishing, life-giving ways. And of course this relies on a certain kind of creature within the decomposing community, which often provokes in us humans feelings of aversion, disgust. These detritivorous *paroikoi* include bacteria, insects, woodlice, fungi, worms and, yes, our friends the slugs.[8]

I have suggested here that we can discern an *ecology of worship* permeating the root systems of our neighbourhood: gathering us together with our gifts and wounds, enabling mutual transformation between our entangled stories, reshaping the way we see, and redistributing the new gifts released through processes of decomposition. Worship within our neighbourhood ecology is the daily invitation *to live together*, to embrace the dying that is part of the living, and to learn to inhabit a kind of *loving-together* – Albrecht's sumbiophilia – that acknowledges this patch of earth that we share, intimately entangled with this *planet* Earth that we share, not just as common ground but as *holy* ground. And if we can recognize the Spirit of God descending like a dove, perhaps we can also learn to recognize the Spirit of God approaching like a slug, and exclaim: 'Surely YHWH is in this place – and I did not know it!'

Notes

1 See Grinnell, 'Beyond "Assets and Deficits" to "Gifts and Wounds"', for a rich exploration of how our wounds can often be gifts (and, conversely, how sharing gifts can sometimes be wounding).

2 This differs from Michel de Certeau's technical deployment of the two terms but is closer to our usage locally.

3 Norman Wirzba (drawing on Ecclesiastes 9.4) seeks to redirect the question about 'grounds for hope' towards the 'grounds for love': 'what do you love, why do you love it, and what do you need to sustain your love?' (pp. 177–8).

4 Here I am approaching from a different angle the work I have done elsewhere of reversing and reframing the focus of missiology, from Christian *agency* to Christian (and human) *receptivity*. See Al Barrett, 'Re-wilding the 5 Marks of Mission': Keynote talk at USPG 'Justice and the Church' conference, 17 June 2023, on *This Estate We're In* [blog], 25 October 2023, https://thisestate.blogspot.com/2023/10/re-wilding-5-marks-of-mission.html (accessed 30.05.2024).

5 We use Shakespeare's *The Earth Cries Glory: Daily Prayer with Creation*.

6 See the work of Nancy Kline, e.g. https://www.timetothink.com/thinking-environment/the-ten-components/.

7 The terms are psychologist Bruce Tuckman's. See, for example, https://en.wikipedia.org/wiki/Tuckman%27s_stages_of_group_development.

8 See, for example, https://treesforlife.org.uk/into-the-forest/habitats-and-ecology/ecology/decomposition-and-decay/.

References

Albrecht, Glenn, 2019, *Earth Emotions: New Words for a New World*, New York: Cornell University Press.

Barrett, Al, 2019, 'Street Parties, Hosting, and the Emergence of "Commoning" on a Multi-ethnic Outer Estate', *Crucible: The Journal of Christian Social Ethics*, October, pp. 23–35.

Barrett, Al, 2020, *Interrupting the Church's Flow: A Radically Receptive Political Theology in the Urban Margins*, London: SCM Press.

Barrett, Al and Ruth Harley, 2020, *Being Interrupted: Reimagining the Church's Mission from the Outside, In*, London: SCM Press.

Cassidy, Laurie and M. Shawn Copeland (eds), *Desire, Darkness, and Hope: Theology in a Time of Impasse*, Collegeville, MN: Liturgical Press.

Coles, Romand, 2005, *Beyond Gated Politics: Reflections for the Possibility of Democracy*, Minneapolis, MN: University of Minnesota Press.

Coles, Romand, 2016, *Visionary Pragmatism: Radical and Ecological Democracy in Neoliberal Times*, Durham, NC: Duke University Press.

De Certeau, Michel, 1984, *The Practice of Everyday Life*, Oakland, CA: University of California Press.

Grinnell, Andrew, 2019, 'Beyond "Assets and Deficits" to "Gifts and Wounds"', *Crucible: The Journal of Christian Social Ethics*, October, pp. 9–22.

Haraway, Donna, 2016, *Staying with the Trouble: Making kin in the Chthulucene*, Durham, NC: Duke University Press.

Kimmerer, Robin Wall, 2013, *Braiding Sweetgrass: Indigenous Wisdom, Scientific Knowledge, and the Teachings of Plants*, Minneapolis, MN: Milkweed Editions.

Locke, Toby Austin, 2020, 'Fields of Commoning: Attempts at Creating (Un)-Common Worlds in New Cross', unpublished PhD thesis, Goldsmiths, University of London, https://research.gold.ac.uk/id/eprint/28399/1/ANT_thesis_AustinLockeT_2020.pdf (accessed 6/06/24).

Rumsey, Andrew, 2017, *Parish: An Anglican Theology of Place*, London: SCM Press.

Shakespeare, Steven, 2019, *The Earth Cries Glory: Daily Prayer with Creation*, London: Canterbury Press.

Shaw, Martin, 2021, *Smoke Hole: Looking to the Wild in the Time of the Spyglass*, London and White River Junction, VT: Chelsea Green Publishing.

Simpson, Ray, 2009, *High Street Monasteries: Fresh Expressions of Committed Christianity*, London: Kevin Mayhew.

Smith, E. T., 2024, 'Practising Commoning', The Commons Social Change Library, https://commonslibrary.org/practising-commoning/#Introducing_%E2%80%98Commoning (accessed 5.06.2024).

Stone, 2023, Selina, *Tarry Awhile: Wisdom from Black Spirituality for People of Faith*, London: SPCK.

Wirzba, Norman, 2022, *Agrarian Spirit: Cultivating Faith, Community, and the Land*, Notre-Dame, IN: University of Notre Dame Press.

3

Being Worship, Being Eucharist

ALISON MILBANK

We live in unprecedented times in that the centrality of Holy Communion is being questioned in the Church of England as never before. This contrasts with the great Protestant reformers, who sought to establish more frequent reception of the sacrament, a desire also at the heart of the Evangelical Revival of the early nineteenth century, following in the wake of John Wesley, who believed that 'It is the duty of every Christian to receive the Lord's Supper as often as he can' (Wesley, vol. II, p. 106). The statement produced by the evangelical Keele Congress of 1967 laments that: 'We have failed to do justice in our practice to the twin truths that the Lord's Supper is the main service of the people of God, and that the local church, as such, is the unit within which it is properly ministered' (Gray, p. 147).

Yet since the *Mission-Shaped Church* report of 2004, mission and the traditions and practices of the Church, of which the Eucharist is one, have been seen as disconnected or even at variance. In Robert Chapman's 2014 doctoral study on the Eucharist in the wake of the report, one of his interviewees remarked: 'I think at times eucharistic-based worship can be at the exclusion of proclamation ... Holy Communion is more to do with fellowship and community, and a unifying act, rather than a missional act' (Chapman, p. 209).

In 2014, Chapman found a number of Anglican clerics for whom the sacrament was personally meaningful, but who denied its value as evangelism. I wonder whether this personal devotion still holds, since it appears that many resource churches do not advertise the Eucharist at all, while in the Truro diocese pastoral reorganization, Communion by Extension is being rolled out as a substitute, 'for those who would benefit from this spiritual food', which assumes some people do not (Kerrier Deanery Plan, p. 6).

For at least one diocese the Eucharist is seen as 'maintenance' rather than mission, and since mission has become so central a feature of Anglican policy, this sidelines the Sacrament completely. This situation is concerning, for no institution can flourish if it denigrates its central activity and it creates a gulf between congregations and the hierarchy. For ever since the 1950s Parish and People Movement, most parishes have enjoyed the Eucharist as their central rite and seen their identity as liturgical communities. Moreover, prior to that Holy Communion was available regularly at the 'early service' or as an add-on to Matins in all traditions.

While it is possible to deform the Eucharist into a horizontal event of communal bonding as Chapman's interviewee suggested, or over-emphasize its ritual performance at the expense of its proclamation, I want to argue in this chapter that in its essential character, the Eucharist is a wholly evangelistic act and, indeed, a protection against the instrumentalization of mission. I shall explore this through the idea of gift, which is both biblical and central to the liturgical movement of the later twentieth century.

The Eucharist makes the Church

Embedded within St Paul's first letter to the Corinthians is the earliest formula of the words of institution:

> For I received from the Lord what I also handed on to you, that the Lord Jesus on the night when he was betrayed took a loaf of bread, and when he had given thanks, he broke it and said, 'This is my body that is for you. Do this in remembrance of me.' In the same way he took the cup also, after supper, saying, 'This cup is the new covenant in my blood. Do this, as often as you drink it, in remembrance of me.' For as often as you eat this bread and drink the cup, you proclaim the Lord's death until he comes. (1 Cor. 11.23–26)

The first point to make is that the Eucharist is received 'from the Lord'. It is his command – 'do this' – and we must obey. Unless we think that Our Lord's actions and instructions are to be separated out between the missional and the communitarian, which would be nonsensical, this is the strongest possible authority for the importance and centrality of the Eucharist to the life of the Church. Second, we know from Acts, Paul's writings and the *Didache* that the early Christians were, indeed, constituted as the Church by their meeting for 'the breaking of bread and the prayers ... And ... the Lord added to their number' (Acts 2.42,

47); by observing this common life, people were drawn to faith, and can be today. Third, and following on from this, the passage demonstrates that eucharistic tradition is evangelism because it is a handing on of the divine command and proclamation that we have received. Fourth, Paul reveals here that the gospel proclamation was enacted in the Church long before the New Testament existed. Indeed, the biblical critic Etienne Trocmé argues that the passion narratives emerge from early Christian ritual practice, not vice versa (Trocmé, p. 82).

Henri de Lubac's celebrated adage that 'the Eucharist makes the Church' (de Lubac, p. 37) is then really biblical. We find out who we are and our missional task through this sacrament, as those who 'proclaim the Lord's death until he comes'. The Eucharist *is* proclamation. In the words of Cardinal Toppo, Archbishop of Ranchi, it is 'the symbolic recapitulation of Jesus's life which reached completion in the total self-gift of himself by dying on the cross' (Toppo). The salvific acts of God in creation and redemption are proclaimed by word and by action, as the story of self-giving is told through that same gift which is offered to us here and now. The Eucharist takes us deeply into the paschal mystery in which the Church was birthed from the cross through the blood and water that poured from Christ's side: our life flows from the waters of baptism and the blood of the Eucharist.

Moreover, two key resurrection appearances in Luke and John make quasi-eucharistic actions the mode of recognition of the risen Christ. In Luke 24, the two disciples travelling to Emmaus receive an explanation of Christ's death and how it fits with the Jewish Scriptures from Christ himself, but they do not recognize him until he breaks bread with them. In John 21, Christ calls from the lakeside, '"Come and have breakfast." Now none of the disciples dared to ask him, "Who are you?" because they knew it was the Lord' (John 21.12). They recognize Christ in that eucharistic invitation. If we too therefore seek an encounter Christ, we must come to the Eucharist. As on the way to Emmaus, biblical proclamation is incomplete without this participation. We must, if you like, show as well as tell.

Jesus continues his mission of self-giving love then through the Eucharist, which makes the Church and offers us, in Richard Hooker's words, 'a real participation of Christ and of life in his body and blood by means of this sacrament' (Hooker, vol. II, p. 81). It is the means whereby we are made one and re-membered as his body. For in remembering him we ourselves are remembered. Jessica Martin finishes her moving series of meditations on the Sacrament in modernity by speaking of death as the point when all that is left is 'the remembrance God makes of us' (Martin, p. 116). All that can sustain us then is the body and blood of Christ and how far we have allowed our imperfect, fragmented experiences to be caught up into his action. The Church today is vulnerable and divided, but all that can be taken up into the breaking of the bread and our unity shown in that very acknowledgement of brokenness.

Eucharist as gift

Gift-giving in some form is a part of every human society and is readily understood. If we give well, we offer something of ourselves in the present we choose; the gift of a handmade card makes it doubly precious to the recipient. We also seek to match our own tastes and preferences with those of the person to whom we make the present. The Eucharist describes and enacts the gift of Christ to the world, in his incarnation fitted to our need and in its culmination in the death on the cross. In this gift, the giver gives his whole self in the act of donation, and thereby Christ reveals the self-giving nature of the holy Trinity. And what is God's mission but this act of self-donation, which we must share? There can be no lack in God, so his mission can never have the anxiety and functionalism that can too easily shape our own evangelism. 'Father, forgive them', is all Christ says about those who crucify him as his self-giving flowers in the grim theatre of Calvary.

If we want unbelievers to learn anything of God it is surely this unfailing action of self-offering love towards us, and nothing reveals it so powerfully as the Eucharist. Prayer B of *Common Worship* expresses it beautifully: 'He opened wide his arms for us on the cross', words that elaborate 'he extended his hands in suffering' from the anaphora in the *Apostolic Constitutions* (*Common Worship*, p. 188; *Constitutions*, p. 489). New Atheism seeks to present Christianity as an instrument of power and subjugation, while followers of Nietzsche by contrast call Christianity's embrace of humility manipulative and a kind of wallowing in suffering for the guilt it can engender. The Eucharist answers the argument of New Atheism by the force of its enactment of Christ's serene putting aside of power, and the Nietzschean by the fact of a sacrifice that is an act of pure donation and no transactional bargain. There is, moreover, no guilt engendered by the eucharistic prayer; it is rather a piece of work in which Christ's pain is not dwelt on but part of the flow of self-giving. Even in the more penitentiary language of the Book of Common Prayer, the absolute nature of Christ's action – 'a full, perfect and sufficient sacrifice, oblation and satisfaction for the sins of the whole world' – with its weighty tread allows no room for guilt because the job is done. The Sacrament is effective enacted apologetics.

So far we have been considering the human side of Christ's self-offering: the gift to us. Yet the heart of Christ's life is primarily one of self-giving to the Father. That is the nature of the life of the second Person of the Trinity, which finds its way into historical expression in the life of Jesus, completed in the words, 'Father, into your hands I commend my spirit' (Luke 23.46). The Greek word for 'commend', *paratithemi*, can mean 'entrust', but also 'lay before' or 'offer', and so continues the sense of donation (Liddell and Scott, p. 603). The Catholic theologian Maurice de la Taille ecumenically cut across the division between a post-Tridentine conception of Christ making a new sacrifice each mass and the Protestant insistence that the sacrifice was a once-for-all event, by stressing that Christ is always offering himself to his Father: his is an eternal action and one we rely on when we offer our prayers in the name of Jesus, who lives always to make intercession for us (de la Taille, p. 47; Heb. 7.25).

Our participation in the gift

It is here that we begin to see how Christ's gift of himself shapes the mission of his Church. Modern understanding of eucharistic action has returned to Thomas Aquinas's insight that the offering made is Christ's self-giving in which we all as his body also have a part. As the Book of Common Prayer has it, we offer 'ourselves, our souls and bodies, to be a reasonable, holy and lively sacrifice' (p. 309). We do not passively receive the sacrament but rather enter the very dynamic of Christ's self-giving. Here we are part of the self-offering that Christ makes to the Father, which is a costly participation. For the gift we receive is Christ's life, which is one of oblation. The logic of this is that the Eucharist is the conduit and expression of a gift of self-giving that calls us to go beyond ourselves, and again we see the missional nature of the event. As Christ said to Peter after that breaking of bread by the shore: 'feed my sheep' (John 21.17). Our motive for mission is an outworking of this eucharistic participation.

It is something people can understand from the logic of ordinary present-giving. When we give, we expect some return in the form of thanks, not just because it is 'meet and right' to show appreciation of generosity but because a gift has to be given and received. A gift is a mode of connection between giver and receiver, which is embodied in the act of thanksgiving. And the word 'eucharist' means thanksgiving. The journalist G. K. Chesterton found his way to Christianity partly because he felt a need to say 'thank you' for existence. He wrote:

> The test of all happiness is gratitude; and I felt grateful, but I hardly knew to whom. Children are grateful when Santa Claus puts in their stockings gifts of toys or sweets. Could I not be grateful to Santa Claus when he put in my stockings the gift of two miraculous legs? (Chesterton, p. 82).

It is significant that even the most secular junior school will want to request a Christian assembly for harvest because it is a human need to exist in a relation of gratitude. To be eucharist is our human fulfilment.

And part of our thanks in the Eucharist is to accept the gift of being loved by God and our dependence on him for his acts of creation and redemption. This acknowledgement makes us recipients as well as sharers in the offering; we are also the gift received. In his upper room discourse Christ says: 'Father, I desire that those also, whom you have given me, may be with me where I am' (John 17.24). So we are called to give ourselves away and this begins in worship which, as Rowan Williams, puts it, is 'the culminating and fulfilling form of self-dispossession or self-giving' (Williams, p. 50) in an exchange where we are caught up in generative acts of giving and receiving.

The Spirit's gift of Communion

The last quotation from Christ's priestly prayer reminds us how eucharistic theology pervades John's Gospel, expressed often through Christ's complex weaving of chains of interconnection: 'As you, Father, are in me and I am in you, may they also be in us, so that the world may believe that you have sent me. The glory that you have given me I have given them, so that they may be one, as we are one' (John 17.21–22). The union in Christ of the eucharistic community is here shown to be a witness, 'so that the world may believe'. Local churches have this unity of interdependence in their bones. They may not be able to articulate it, but it lies behind their distress at eucharistic infrequency or removal.

It is what renders a disparate group of people one, as their group identity is 'in Christ'. The truth or 'message' of Christianity is inextricably bound to a form of life, which is why the practices that form us are the gospel we proclaim.

The unity brought by Holy Communion is brought by the Holy Spirit and it begins the rite as priest and people exchange greetings within the Spirit: 'The Lord be with you / and also with you.' It is, of course, in the Spirit that we pray at all, and modern liturgies have brought out the importance of the eucharistic *epiclesis*, in which the Spirit is invoked to actualize the transformation of the elements. The Holy Spirit moves upon the bread and wine as at the Creation, to bring life. And it is the Spirit who acts dynamically in the soul to reorder our desires under Christ's headship to divinize us: to make us holy and unite us ever more closely to Christ. And while only full participation can effect these things, they are proclaimed and enacted in full sight of everyone. The first invitation Jesus makes in John's Gospel is 'Come and see' (John 1.39), and if seeing provokes in an unbeliever a hunger for a deeper participation, the Spirit will have done her missional work.

The Eucharist as justice

The act of communion is not given us just for our personal sustenance but for a union in which we become the gift. I have argued that the whole of the Eucharist is missional, but it culminates in our being sent out in the power of the Spirit. Stanley Hauerwas has long taught that done properly, the Eucharist is a witness against the powers of this world. This belief that eucharistic participation prompts us to further transformative action goes all the way back to John Chrysostom in the fourth century:

> Do you want to honour Christ's body? Then do not scorn him in his nakedness, nor honour him here in the church with silken garments while neglecting him outside where he is cold and naked. For he who said: 'This is my body', and made it so by his words, also said: 'You saw me hungry and did not feed me, and inasmuch as you did not do it for one of these, the least of my brothers, you did not do it for me'.
> (John Chrysostom, p. 313)

Seeing this social action as an outworking of our participation in Christ's self-offering prevents it from being mere social work but makes it rather a continuation of worship. There is a danger in these times when social justice initiatives form such a central part of mission strategies that we can baptize almost any activity as 'Kingdom building'. We forget that human beings cannot build God's Kingdom; if they try, they will end up with the tower of Babel. Any real transformative actions or services to the community must be outworkings of our eucharistic giftedness to prevent them from being transactional, idolatrous or secular. Intercessory prayer, a central part of the Communion, is where the impetus to action should begin, for it is there that we begin the hard work of understanding the needs and concerns of our locality and imagining what help we can give. I have witnessed this in action in a number of ordinary Anglican churches, and studies such as the *Holistic Mission* report of 2013 reveal that 81% of those regular worshippers surveyed were engaged in such work (Blond and Noyes, p. 3). Liturgical community naturally finds its fulfilment in works of mercy. But the Eucharist, in enacting an act of injustice that is taken up into God's just purposes, which far exceed it, reveals that justice is more than giving everyone their due: it is God's own righteousness, which alone can restore disordered relationships. Benedict XVI compared this eucharistic justice to:

> A sort of 'nuclear fission', to use an image familiar to us today, which penetrates to the heart of all being, a change meant to set off a process which transforms reality, a process leading ultimately to the transfiguration of the entire world, to the point where God will be all in all. (Benedict XVI, #11)

Missional suggestions

Part of the reason why some Anglicans fail to celebrate the Eucharist is that they do not acknowledge this transformational potential and therefore believe the rite has no meaning for outsiders, as it is too alien. And yet I know individuals whose faith has been woken by attending a Eucharist, a tendency that goes all the way back to those tenth-century Russian emissaries who were sent to find the best form of religion to embrace and were transported by the worship in Hagia Sophia in Constantinople: 'We did not know where we were, on heaven or on earth; and do not know how to tell about this. All we know is that

God lives there with people' (Hatzidakis, p. 50). In our secular world, all worship is as strange to outsiders as that Orthodox liturgy, but its very mystery and otherness can be transformative. A peaceful simple Communion in the round can be experienced as just as transporting and as 'other' as a glorious sung mass, for both are about the business of God, intent on doing the work. This confidence in something that we just do because Christ told us takes the attention away from us and our liturgical creativity and puts the focus on God himself, the true actor of the drama. And there are ways we could bring out some of the more missional aspects of the Eucharist, both for the understanding of the faithful and to make the Eucharist more meaningful to those as yet unbaptized.

1. Defamiliarizing the secular

Defamiliarization is a term used by Russian formalist critics to talk about the way a literary text can make language strange and help us to see the world in new ways, and which, I have argued, is also a key evangelistic strategy to disturb people's assumption that the material world is all there is (Milbank, p. 31). We can use liturgy creatively to make people see things differently; for example, by celebrating Holy Communion in unexpected or secular settings. In the USA, where capital punishment is still legal in some states, Anglicans gather to celebrate the Eucharist outside the prison gates on the morning of an execution. A priest told me how he was moved to celebrate it while on holiday in Ibiza, when everyone comes out to view the glorious sunset over the sea. He and a friend celebrated it on some rocks on the beach and over 30 people joined them. A local church in Wantage took the Eucharist outside to the market square by the statue of King Alfred, to mark Alfredfest, using bread baked (and burned) by a local bakery. In all three cases, the unexpectedness of the event served to allow the sacred to break the limits of the secular, to demonstrate that there is nowhere God is not. These are small examples of that 'nuclear fission' that transforms reality and begins to win back the world for Christ, and which is incalculable in its reach and effect.

2. The Eucharistic bread and the holy loaf

One reason the Eucharist is considered non-missional is that the non-baptized are excluded from receiving the sacrament. I think this argument fails to realize the multiple ways in which someone from outside the faith might feel an outsider in the most informal, non-sacramental worship. It also ignores the fact that this very exclusion can be evangelistic in evoking a desire for something so meaningful to those who participate in it. Indeed, it offers a gateway into belonging. Moreover, in the Christian eucharistic tradition there are also resources to include everyone in some kind of participation through various kinds of blessed bread. In the medieval Church, each household would take it in turns to bring a loaf to be shared at the end of the service by everyone. Special prayers were said for the family, the loaf was blessed and then cut up and distributed (Duffy, p. 125). In the Greek tradition, one large loaf, the *prosphora*, is used for multiple purposes. One section is used for consecration, while others are offered to the saints, with a final part reserved for everyone at the end of the service, or those who do not receive communion. These breads may have been developed for situations of infrequent communion but they have a particular value in our own secularized age, because it means that we can offer bread to everyone to share, without giving Holy Communion to those who have not been baptized and prepared. It also brings back something of the ancient love feast to our eucharistic practice.

Indeed, to accompany the Eucharist once again with a meal on occasions would bring out its importance in expressing the hospitality and gift-giving of God. The genius of the Alpha course lies in its meal setting, which bonds people as they learn together, and the Common Table movement has the same powerful message of hospitality and inclusion. We have lost something of the abundance of the love feast in reducing it to instant coffee and indifferent biscuits after a service. The parish I attended in Virginia always had fruit punch out of a big silver bowl, which was much more festive and not expensive, with regular Sunday bring-and-share meals, which also embody that reciprocity of giving and receiving.

If the Eucharist is to speak missionally beyond its immediate participants, then we might also consider reviving the use of actual bread, which tastes and smells good and embodies the nourishing nature of the sacrament, fulfilling Psalm 34.8: 'O taste and see that the LORD is good.'

Traditionally, the Western Church used unleavened bread in imitation of the Passover, with which several of the Gospels associate the Last Supper, while the Eastern Church continues to use leavened bread, recalling the teaching of Christ that his disciples should be yeast in the social loaf. Whether leavened or unleavened, a commercial white-sliced loaf, however, will not do. We should use nourishing home-baked bread, which could be offered by anyone. Indeed, its provision can become a way of drawing newcomers into closer relation, with recipe and prayer instructions provided to them. Or in imitation of Coptic churches, which often have an oven near the sanctuary, we could use the church kitchen to bake the bread, so that the smell fills the building.

3. Extending the offertory

It would be symbolically powerful to bring up a freshly baked loaf in an offertory procession. This custom is an important development from the Parish and People movement in which the Church's participation in Christ's offering of himself to the Father is expressed by lay people bringing up the bread and wine as representative of our priestly returning the world back to God. This ritual could be deepened in meaning by extending what is brought up. People might bring up symbols of their work, for example, or their creativity in the form of arts and crafts, including work made by children of the congregation. Symbols of the local church's outreach could also be brought forward, like the week's offerings to the food bank and perhaps even items representing the challenges faced by the community. Individuals can announce briefly what they bring as symbols are handed over. The important idea that this conveys is that we are part of the gift of Christ's offering to the Father and that there is nothing we cannot bring of ourselves. For that which we bring, whether bread or person, comes to be remade, reordered by the Spirit's action.

There are many other small ways, particular to context, in which the local Eucharist can develop its own missional potential, but they will naturally express the giving, receiving and handing on of the divine economy of gift that I have described. And although it is the Eucharist that is put under missional scrutiny today, perhaps it should be the other way round. Do we consider what mission is for? The Eucharist is there to proclaim, to transform us and the world and to witness to Christ's saving action, and these are also the purposes of mission. Furthermore, mission will be strongest when it is eucharistic, full of gratitude for what God has done, and rooted in the sacraments that Christ has given us, which form us and make us the Eucharist we proclaim. Secularization and church weakness should turn us back to the Eucharist as embodying our mission, for as Stanley Hauerwas and Sam Wells remind us:

> When serious challenges arise, which the Church must face together, it is to ... the pattern of practices called the Eucharist, that Christians turn. And what they find is an enacted prayer, a prayer that articulates the call to God to rend the heavens and pour down righteousness, and a prayer that at the same time embodies his response. His response is the presence of his Son, the empowerment of his Spirit, and the encouragement of his Word. (Hauerwas and Wells, p. 26)

And they conclude unanswerably: 'Who could ask for anything more?'

References

Benedict XVI, 2007, *Sacramentum Caritatis*, https://www.vatican.va/content/benedict-xvi/en/apost_exhortations/documents/hf_ben-xvi_exh_20070222_sacramentum-caritatis.html.
Book of Common Prayer, 1974, London: Eyre & Spottiswoode.
Blond, Philip and James Noyes, 2013, *Holistic Mission: Social Action and the Church of England*, https://www.respublica.org.uk/our-work/publications/holistic-mission-social-action-church-england/ (accessed 21.05.2024).
Chapman, Robert, 2014, 'Eucharistic Sacrifice as Missionary Gift in Mission-Shaped Church', PhD Dissertation, Archbishop's Examination in Theology.
Chesterton, G. K., 1957 (1908), *Orthodoxy*, London: Bodley Head.
Common Worship: Services and Prayers for the Church of England, 2000, London: Church House Publishing.
Constitutions of the Holy Apostles, 1994, Anti-Nicene Fathers, ed. Alexander Roberts and James Donaldson, Edinburgh: T&T Clark, p. 7.
De la Taille, Maurice, 1930, *The Mystery of Faith and Human Opinion Contrasted and Defined*, London: Sheed & Ward.
De Lubac, Henri, 2006, *Corpus Mysticum: The Eucharist and the Church in the Middle Ages*, trans. Gemma Simmonds CJ and Richard Price, ed. Laurence Hemming and Susan Parsons, London: SCM Press.
Duffy, Eamon, 1992, *The Stripping of the Altars: Traditional Religion in England 1400–1580*, New Haven, CT: Yale University Press.
Gray, Donald, 1986, *Earth and Altar: The Evolution of the Parish Communion in the Church of England to 1945*, Norwich: Canterbury Press.
Hatzidakis, Emmanuel, 2013, *The Heavenly Banquet: Understanding the Divine Liturgy*, Platanias, Greece: Orthodox Witness.

Hauerwas, Stanley and Sam Wells (eds), 2004, *The Blackwell Companion to Christian Ethics*, Oxford: Blackwell.
Hooker, Richard, 1845, *The Laws of Ecclesiastical Polity*, ed. John Keble, 2 vols, Oxford: Oxford University Press.
John Chrysostom, 1991, *Homilies on the Gospel of St Matthew*, ed. Philip Schaff, Nicene and Post-Nicene Fathers, Edinburgh: T&T Clark.
Kerrier Deanery Plan, 2021, https://trurodiocese.org.uk/resources/our-vision/deanery-plans/ (accessed 22.05.2024).
Liddell, H. G. and Robert Scott, 1991, *An Intermediate Greek–English Lexicon*, Oxford: Clarendon Press.
Martin, Jessica, 2023, *The Eucharist in Four Dimensions*, Norwich: Canterbury Press.
Milbank, Alison, 2011, 'Apologetics and the Imagination: Making Strange', in Andrew Davison (ed.), *Imaginative Apologetics: Theology, Philosophy and the Catholic Tradition*, London: SCM Press.
Toppo, Telesphore, 2008, 'The Eucharist and Mission', https://www.vatican.va/roman_curia/pont_committees/eucharist-congr/documents/rc_committ_euchar_doc_20080620_eucar-missione-toppo_en.html (accessed 21.05.2024).
Trocmé, Etienne, 2012, *Passion as Liturgy: A Study in the Passion Narratives of the Four Gospels*, London: SCM Press.
Wesley, John, 1853, *Works*, ed. John Emory, 7 vols, New York: Carlton & Philips.

4

Being Worship: The Tender-hearted community – Why Inclusion Means Interdependence

SHARON PRENTIS

Recently I revisited a long-standing interest in the heart. Not the heart in a physical sense but the heart as a metaphor of something deeper and more central to human will and purpose. While there are many metaphors of the heart used to describe an individual's inner life, there is less thought given to the heart orientation of a group of people. Most ancient cultures know that it is possible to speak with the heart, and this can be a collective endeavour. In business, it is acknowledged that changing organizational culture is not forced from top-down directives from those in positions of authority but through a shared understanding, the 'collective hearts and habits of people and their shared perception of how things are done', based on trust and conviction (see Walker and Soule, 2017). Regarding the Church, the heart of the Christian community is Jesus Christ and the people who work together in faith to fulfil his purpose.

The mission to live life together in accordance with the Kingdom of God is affirmed through a collective vision and a communal will and intent to live out the gospel. Transformed hearts, as described in Scripture (Ezek. 36.26), share certain collective characteristics. According to biblical teachings, transformed hearts are no longer hardened like stone but have become soft and receptive, like flesh. This transformation involves a change at the deepest levels of a person's being, leading to a shift in attitudes, beliefs and behaviours. It signifies a departure from a state of spiritual desolation to one of renewed vitality and receptivity to the divine will to love others. In this way we appreciate that a good heart reflects the character of God. However, the tendency to see such activity as being primarily in the realm of the individual does not speak to the whole experience of life together. Even if an individual's heart is inclined positively towards others, that is only part of the picture. The reality is that Christian virtues are communicated and embodied as part of our collective formation as part of a community. After all, the plural of disciple is church.

In a church community, made up of different people, our central activity concerns embodying the teachings and character of Jesus Christ, which is foundational to our relationships. As such, the heart of the church, its character, should be known by love, compassion, a spirit of generosity and selflessness. It is a place where people should find acceptance, healing and restoration. It is a community that reaches out to the marginalized, the broken and the lost, embodying the agape love sentiment and divine grace of Jesus Christ. The heart of the church beats with a desire to serve, to share the good news of the gospel and to have influence in the wider world. It is a place of worship, prayer and spiritual growth, where individuals are nurtured and equipped to live out their faith. Despite differences, which can be viewed both as gifts and potential sources of discord, the community heart must beat as one. If we are to encourage a radical welcome that embraces difference, then a keen sense of what it means to be interdependent and to share values is required, listening beyond the surface to others' views, concerns and experiences. As Angie Hong contends, listening within our worship communities to personal struggles and systemic injustices that perpetuate separation is a radical act of reconciliation (Hong, p. 132).

It is crucial to understand that breaking down barriers requires more than just acknowledging who is (or is not) in the group, rather how the group changes to accommodate others. The hard work of living in community means being prepared to bridge the seemingly impossible gap between perspectives, opinions and policies to find out what it means to be the beloved community (Butler, p. 9). While some consideration has been given to being an ally and how those who don't share the same life experiences can be allies through empathy and thereby foster interdependence, being tender-hearted means to feel and understand another's experiences deeply, creating a safe space for listening, being present, genuinely supporting each other and being willing to give away the benefits and deconstruct powers that are so easily assumed by the privileged.

For the theologian Dietrich Bonhoeffer, living in community starts with being attentive. He wrote: 'The first service that one owes to others in the fellowship consists in listening to them. Just as the love of God begins with listening to his word, the beginning of love for our brothers and sisters is learning to listen to them' (Bonhoeffer, p. 97). Bonhoeffer's assertion emphasizes the importance of relationships based on empathy gained from listening to another. In that context, the church community prioritizes building strong relationships with one another and actively seeks to understand and support each other in times of need. In a world that often glorifies individualism, the Christian community is a countercultural force that lives out interconnectedness before God. The collective effort to be one body that listens and learns arises from this desire, a living testament to the interconnectedness God envisions for humanity. However, it's important to note that there is also room for individual and unique contributions as we participate in the body of Christ. This recognition of individuality (as in gifts) *and* collectivity (as those gifts are expressed through the Church and beyond) promotes a deeper understanding of what it means to be in fellowship with one another, where people are attuned to each other's needs. This is a tender-hearted, inclusive and interdependent community.

Vision, strategy and hope

The current strategic priority in the Church of England is captured in the strapline that envisions the future church becoming 'Younger and more Diverse' (see https://www.churchofengland.org/about/vision-strategy/our-priorities/younger-and-more-diverse) and, recognizing that missional priority must focus on these characteristics, resources are aligned to them. What is not acknowledged in the detailed implementation is that there are three groups missing: those who are younger, those who are diverse and those who belong to both groups. Diversity as a characteristic of the Kingdom of God is simply taken for granted with little effort to create contexts that allow people to flourish. Talking about diversity does not bring it about any more than producing data on the current situation. What is known is that the intentional inclusion of people from different backgrounds enriches community life through the sharing of experiences and perspectives to the benefit of everyone (Butler, p. 9).

However, in the current plans the emphasis has been predominantly on 'younger' and relatively little strategic comment has been made about other aspects of diversity. Despite an emphasis by the Church on racial justice, there is a tangible separation between the articulation in the mainstream strategic vision and how it is implemented. Attending to inequity is integral and not an add-on. Strategy involves determining the best course of action based on informed decisions, so a sense of corporate responsibility towards one another is precious. It is often easier to discuss the individual rather than consider our collective responsibility for our collective formation. Dismantling structures, changing cultures that exclude and marginalize, is not usually the first response to what it means to be tender-hearted towards one another.

Searching questions come from deep introspection and the willingness to engage with those who may not already belong to our faith communities. As in the story of the emperor who had no clothes, the temerity of the truth speaks to the reality of our situation. Much of what we do can be seen as superficial, avoiding the difficult conversations about the strength of commitment and the discomfort that inevitably accompanies transformation. How to have these conversations is not part of our strategic plans. For any assembly of believers who do not reflect those who live around them, the question is quite simple – Why? What is it about us that does not convey God's heart? What is it about our collective heart as a Church that cannot speak forth the power of love? How do we hold both the individual requirement to cultivate a heart after God's while at the same time understanding the contribution of everyone to collectively reflecting God's heart? As the Church, the aspiration to be younger and more diverse is part of missional plans and strategies, but is it deep into our collective consciousness and heart?

Over the last 50 years the migration stories of global peoples who entered English churches in the early 1950s, 1960s (and later) still make people shudder. Those early settlers who had been brought up as Anglican communicants in their countries of origin before migrating to Britain did not always receive a warm Church welcome. The hospitality offered was not as they were led to believe, and their reception was lukewarm at best, if not cool. This was the direct opposite of expectations and further propelled a considerable drift away over the years. Subsequent migrants arrived and created their own churches in which they could be authentically themselves. Thus began a separation that only now is being acknowledged and addressed.

As humans we are hard-wired for connection and long for meaningful attachment, not just because of the comfort of being loved, known and accepted as ourselves but to avail ourselves of the opportunity to receive love from someone else. The need to connect is innate; we cannot communicate without it. So the strength and well-being of any group are directly correlated to the level of support provided by one another – we all need a sense of belonging and collective purpose. Those individuals who come together around a common cause have founded social causes and movements whose ripples have made an impact beyond their immediate spheres of influence. The Church, as the communal body of Christ, is deeply rooted in the presence of Christ among the people and the profound connections forged with one another. As the adage goes, 'No person is an island'; this sentiment holds particular significance when contemplating the intricate interconnectedness of our lives. Consequently there is an intention to ensure that the Church reflects everyone and that special efforts are made to welcome those missing groups. This inclusive approach is crucial in fostering interconnectedness and love within the community. Much has been written about why the Church is unable to attract people, explanations ranging from postmodern malaise, lack of credibility and interest, failure to address its own historical involvement in chattel slavery, elitism and specific postcolonial postures that resulted in suspicion and people being disenfranchised. Acknowledging these conditions is part of the work that concerns contrition and repentance and paves the way towards reconciling hearts.

If the heart of the Christian community is indeed its people, then being attentive to what's needed for the diverse family of God to flourish together under God is vital to authentic transmission of the gospel. I grew up in a small community church. It was a place where the disposition of the heart mattered and, more importantly, the notion of the heart not just being singular but collective. As a small church with few resources, sharing was encouraged. The preacher spoke of our hearts for the poor and those on the margins, our hearts for the community and the lost (mission), and our hearts for Christ not only as a solo endeavour but as a collective. We were encouraged to guard our hearts not just as individuals but as the corporate body of Christ – to be responsible for the safekeeping of our most precious aspect, the sensitivity towards God and one another.

I didn't realize it then but, as the child of immigrants, the need to work together due to limited resources and share what we had was our lived reality. We lived in a hostile environment and needed to be aware so that we did not react in ways that internalized rejection causing the opposite of a tender heart. Paying close attention to the dynamics of how power is mediated is of concern to the tender-hearted community because, as Stephanie Spellers points out, those on the margins know the importance of power, mostly because institutional power is so often withheld from them. They know there can be no genuine, radical welcome without a sharing of power (Spellers, p. 145).

One area where promoting a shared perspective is in a collective tender heart, is in worship. In contemporary society, individualism often takes precedence, continually emphasizing the power of one or of a few select people. However, Scripture presents an alternative narrative. We are encouraged to love one another unconditionally and be willing to sacrifice our desires, and even our lives, for the sake of others (John 15.13). This love extends beyond words to encompass the act of setting aside power and privilege to uplift and enable others to thrive. It compels us to walk together at a pace that ensures no one, especially the most vulnerable or young, is left behind. God invites us into a relationship with him and one another, regardless of our diverse backgrounds, cultures and races. This invitation allows us to build genuine connections and learn from one another, ultimately deepening our relationship with God. To truly embrace this invitation we must trust in one another and challenge societal norms that breed racism and prejudice.

Interconnectedness in Christ – towards a tender-hearted community

A tender-hearted community, then, actively seeks to understand its members through cultivating an environment where concerns are heard and addressed. Being our brothers' and sisters' keepers inevitably means engaging deeply with one another's joys and sorrows. As Paul writes in Romans 12.15: 'Rejoice with those who rejoice; mourn with those who mourn.' Mutual empathy is the bedrock of a loving community. The early Church's witness of loving one another so the world would know they were Christ's disciples (John 13.35, NIV) remains a powerful testimony to the Kingdom of God. In a fractured world, Christ's call is to be a beacon of light through living out hope, love and reconciliations, which means continually embodying the gospel in our actions, words and relationships.

This sentiment echoes throughout the Scriptures and the teachings of Jesus, emphasizing that our lives are intertwined in a divine tapestry of relationships and mutual support. However, it's more challenging than it sounds. Wherever there is a group of people, there are opportunities to seriously misunderstand. Consider what it means to overcome suspicion and love unconditionally. It is taken for granted that this will be an easy part of our corporate life together, but we must *work* at living together. There is an assumption that if we hold views that don't concur with those of others we can ignore them and go on to form deep relationships. That is not the case. Unfortunately we live in a culture saturated with notions of superiority that emphasize differences and measure our humanity against idealized standards that aren't biblical. Living in a community requires an openness to alternative perspectives, even when they differ from our own. Jesus exemplified this by washing his disciples' feet (John 13.1–17).

This powerful example of service and humility is an illustration of tender-heartedness to others. By washing another individual's feet, we step into their world, comprehend their struggles and offer genuine support. Building such a community necessitates intentional effort and is not instantaneous. In the Anglican tradition we emphasize the collective efforts of the 'whole people of God' to embody the gospel afresh in every age. The early Church, as depicted in the book of Acts, adapted accordingly shared their possessions, supported one another and loved so profoundly that individuals were drawn to them daily (Acts 2.47). Although the New Testament does not provide a specific cultural model for the contemporary Church, it does emphasize the authority of the apostolic witness as having a heart for others. We should be careful not to rigidly replicate ancient structures but rather to adapt and innovate under the guidance of God's Spirit. The theologian Carl Braaten suggests there is no normative biblical church order into which they all fit. He highlights the danger of replicating and absolutizing ancient structures and forms for today's churches and fellowships, and argues that the early Church was granted freedom to adapt and innovate under the guidance of God's Spirit (Braaten, p. 132).

Ultimately, by prioritizing love, acceptance and trust within our communities we can work towards the realization of God's Kingdom on earth. This requires continuously examining and challenging the disparities and divisions within our congregations and actively seeking reconciliation and unity among believers. As Paul wrote (Eph. 4.15–16, NIV): 'Instead, speaking the truth in love, we will grow to become in every respect the mature body of him who is the head, that is, Christ. From him the whole body, joined and held together by every supporting ligament, grows and builds itself up in love, as each part does its work.'

Essentially, the term 'reconciling' is a progressive verb to indicate this is something that will have to continually be worked out because the tendency towards marginalization is so profoundly ingrained; however, the whole story of redemption means that continuing act of reflection of repentance can help to be a posture of working towards the ultimate realization of all groups of people. This is why worship is so important: because God together leads to healing. The heart of a Christian community is Christ and his people. It is a community that mirrors the interconnectedness God desires for humanity, marked by self-sacrifice, vulnerability and intentional relationships.

Affirming identity in the tender-hearted community

Guided by the African viewpoint that 'There is no me without us', we come to a profound understanding that our identities are not isolated entities but are deeply intertwined with communal relationships. These relationships, which foster mutual flourishing and build interdependence, teach us that we are being built together. Whatever affects one affects all, and our welfare is intricately tied to the well-being of others. This is the enlightening nature of fellowship. A general appreciation that all people bear the image of God but are not treated equally, and that some are subject to injustices that permeate social relationships and structures, is key. A practical example is the Church's pivotal role in advocating for social justice. A community that stands against all injustice and acknowledges that disparities that diminish another human being are not of God demonstrates its commitment to the collective good. Moreover, in the affirmation of identity as God's creations wonderfully made, a willingness to bring ourselves as a gift to the community is implicit, which is about acceptance – environment which accepts that gift – no matter how outside our normal sphere of experience. Our differences are a source of strength but they require us to keep our hearts open to all diligently. In doing so a church's emphasis on acceptance and inclusivity makes each one of us feel valued and included.

Drawing near to Christ and one another

As we draw near to Christ we inevitably draw closer to one another. Christ's love compels us to break down barriers, build bridges and seek unity in diversity. This transformative love reshapes our relationships, making us more empathetic, compassionate and committed to one another's well-being. The early Church's profound love for one another was so exceptional that it became evident to the world that they were, indeed, disciples of Jesus (John 13.35). How did they do this? The clue is in their life together as a worshipping community. Bible study and preaching further shape the communal identity of the hearers who hear as a group.

As a result, a better collective understanding in community develops. Without communal formation, personal formation is affected: development as a disciple is limited without others. In the storytelling process described by Chris Howson, participants are asked to remember and share their thoughts and memories about a story. This technique allows for different interpretations and outcomes, leading to deep insights based on the fact that Jesus used stories to provide insight into the Kingdom of God and provoke reactions from the disciples. All aspects of the text are open to question, allowing for the exploration of long-standing difficulties and questions. People are respectful towards each other, often engaging with new perspectives and making discoveries (see Howson, 2011).

The individual, organizational and institutional, though different, are linked. All aspire to reflect the love of God and witness to a greater reality of the Kingdom, but to what degree? Institutional ways of being and culture may attempt to, by their process, procedures and structures, implement ways that develop, but if at the individual level the heart does not see the need or is unwilling, things will stay the same. Likewise, suppose the individual perceives the need for transformation and is willing to change heart but the organization, in its rigidity of attitude and thought, can't extend the grace. In that case, it thwarts attempts to usher in something different, and nothing changes. Organizations are not neutral; therefore, the heart or core values must move from maxims and words on paper to embodied reality.

Intentional relationships and embracing the unfamiliar

Nevertheless it is crucial to move away from any view of community that emphasizes uniformity and assimilation of difference. Preferable is an approach that is intentional in cultivating diverse relationships and is comfortable embracing the unfamiliar and eagerly listens to God with and through others. A Christian community is intentional in its relationships, determined to discern the mind of Christ among its people. Doing this together is a challenging task for the group. God does not discriminate. This means appreciating that divine wisdom is a quality anyone can possess and being willing to encourage, arbitrate and hold each other accountable.

The Church's role in advocating for social justice is paramount. A community that stands against racial injustice or economic disparity demonstrates its commitment to the collective good while respecting individual identities. Striking this balance is integral to cultivating a community that faithfully mirrors Christ's heart. For example, consider a church community where different people are welcomed. A tenderhearted community feels keenly what is required to increase a sense of belonging. Such radical welcome is held collectively but enacted individually as everyone takes responsibility for living radical welcome beyond the personal and interpersonal level that goes deep into the very marrow of congregational life, thus living out faithfully what it means to make room for others (Spellers, p. 157).

In Acts 2, there is an example of a community coming together and anticipating a supernatural encounter, which resulted in them gaining the ability to understand and communicate in different languages. While we may not anticipate miraculous translations today, we can aspire to attain a deep understanding of one another inspired by the Holy Spirit. The ability to truly listen and comprehend was bestowed upon everyone, leading to a deeper understanding that transcended everyday human experience. This raises the question of what this means for us today. As we come together to worship and seek to understand what it means to be connected as brothers and sisters, we also strive to share the good news with others.

The ability to envision arises from our hearts, allowing us to reimagine different possibilities surpassing our current reality's limitations. Individually, our dreams will be confined by our limited imaginations. However, when a group shares a collective dream and vision, it has the power to bring that vision to life. To achieve this, everyone must be willing to play their part and support the shared vision. Unfortunately this doesn't always happen, as a few individuals can unintentionally hinder the dream due to expectations and the apathy of the majority. To make the shared vision a reality it is essential for everyone involved to understand that it is not just about achieving specific outcomes but also about believing that equity, diversity and inclusion are not only possible but are the reality of the Kingdom of heaven. God acknowledged being amid all peoples' expressions of love and solidarity and said that being a disciple is not just an individual adventure but one done in a relationship with others. Therefore the Trinitarian aspects of mutual, reciprocal love come out.

An African saying is that to travel fast, one travels alone and to travel far, one travels together; but travelling together also means being aware of each other's needs. This journey is done with a sense of being led by God, following Christ inspired by the Spirit and being attentive to those around us on the journey. A diverse congregation is more aware of this than one that's made up of similar people because diversity provides an opportunity to be attentive to difference and see it not as an impediment but as a way for people to learn what it is to understand those elements of humanity that shape our selves, elements that have been given as part of our ways of being and which can be offered to God. Communities are created only by what they have in common. Still, those things that are different and the attempts to empathize with one another and develop a sense of value, which ultimately come in, have value for everybody concerned. However, it is not easy or taken for granted that this automatically happens. It requires a level of awareness and understanding so that an intentional approach can be part of the relationships that develop and the maturity that comes with appreciating what God might be doing through various members of the Church as the body of Christ.

How we worship together is also an opportunity to be exposed to what God might be saying through different people. In her book *The Next Worship: Glorifying God in a Diverse World*, Sandra Maria Van Opstal speaks of why it is important to worship together and some of the tensions and difficulties that can arise. When it comes to worshipping together, she tells the story of leading worship for a group. She introduces some songs from Swaziland, where she had worshipped with those who had worked with people living with HIV. Such a collective act of worship across cultures was a way of connecting deeply with citizens and brothers and sisters who are doing ministry and mission in challenging circumstances. Yet there was a sense of hope because they followed their saviour by working together and supporting working in a particular area as a sense of collaboration and partnership, which is both honouring and not paternalistic. Still, it's a way of sharing in ministry together, so learning songs in a native language engenders a sense of interdependence and mutuality, which singing songs in one language would not. It is an opportunity to acknowledge the pain and the justice of the world and respond with Christ and hope by the willingness to speak in another language, not because it is a fad or seems like entertainment but as a sincere attempt to identify and empathize with global situations, standing in solidarity, prayer and hope. The reality is that some people might find attempts to do this superficial and a bit clumsy, but the ethos and principle behind it are an attempt to think of and roll alongside another. Sometimes worship should involve everyone; therefore a common language or a liturgical stance is critical. There are times when the effort and the attempt to fully embrace others and acknowledge their own struggle across the world is consistent with being a part of the universal Church. Van Opstal responds to the concern that not everyone can join in singing in different languages with this response: 'We come together as a community for corporate worship so that we are not so focused on our own personal worship ... sorry if it feels authentic to you, it will be the authentic way of the kingdom' (van Opstal, p. 23).

Learning another's heart language or ways of expressing themselves is most evident in worship, and it is an act of humility. The need to forgo our own proclivities and preferences to move beyond our fears and to fully embrace different perspectives in a different way of being, irrespective of the tradition we may have from becoming acquainted with another way of prayer and reverential posture to God, enables us to fully embrace one another in ways that would not usually occur. As Hong, another proponent, asserts, worship also reinforces a sense of identity allowing the expression of unity in 'Divine Love', making justice and reconciliation achievable. When structural divisions persist, Christ's transformative influence motivates us to examine the power dynamics and oppressive systems that strive to keep people apart.

The heart of the Church is people, the diverse community of believers who gather in love and unity; the community that reflects the heart of Jesus, who taught us to love one another as he has loved us. Diverse congregations contribute to a rich tapestry of worship experiences. Worship represents not only the opportunity to come together but also to confront and, to some extent, undermine some of those prevailing notions of what it means to be people who worship God.

References

Bonhoeffer, D., 1954, *Life Together: The Classic Exploration of Christian Community*, trans. John W. Doberstein, New York: Harper & Row.
Braaten, Carl E., 1985, *The Apostolic Imperative: Nature and Aim of the Ministry*, Minneapolis, MN: Augsburg Publishing.
Butler, Amy, 2017, 'Becoming the Beloved Community', in Grace Ji-Sun Kim and Jann Aldredge-Clanton (eds), *Intercultural Ministry: Hope for a Changing World*, Valley Forge, PA: Judson Press, pp. 9ff.

Hong, Angie, 2017, 'Equals at the Table', in Grace Ji-Sun Kim and Jann Aldredge-Clanton (eds), *Intercultural Ministry: Hope for a Changing World*, Valley Forge, PA: Judson Press, pp. 124–33.

Howson, C., 2011, *A Just Church: 21st century Liberation Theology in Action*, London: Continuum.

Spellers, S., 2006, *Radical Welcome: Embracing God, the Other and the Spirit of Transformation*, New York: Morehouse Publishing.

Van Opstal, S. M., 2016, *The Next Worship: Glorifying God in a Diverse World*, Downers Grove, IL: InterVarsity Press.

Walker, Bryan and Sarah A. Soule, 2017, 'Changing Company Culture Requires a Movement, not a Mandate', *Harvard Business Review*, 20 June.

5

On the Ground: Being Worship in the Parish

ANDY SMITH

In his book *The Household of God* the missionary bishop Lesslie Newbigin argued that the identity of the church is both eschatological and missionary (Newbigin, pp. 111–25). He made the case that if a church ceases to be missional it loses its ecclesial identity. The church's missionary identity, as God's instrument in the world, cannot be removed without risking its very nature as church.

Newbigin's work is one of the key theological sources underpinning fresh expressions, pioneering and a fresh call to mission outside the church in the world. The church must be missional. Forty years ago such a statement may have been controversial; now it is widely accepted within our ecclesiology.

In the midst of this argument Newbigin made another point, less referenced but equally significant. He not only stated that the identity of the church is that it is missional but argued that the reverse is also true. He stated: 'An unchurchly mission is as much a monstrosity as an unmissionary church' (Newbigin, p. 148). Newbigin argued that mission (in its broadest sense) must result in ecclesial Jesus communities forming. Mission invites others into a new reality, into a new way of living, as followers of Jesus. The result is the People of God; it is church forming.

So sure, the church must be missional but mission must be 'churchly' too. Seventy years on from this book's publication, we may want to rephrase Newbigin's language but his argument is perhaps more poignant now than when the words were originally published. The church in the UK has lived through a time of great change, as it is responding to a context that is post-colonial (Heaney, pp. 1–10), post Christendom (Brown, pp. 1–15; Newbigin, p. 13) and perhaps now emergingly post-truth (Davis, 2017; Ball, 2017) context. The theological response to this is a fresh understanding that mission is first and foremost an 'identity of God', the *missio Dei* (Bosch, pp. 389–93), rather than a task of the church as it 'sends missionaries across continents'. The church has discovered a new missional need in Western Europe, including within England. The church in the UK is now beginning to receive missionaries from the places it used to send them (Kwiyani, pp. 15–18). There is a fresh emphasis on going out from the church to see where God is at work in the world (Ross and Baker, pp. 5–7, 22–4); there is a new emphasis on contextualization or inculturation into the multitude of subcultures within an atomized society.

Alongside the increased focus on mission in the UK, church attendance continues to decline. In some places the church has become tired; at worst, faith communities are perceived as just about surviving and limping on. Mission has been rediscovered, re-emphasized and celebrated. We commend mission that reflects Kingdom values. But sometimes this means the emphasis on the church and its worshipping life gets lost. The gathering of God's people can become an aim for tomorrow, not a reality for today. Perhaps we are even, in some circumstances, a bit embarrassed about 'church'.

It is now not uncommon to hear about new, exciting pioneering that is focused upon mission and Kingdom, but yet these same initiatives lack a gathered worshipping life. There is often no urgency to this or any concern that this is the case. The necessity becomes for mission to reflect Kingdom values and so no one is really worried if worshipping ecclesial communities of faith ever really develop. Some who feel called to mission are beginning to describe themselves as 'post-church'.

Has the pendulum swung too far? In seeking to discover a call to mission in the UK, have we become a bit embarrassed about the church's core identity as a community at worship? And what does this actually do to the church's mission? Have we lost a sense of expectation that God is still at work in and through the church? Have we lost a sense that the church in worship, frail as it may be, is a sign of the Kingdom and a foretaste of a future reality (Bosch, pp. 374–6)? Have we lost the beautiful eschatological vision of the people of God as the Bride of Christ faithfully waiting for his return (Bosch, pp. 373–4)? If so, Newbigin would say, this is as much a monstrosity as a church without a mission.

David Bosch developed this ecclesiology further. For Bosch, the church is shaped by two centres of gravity. First, it is a community at worship for no other reason than that God is worthy of worship. Second, it is a community of mission that exists for the other. In his seminal book *Transforming Mission*, Bosch described the church as an ellipsis with two foci: 'worship and prayer' and 'mission, service and evangelism' (p. 385). At the heart of the contemporary church you find not a singular purpose but two equal yet distinct identities. Bosch stated that Christian mission has to be 'moored to the church's worship' (p. 385); he was clear that integral to its mission is the gathering around the word and sacrament. He quoted Jürgen Moltmann in arguing that 'without the actual, visible procedure of meeting together, there is no church' (Moltmann, p. 334; Bosch, p. 385). Mission, the visible gathering of the people of God, and worship (including sacraments), are intrinsically linked and inseparable.

During my time as vicar of Ascension, Southampton, we consciously sought to be a community that embodied this dual purpose of *mission* and *worship*. Like a planet orbiting two stars, where there is no singular gravitational centre, mission and worship were central to our shared life. One was not a means to the other or a route to the other; both were of equal importance and significance. This brought a sense of priority to both of these identities. In an era within the wider church marked by anxiety over institutional survival and a targeted focus on growth, an approach that held mission and worship as two equal priorities was liberating for the worshipping life of the church. My experience was that holding these two ecclesial aims in tension within a local parish church community led to health, life, fruitfulness and flourishing.

I served as vicar of Ascension from 2013 until 2020. This was a suburban parish church two miles from the city centre with a population of about 14,000 people. The demographics of this area were diverse but included young professionals, young families and retirees. The parish included part of a large outer urban estate.

The Church of England has the aim of planting 10,000 new worshipping communities as part of its vision and strategy for the 2020s. Alongside this it wants to become a church where *mixed ecology is the norm*. For some, the emphasis on mixed ecology and planting is perceived as a threat to the sustainability of the local parish church. Our experience in Ascension was quite the opposite. Taking an approach of congregational planting and then later church planting within the estate enabled significant cultural change within a local parish. This was urgently needed and would not have been possible with a methodology of incremental change. Planting breathed fresh life into a local community-focused church, resulting in a 'younger and more diverse' church community. It brought renewal and fresh missional life to an ordinary suburban parish church. But primarily what was crucial in this was aligning what was planted as a new congregation with both *mission* and *worship* as its central DNA.

The planting process was integral to all God had in store for the community. During my time as vicar, I witnessed the flourishing of a Jesus community. Like many churches in a post-Christendom context, Ascension had experienced significant decline. Evidence of this could be found in poor Sunday attendance, a significantly ageing congregation, a cultural profile that did not reflect the wider parish, major financial concerns and a retreat from engagement with wider society. There was an urgent need for growth and culture change. The first task was to restructure resources for future mission and ministry. This process wasn't easy. Part of the initial re-ordering process was a detailed review with key stakeholders. Difficult decisions had to be made, which included a daughter church building being closed and sold. This was a risk within this fragile community but entirely necessary for what followed.

Following the restructuring a new worshipping community was planted in the parish. This began to change the narrative of steady decline. The new community grew from 14 people to over 150, in addition to the existing congregation seeing growth. The church became a multigenerational community that included many children, families and students. Over time a new ministry team was recruited (two curates, a Church Army evangelist, three ordinands, a children's and youth worker). A small group structure was established for discipleship, mission and community. We saw fresh engagement with wider society, both locally and internationally; eight individuals within the community explored God's call to ordained ministry and are now either leading churches or training for ordination; the church finances were transformed, allowing new mission and ministry opportunities; fresh engagement with millennials, with schools, with children, with students and with wider society. In addition we re-established the parish partnership with the link parish in rural Uganda.

Our approach as a community is most succinctly described by the mission statement and values. Ascension had as its mission statement: 'Inviting those around us to encounter the living Jesus and be transformed to a life captivated by him.' We based ministry and mission on five values:

Jesus is the definition. We look at Jesus to see fully who God is, what it means to be human and how it looks to be fully alive.

Prophetic interruption. We expect that the Holy Spirit will interrupt our plans, as he leads us as a community. We make space to respond to this as we follow him together.

Empowering vocation. We are committed to helping people discover who Jesus has made them to be and empowering them to play their role in his rescue plan for creation.

Jesus encounter. We expect to encounter Jesus as present with us and to be changed through this. We intentionally shape our gatherings to make space for this.

Dependent prayer. We seek to engage deeper and more often in prayer; only with this foundation will we see the impossible happen and lives transformed by Jesus.

Soon after congregational planting we pioneered an intentional residential Christian community, the Ascension Mission House. We invited four young adults to live in a parish-owned house. They met for community meals, prayed and worshipped as a community and sought to make Jesus known in the wider parish. The community house collectively, and the leadership of the individuals within it, modelled the commitment to mission and worship to the wider church and, in doing so, embedded this core identity. It was pivotal, especially in the early days.

In addition, with the support of the newly planted congregation and longstanding church members, we partnered with the Church Army to pioneer a new contextual Christian community on the outer urban estate. This has since developed into the new home of the Church Army's Southampton Centre of Mission, with a contextual estate worshipping community emerging. It has seen people coming to faith from within the estate and allowed for innovative community engagement. This new ministry replicated the theological imperative from Ascension for mission and worship to be two centres of gravity for the new community, while also seeking to be contextual to the new social context. Our experience was that it was possible to do both from the outset. It is an example of the mixed ecology being worked out locally and of contextual pioneering, gathered church and a parish structure genuinely enabling and bringing life to one another.

The mixed ecology being worked out locally, through the community mission house and the contextual estate planting, but within a local church community rather than across a deanery or diocese, allowed for mutuality and interdependence between gathered church and a pioneering/fresh expression approach. The mixed ecology was normal; both expressions of the church depended on one another yet were held together by our shared values, our geography and our shared ecclesiology rooted in mission and worship.

Parish, pioneering, fresh expressions and church planting can often be seen in competition with one another and there is, at times, animosity between these approaches (Davison and Milbank, pp. 64–118). A clear, confident understanding of a shared ecclesiology that was rooted in both *mission* and *worship*, always attempting to balance both as equal priorities, created fertile ground for each of these to flourish with a local parish church.

References

Ball, J., 2017, *Post-Truth: How Bullshit Conquered the World*, London: Biteback Publishing.
Bosch, D. J., 1991, *Transforming Mission: Paradigm Shifts in Theology of Mission*, Maryknoll, NY: Orbis Books.
Brown, C. G., 2000, *The Death of Christian Britain: Understanding Secularisation 1800–2000*, London: Routledge.
Davis, E., 2017, *Post-Truth: Why we have Reached Peak Bullshit and What we can Do about it*, London: Little, Brown.
Davison, A. and A. Milbank, 2010, *For the Parish: A Critique of Fresh Expressions*, London: SCM Press.
Heaney, R. S., 2019, *Post-Colonial Theology: Finding God and Each Other Amidst the Hate*, Eugene, OR: Wipf & Stock.
Kwiyani, H. C., 2017, *Mission-shaped Church in a Multicultural World*, Cambridge: Grove Books.
Moltmann, J., 1977, *Church in the Power of the Spirit*, London: SCM Press.
Newbigin, L., 1953, *The Household of God: Lectures on the Nature of Church*, Eugene, OR: Wipf & Stock.
Ross, C. and J. Baker, 2014, *The Pioneer Gift: Explorations in Mission*, Norwich: Canterbury Press.

6

On the Ground: Life, Death and Resurrection in Church Planting

SARAH MCDONALD HADEN

The Christian story is one of life, death and resurrection. As followers of Jesus Christ we embark on a journey, discovering the power of Christ's death and the hope of his resurrection. To be a disciple of Jesus means embracing this path of life and death, knowing deep in our hearts that because of the gospel, death will never have the final word. To be a church planter is to live this story alongside the life, death and resurrection of church communities. It's a calling to walk with church communities through their own cycles of dying and rising, holding on to the promise that, in Christ, new life always springs forth.

I've been involved in church planting in the Anglican church since beginning mixed-mode ordination training 12 years ago. Along the way I've worked with a range of different types of planting, from beginning a wholly new congregation in a new area to revitalizing a congregation in an existing church building. Whatever the type, whether revitalization or forming a new congregation or Bishop's Mission Order (BMO), church planting, at its best, seeks to engage those who do not currently engage with church in new ways alongside and apart from existing structures. People who plant and pioneer seek to bring new life in places where worshipping life is fading or no longer present.

In my own journey I have witnessed both the bloom of new life and the farewell of communities. Within the rhythm of church planting, death is as intrinsic as birth. This reality challenges our theology, urging us to embrace the fact of the coexistence of life and death within the ecclesiastical landscape. As Anglicans we are not very good at this. As a church whose ministry often centres around supporting people through life's pivotal moments – birth and death – we can struggle to acknowledge and cope with the birth and dying of church communities. It is

LIFE, DEATH AND RESURRECTION IN CHURCH PLANTING

indeed a curious spectacle: a community well-versed in the rituals of farewell grappling with the concept of closure. I wonder why this is.

Of the communities I have been involved in planting, some are very much alive and others are not. We must not shy away from acknowledging that not all seeds will take root, nor all congregations endure through the ages. For just as a gardener tends to both budding blossoms and withering leaves, so too must the church planter; those who seek for new life acknowledge where there is also decay and death.

My initial foray into church planting began during my time as an ordinand. Freshly selected, I found myself training mixed mode on placement at a two-buildings HTB network parish in north London. I arrived amid the crescendo of a £4 million construction project, re-opening a revitalized church building, buoyed by the naive notion that 'If we build it, they will come.' But reality proved a stern teacher: the congregants did not materialize as swiftly as anticipated. It took several years of concerted effort to foster both congregations and communities while maintaining a complex church structure. But slowly and steadily, growth did happen. In particular, a 5 p.m. service planted by a final-year ordinand focusing on those in their 20s and 30s began in a flat and grew into a healthy-sized congregation. Perhaps the greatest gift we can give to people seeking to plant new communities is an undivided focus and space to pursue the 'new' without the struggle of dual identity roles and numerical targets.

I remained in north London for my curacy and was entrusted with the task of establishing a new worshipping community within a shopping centre just beyond our parish bounds – the Nags Head area of Holloway. The vision was to create a worshipping community within the shopping centre for those who wouldn't engage with traditional church of any kind.

Supported by the funding of our sending church and bolstered by the prayers and blessings of the local parish community, we gathered a small team of six who would form the beginnings of a new community. We embarked on a journey of prayer walks and Wednesday-evening gatherings at the local Costa Coffee. For the first month no one came and yet, painfully slowly, a small community began to grow over the first year, although never more than 12 or so per week. As the community grew alongside a simple Bible study on Wednesday, we began to meet monthly at the local Wetherspoons to share a meal and communion. I led the community one day a week alongside my role as curate and then associate vicar of the sending church.

The Nags Head church community journey was a beautiful mess, woven with threads of joy and chaos. The community we nurtured was diverse and chaotic, made up of almost entirely unchurched people, many on journeys marked by struggles with mental health, past convictions and addiction. Each Wednesday was unique – some weeks there were deep moments of prayer and encounter with the Holy Spirit, some weeks it was a success if a fight hadn't broken out!

Our journey as a worshipping community lasted five years until circumstances changed. The pandemic closed the doors of the Costa Coffee we met in. Online worship was not viable for the needs of the community. Economic changes led investments away from the area towards Finsbury Park. Many of my team, including myself, moved away and the community came to a natural close.

Yet despite the bittersweet farewell our brief yet impactful church plant did not feel like a failure. Lives were transformed, hearts were touched and people were confirmed in their faith. Many found new spiritual homes, though I often find myself pondering their whereabouts today. The community lasted for a season then reached its end. Most of us who are practitioners of church plants will have similar stories of life and death – things we tried that worked for a while or didn't work at all. I wish we heard more about these stories and churches, as they are as common to church planters and planting as the 'success stories'.

My next venture into church planting commenced a mere six days into the fateful month of March 2020, just before the world was plunged into the throes of a global pandemic. In March 2020 I was licensed as the leader of Cheltenham Network Church, a BMO in Gloucester diocese. The church I inherited was 30 years old and had led a nomadic existence in Cheltenham, moving around local schools to gather, never growing bigger than 60 or so adults. At the point of my arrival, the congregation, meeting in a secondary school, was struggling to sustain both its physical sanctuary and the volunteer manpower required to keep afloat. The onset of the pandemic offered an unexpected reprieve – a chance to pause, to breathe and to reassess. It was evident to some, if not all, that a return to the pre-pandemic status quo was untenable, financially and otherwise. Yet amid the uncertainty a glimmer of hope flickered on the horizon, albeit faint and indistinct.

In the midst of the second lockdown I was invited to offer some support to a neighbouring parish church grappling with its own set of challenges. Their beloved vicar had succumbed to illness and died during the pandemic, leaving behind a small congregation bereft and grieving inside a vast building. Thus began an unexpected alliance – a graft born of necessity and mutual support. Invited by the churchwardens, our BMO began to gather alongside their faithful on Sunday mornings. What began as a tentative collaboration slated for six months evolved into a year-long partnership, and now, as the dust settles, we find ourselves committed to walking this path together indefinitely. I was duly licensed as the vicar of both the parish and the BMO, a testament to our shared journey and collective vision for the future.

As the two churches joined forces almost immediately, signs of life began to appear. With a larger pool of resources and a surge of collective energy, our capacity to effect change multiplied exponentially. We were not just the sum of two parts and were able to do and resource much more. Some of those who had spent 30 years 'wandering' relished the opportunity to engage in local community mission. Some of those who had worshipped in the local parish joined groups focused more on networks rather than neighbourhood. The youth work flourished, the building offering space for youth ministry that resourced the south of the town.

However, amid the joy of life and growth, for both communities, a sombre undertone of trauma and grief lingered. For some members of the BMO, the newfound stability brought with it a sense of loss – a departure from the nomadic lifestyle that, though challenging, had become a familiar companion. The worship style of the parish underwent a metamorphosis, moving to a more informal style. They still grieved the loss of their priest and what had been. The two smaller churches became a larger community unsettling the power and group dynamics that existed before. Alongside the newness of life and growth sat the grief that life would never be the same again.

As the two churches continue to grow together we continue to exist in this place of life and death, where grief and new life coexist. In the delicate balancing act of operating within two distinct structures, we strive to move forward with grace, avoiding the pitfalls of becoming ensnared in the minutiae of administrative detail. We are keenly aware of the danger of losing our mission because of the complexities of organizational dynamics. As a leader, often this hasn't been easy – and has required a huge amount of emotional awareness and diplomacy (in which I have often failed) as I seek hold some people's frustrations and grief alongside the joy of new life. It is costly to hold pain and life together. Perhaps this is the eternal tension of the priest, where church life is always embracing both joy and sorrow together.

In church planting, as in the gospel story, life and death walk hand in hand. It is not a binary choice between one or the other but a delicate dance between the two, intertwined and inseparable. Our newness is always interwoven with our history and the history of the places we minister in. New growth often lives alongside grief. For those of us who live and lead worship, we must understand this tension as we treat our communities with empathy and curiosity. It is in the tension that we discover the richness of our shared pilgrimage and gain humility – knowing that others will follow us with the next 'new thing'.

In the face of this complex reality one might wonder: Why embark on such a journey? Why devote yourself to the task of nurturing new life within the established framework of tradition and ritual? The answer lies in the profound belief that every person, cherished and known by God, deserves a community of faith – a sanctuary where they can find solace, support and belonging. God is not finished with the Church of England.

To be a church planter, to be one who dares to usher forth new life, is to embrace a path fraught with pain and sacrifice, often disappointing those both inside and outside the church. Yet it is a pain that becomes bearable, even purposeful, when the object of worship is deemed worthy. For in the pursuit of building communities of faith, ego and personal desires must yield to the greater calling – that Jesus is worthy of following entirely and absolutely wherever that leads.

In the end, the journey of church planting within the Anglican tradition is not about constructing (or reconstructing) church communities or implementing strategic initiatives. It is a vocation – a call, born out of a deep-seated conviction that every person is deserving of the hope and healing that Jesus offers and a church to call home.

7

Being Worship: To Proclaim Afresh in each Generation

ISABELLE HAMLEY

At every ordination service and in every licensing service, ordained and lay ministers affirm their loyalty to the inheritance of faith held in the Church of England in the Declaration of Assent. The declaration speaks of the faith of the church, which ministers are called to 'proclaim afresh in each generation'. At the centre of this commissioning therefore lies a dual imperative – to nurture the faith of the church and to proclaim it afresh. It is both internal and external, it holds together the need to nurture the identity and markers of worshipping communities, and the need to step beyond the boundaries of the community, to be in conversation with the wider world so that the ways of proclamation, the ways of gathering those who are not yet part of a common journey of faith, can continually evolve and make themselves intelligible in changing contexts.

Current conversations about mixed ecology and the tensions between different forms of church and mission can be seen as a destructive conflict between competing traditions; or we could view them as potentially fruitful conversations about the different ways in which we can discern together how to proclaim our faith afresh. The symposium that gave birth to this book explored mission, Kingdom and church. Speaking of mission and Kingdom was marked by diversity and richness. There was a common sense of calling expressed in a multitude of richly varied ways. Speaking of church was far more fraught: the place of gathering, of worship, of where and how this happens seemed to be far more controversial than the idea of doing mission. Somehow the interplay of church with Kingdom and mission was difficult to articulate and agree on, and at times led to a battle of stereotypes between different traditions and expressions.

All was not negative however, and this section of the book draws on the richness of these conversations, the different languages they represented, and each chapter in its own way seeks to undermine a sharp distinction between worship and mission but argues that they are an indissoluble whole. The language and imagination of different parts of the church are expressed in different ways and using different concepts, and yet there is a common vision and calling – to worship and to reach out, with a continuous movement between these two poles, and an understanding that they cannot be separated.

The tension in speaking of 'worship'

Worship and church may have been difficult because they are 'home' in a profound way: they are the place and practices that resource, shape and send us; they set the parameters for our belonging. Conversation between traditions is shaped by this belonging and the deeper underlying structures and values that shape faith. Just like conversations across cultures, it is easy to stumble on different languages, on different concepts, or to think that the same word or symbol can mean the same thing, when its roots and connotations are steeped in completely different social imaginaries. Being able to interpret one another's language is part of the journey of living out a mixed ecology well, caring for every part of the ecosystem – rather than seeing a different plant and calling it a weed.

To speak of ecosystem is to recognize some of the tensions that give rise to competition rather than mutual respect: in an anxious climate, where the discourse is one of scarcity, decline and limited resources, the ecosystem is under strain and different parts of it see themselves in competition with one another, especially when funding becomes tied to shorter-term projects that need to demonstrate their value by being innovative and high-yield. The rationale for these is often set against longer-term, organic models that may evolve rather than effect a step-change or a more radical rupture from existing patterns. In a competitive model, difference becomes value-laden, and different dynamics of power take centre stage in both decision-making and in the evaluation of different models.

And yet despite this overall anxious climate, the different chapters in Part I show the vitality, creativity and innovative power of each tradition – as well as hint at the challenges they all face. Alison Milbank explores missional expressions of the Eucharist for our contemporary culture; Andy Smith reflects on the symbiosis between parish and church plant; Sarah Haden on the complexity of the new in places with existing stories; and Al Barrett on the porous and pervasive nature of worship seen as taking in the whole of life.

All these chapters take for granted that worship and mission belong together, and that one does not, and cannot, exist without the other; indeed, they go a step further and suggest that it may not even be helpful to have a sharp boundary between both, as worship can be mission, and mission worship. Within this guiding thread we see a pushback against an understanding of both mission and worship that becomes utilitarian. Both are a reflection of God's heart, rather than a means to an end or an end in themselves. In the final chapter of the Gospel of Matthew we find the Great Commission, often seen as a mandate and manifesto for mission. In John's final chapter, Jesus gives the command 'Feed my sheep' to Peter, often considered foundational for the church – after welcoming Peter back following his denial. These two Gospel accounts are not in tension, they are complementary. One cannot endure without the other. Inward and outward movements strengthen and shape one another in a seamless whole. But Peter is not told to feed the sheep so they can bring in other sheep. And the disciples are not told to go and make disciples so that they can form a megachurch. Neither command is utilitarian; both reflect the heart of God and the way God cares for every person and every community: seeking, caring, feeding, sending, welcoming back.

Honouring complexity

Another striking feature of the contributions in Part I is their attention to complexity and the pushback against simple caricatures of different traditions. To have a good conversation about mixed ecology and proclaiming the gospel afresh, we cannot be reductive about the different traditions, what they each bring and how they take their place within the overall ecosystem. Alison Milbank draws attention to the way eucharistic communities have sometimes been dismissed as uninterested in mission and focused on maintenance; in the same way, church planting and fresh expression have faced criticism for not being 'proper church' or undermining local congregations. The only way to avoid this type of reductionism is to listen to the way each tradition understands itself, and the way within its own life it seeks to proclaim afresh and, to a degree, how far it is ready to accept and integrate wisdom from the wider church.

There is striking agreement among contributors about the unity of mission and worship; the more difficult question is one of incarnated practice and how one understands one's practice. Both Hannah Steele and Andy Smith speak out against setting up a dichotomy between the two, arguing from a *missio Dei* perspective that all worship and church are part of the movement of God's action and blessing in the world. From a different angle, but with similar conclusions, Alison Milbank argues that worship fundamentally shapes a community and is within itself missional. Agreement across traditions on this point illustrates the need for engaging with the complexity of discourse around mission and worship. A striking feature of the symposium was the difference in language between different traditions, and how different language can actually mask strikingly similar commitments. A lack of attention to complexity easily gives rise to destructive dichotomies – like the characterization of worship, particularly eucharistic worship, as 'maintenance' (as Milbank recounts) or the dismissal of all church planting or fresh expressions as inimical to parish life.

This is where biological images can serve us well. The metaphor of mixed ecology, controversial as it may be, points to complex interdependent life. Different church traditions and expressions of church life exist within an ecosystem, rather than in independent units each pursuing their own goals. Or, at least, within an ecosystem it is not possible for independent units to pursue their own goals without having an impact on the health of the whole – which is where tensions arise: dominant organisms could easily kill an entire ecosystem, like Japanese knotweed; conversely, parts of the system struggling to flourish may need pruning or strengthening for the sake of the whole. In conversations on social media, and at times in the symposium, 'death' was a concept lurking behind conversations around church 'life'. Life and death are natural parts of ecosystems and essential to their renewals. However, it can be easy, in the context of the Church of England, to argue for the death of the 'other' form of church and the renewal/strengthening and ongoing life of one's own. Yet it stands to reason that different forms of church reach out into different parts of our culture and society, attract different personalities and resonate in different ways. A rich ecosystem has the potential to reach out further and be more sustainable than the type of one-crop agriculture that impoverishes the soil: biodiversity may be a better metaphor than 'mixed ecology', as it keeps a sense of interdependence within a common system.

Among tensions about forms of worship it may therefore be wise to attend to an underlying ecclesiology in the Church of England, one that is not purely congregational but translocal and connects parishes to deaneries to dioceses to the Anglican Communion, and sets the Church of England as part of the universal church – hence in relation to ecumenical partners. This ecclesiology sets interdependence as a given, but tensions arise when the interdependent members are members of vastly different sizes and shapes. The very interdependence of churches within the Church of England is an ecclesiological strength, and yet it is at the heart of current tensions as competition for project funding and resources risks moving local relationships away from interdependence and towards competition, and does not necessarily pay enough attention to the need for a complex ecosystem where biodiversity is key to health and growth. Sarah Haden helpfully points out the additional complexity of the tension between institutional expectations and those of her nomadic congregation; while this is particularly true of new missional initiatives, it is fair to say that inherited forms of church also struggle with conflicting expectations from above and below. These 'expectations' are particularly acute when it comes to worship because even though worship is unquantifiable in itself, it is the place where the institution often seeks to quantify growth and success by counting regular worshippers. If wider, more holistic, more complex, measures were used, would the tensions between different traditions and forms of worship lessen somewhat?

Embodiment and integration

Unity is a running thread through every chapter, not just about mission and worship but also between worship, discipleship and mission. Throughout Part I, worship is repeatedly said to be about the whole of life. Worship and mission are the embodiment of God's action in the world; there can be no Christian life unless it is rooted in and shaped by worship. Christians in worship embody the witness of the church; Christians at work embody the witness of the church; Christians in conversation embody the witness of the church. To divorce worship from mission risks creating a sacred/secular divide that separates different parts of life into different activities, or at least modes of presence. Al Barrett's chapter explores powerfully how the blurring of boundaries within a neighbourhood ecclesiology serves to extend worship and embody witness and mission in a seamless, joined-up manner.

Al Barrett, Hannah Steele and Alison Milbank all point to the centrality of worship in shaping Christian discipleship and witness, and the power of words and rituals to shape us and how we see and understand the world. This is the deeper connection between worship and mission: worship shapes the Christian imagination in a way that shapes mission; and, one might add, mission returns to worship and enriches it in a never-ending cycle. If worship is seen as communication with God, it is the place where we find our place and identity in Christ, where we are taken up into the movement of God within the world; in this sense mission cannot be fully distinct from worship, as this would empty mission both of power and content, and worship cannot exist independently from mission since it would take away an essential shape to our worship by divorcing it from life in the world.

Worship should form within worshippers the habits and imagination that sustain and give shape to missional life in the world. Christian tradition has long thought of the Eucharist in this way, as shaping the people of God for lives of interdependence, justice and service. Yet the shaping that worship effects is a slow shaping, and maybe this is another crack underlying the false dichotomy between mission and worship. Mission can (wrongly) be seen as active, quantifiable, something that can be seen as productive. The slow shaping of discipleship and mission through worship stands against the mores of an instant society looking for an instantly packaged Christianity, as Hannah Steele points out in Chapter 1. But yet again this is a false dichotomy. Mission both needs and makes disciples, and disciples are formed in worship, in conversation with God. Worship at its deepest calls for hard, slow transformation, the kind of transformation that walks hand-in-hand with mission.

Mission that is not shaped by worship is at serious risk of being misdirected. Hannah Steele, and Sharon Prentis in Chapter 4, both highlight the point. Mission can easily be turned into empire-building or a power exercise over the other. It is only in being transformed that mission can take its proper shape, by calling for service, justice and obligation to the other. Neither worship nor mission are individualistic enterprises, as Sharon Prentis reminds us: they are about the formation of God-shaped communities, something that takes time, effort and intentionality. But more than anything, the shaping of community takes a fundamental transformation of the human heart, so that what needs to change is recognized at the deepest level. God-shaped mission starts with the compassion of a tender-hearted community, whose heart beats alongside the hearts of those who suffer, in harmony with the heart of God.

PART II
Being Witness

8

Being Witness in a Global City

ANA FRANÇA-FERREIRA AND ANGUS RITCHIE

Introduction

St Paul's letters to the Corinthians are texts we both draw on regularly (in our training and our personal reflection), as Christian leaders engaged in community organizing with churches in east London. In this chapter we will share something of that dialogue between Scripture and context as we reflect on how to be a faithful witness in our global city.

As Frances Young and David Ford explain, in writing these letters St Paul is engaged in a process of spiritual improvisation – applying the good news of Jesus Christ to this particular time and place: 'There is no gospel in general, it is always rooted in particular contexts, language, conflicts, interests' (Young and Ford, pp. 201–2). To apply these texts to our own situation involves attending to the 'concrete social conditions and relationships' in first-century Corinth and twenty-first-century London. They have a number of striking resonances.

First, Corinth was a centre of trade. This was driven by its geographical location on the isthmus that connected the eastern Mediterranean with Rome. By AD 55, Corinth was a financial centre as important as Athens or Patras, and had also become a centre of manufacturing and of political power (Collins, pp. 21–3; Furnish, pp. 7–10).

Second, Corinth's power was built on the labour of a range of migrant peoples. While most Roman colonies were settled by army veterans, Mary Gordon writes that those sent out in 44 BC to refound Corinth were migrants from the eastern Mediterranean, probably for the most part Syrians, Egyptians and Jews, now living as people 'in a civilization not their own' (cited in Furnish, p. 7)

Third, Corinth was a place of striking social and economic inequalities. Even within the Eucharist, wealthier worshippers felt comfortable feasting in the presence of fellow-Christians who went hungry. The dominant religions of the day offered a theological rationale for such inequalities (Furnish, p. 15). St Paul is scandalized because the gospel asserts the opposite, locating the power of God in the very people and situations the dominant culture belittles and oppresses (1 Cor. 1.26–29).

Community organizing and faithful witness

The practice of broad-based community organizing was pioneered by Saul Alinsky in the slums of Chicago in the 1930s. At first glance, Alinsky seems an unlikely dialogue partner for St Paul. However, the often provocative and cynical language he used to describe his approach belied the depth of his spiritual commitments.[1] Alinsky's approach involved a transition from paternalistic social work that sought to do good to those experiencing injustice, to the development and recognition of those very people as the agents of change.

Alinsky founded the Industrial Areas Foundation (IAF) to develop and promote this approach. Under Christian organizers such as Ed Chambers, Ernesto Cortés, Sr Judy Donovan and Michael Gecan, the work became more deeply rooted in the life and witness of local churches. With the development of Citizens UK as a sister organization to IAF, Christians in east London founded the Centre for Theology and Community (CTC). The Centre seeks to ground churches' organizing more deeply in the faith and worship, and to harness the approach to help them grow in number and in depth as well as social impact.

Within the Citizens UK alliance there are community organizing alliances in a growing number of towns and cities across the country. Each alliance includes churches, mosques, schools, trades unions and other membership-based civic organizations that have agreed to work together for social change in a particular place.

In practice, community organizing involves lay and ordained leaders within each institution undertaking one-to-one meetings within and beyond its walls. Out of these many conversations come the actions and campaigns that deliver change. Member institutions join together at regular intervals in 'assemblies' to share the results of their conversations and to agree shared priorities for action. The actions may start small: a campaign for a sign outside the church, a zebra crossing in a housing estate or lighting in a park. As well as being valuable in themselves, these actions build the confidence of individual leaders and the wider community to imagine more substantial changes.

While an organizing alliance will consist of diverse groups – Christian, Muslim, Jewish, secular – that does not mean they need to leave their distinctive beliefs at the door. A Christian congregation that takes organizing seriously will root this external action in the gospel. Christian participation in community organizing embeds this in a holistic process of discerning and responding to action that is God's before it is ours. This is expressed in the Cycle of Prayer and Organizing.[2]

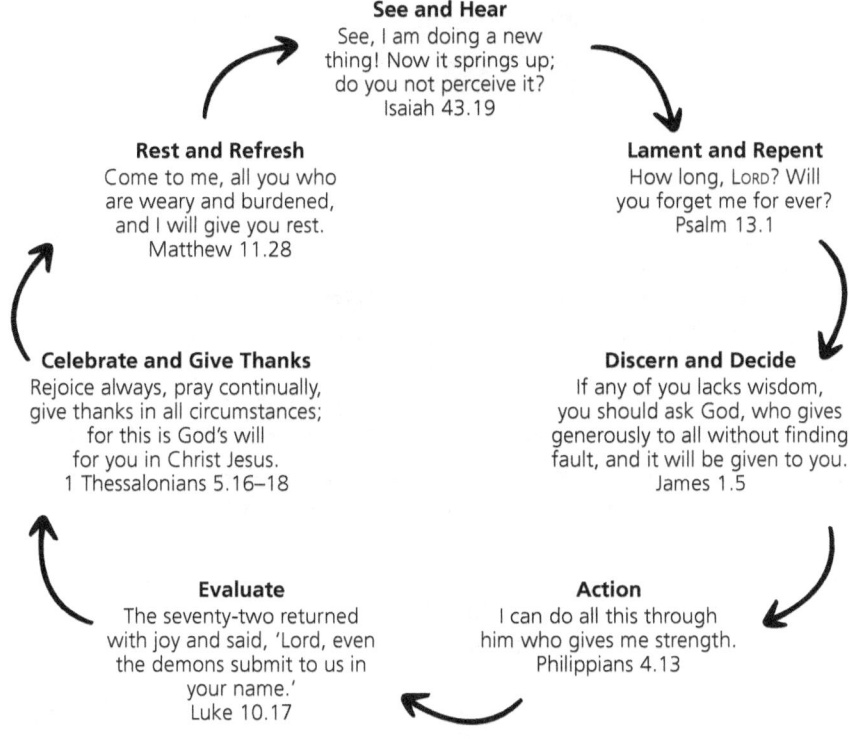

Figure 1: Cycle of Prayer and Organizing (NIV)

What light, then, do 1 and 2 Corinthians cast on how we might be a faithful witness in this global city? And how might the practice of community organizing help us to live this out?

Beyond worldly hierarchies: organizing and power

Power relationships are a key theme in both letters to the Corinthians. In the first epistle, after the opening greetings St Paul immediately moves to address factionalism within the congregation (1 Cor. 1.11–17) and connects it to the way the Corinthians continue to live by the values of the world (1 Cor. 1.18—3.23).

His appeal is not to an ethical standard but to what has been revealed about God through his actions in the world. In the triumph of Christ crucified and in the humble status of those God has called in Corinth, he reveals a 'wisdom' that is a 'scandal' and 'foolishness' to the wider world. In the words of Fr Kenneth Leech:

> Religion goes disastrously astray when it ceases to be a sign of contradiction and becomes the cement for social conformity. The foolishness of God is then replaced by capitulation to the values of the world ... Conformity to the world is the betrayal of its foundation in folly and contradiction, and of its necessary role as a community of contrast and of dissent. (2006, p. 10)

In 2 Corinthians the focus is more directly on the nature of St Paul's own authority. We are told that he too is judged by worldly standards; dismissed because of his unimpressive physical appearance (2 Cor. 10.10), his lack of impressive oratory (2 Cor. 11.6) and his refusal to demand payment for his ministry (2 Cor. 11.23).

He cannot remain silent in the face of this contradiction of the gospel. But he does not want to reinforce the patterns of this world by the manner in which he asserts his authority. As Young and Ford observe:

> [Paul's] chief concern in 2 Corinthians might be described as theological purification of authority through the gospel. Is it possible to have a specifically Christian conception of authority which, in community, unites the freedom 'where the Spirit is' (2 Cor. 3.17) with 'the love of Christ constraining us' (2 Cor. 5.14)? Only, Paul suggests, if the vision informing that is of the authority of God, his glory known 'in the face of Christ' (2 Cor. 4.6). (pp. 231–2)

These themes resonate deeply with the community organizing method. While organizing is best known for its campaigns (perhaps most famously the movement for a living wage), what is most distinctive about the method is its focus on the dignity and agency of those the world overlooks and indeed oppresses.

This is why the community organizing method begins with the one-to-one relational meeting. The 'one-to-one' is a conversation that does not seek to enlist the other party into a predetermined activity but rather explores their gifts and passions. It explores questions such as:

- What relationships are central to this person's life?
- How do they spend their time and money, and why?
- What are the motivations for key decisions they have made?
- What institutions are they involved in, and why?

Alongside the one-to-one, churches engaged in community organizing are taught to conduct a 'power analysis'. The tool is used as a way to understand the dynamics of an organization and identify the people to have one-to-one meetings. By intentionally reflecting on how our organization operates we can see the different activities and who are the people at the centre of such activities. The power analysis reflects the following questions:

- Who is officially at the centre of your organization? (Often this is the priest or the person with the most decision-making power.)
- What is the real decision-making process? Does the person at the centre make the final decision? Or is there another process? Are there people close to the official decision-makers who are able to influence their decision?
- Who are the people who can make decisions about money?
- What are the different groups in the organization? (These are often prayer groups, toddler groups, youth groups, senior groups, PCC, particular ethnic or cultural groups etc.)
- Who are the most relational people? (These are the people who are close to different groups of people, are known by everyone and are often invited to participate in different groups.)
- Where are you in this power analysis? What are your most significant relationships?

Power analysis helps us think strategically about our organizations and how to select individuals from various parts of community life for one-to-one meetings and relationship building. It also encourages us to reflect on who we spend our time with and why we choose certain people. Typically, we select those closest to us, people with whom we feel comfortable; while this is not inherently problematic we must consider whether we are fostering a culture of indifference or a culture of encounter (Pope Francis, 2020). Community organizing invites us to foster a culture of encounter, urging us to reflect on how we interact with others, especially those who are not closest to us.

Undertaking such a power analysis ensures that one-to-ones are not only conducted with those who currently dominate the congregation's life. The organizing process ensures that attention is given to the gifts, passions and development of the people whom the dominant culture (and sadly, all too often, the institutional Church) overlooks and marginalizes. In twenty-first-century London every bit as much as first-century Corinth, God chooses these very leaders to be the central agents of his work.

Case study: St Martin's Church, Plaistow

Plaistow is in the London borough of Newham, one of the most ethnically diverse and economically deprived areas in the UK. St Martin's has three Sunday congregations worshipping in English, Spanish and Portuguese respectively. This new season in its life emerged from the ministry of Fr Marco Lopes, who placed his linguistic skills at the service of a vocation to welcome and embrace migrants from more of the diverse communities in the area.

The Portuguese-speaking congregation was founded after Fr Marco's conversations with parishioners in shops and cafés – as people saw his clerical collar and asked if there was a service in their mother tongue. In time, similar conversations led on to the emergence of the Spanish-speaking congregation.[3]

Having been a founding member of The East London Communities Organisation (TELCO, the founding chapter of Citizens UK), St Martin's rejoined the alliance in 2020. As it emerged from the Covid-19 pandemic the church conducted a campaign of one-to-one meetings. These revealed a desire among its congregations for St Martin's to be more rooted in the wider neighbourhood; for the church to create space for young people to lead and grow in their faith and as citizens; for recognition and support for migrants and refugees within and beyond the church; and for better conditions in workplaces (many worshippers being care workers and cleaners on the minimum wage).

As Fr Marco explained, one small and specific ambition that emerged from one-to-ones was for Newham Council to restore the street sign pointing to the church:

> A sign would also symbolise a desire for recognition of the parish church, and its people. Something visible to signal we are here, all are welcome here. We heard too that the local mosque, Ibrahim Mosque, had also hoped for a public sign. What better way to be more rooted and build solidarity across the parish than to work together to win a sign for both institutions? (Lopes and Webster, 2022)

The campaign for a permanent sign was a classic 'small-scale' action, emerging from the immediate concerns of local people and creating an opportunity to identify and develop leaders and to weave solidarity across ethnicity, language and faith.

Fr Marco died very suddenly and unexpectedly in January 2023. In the words of Nuvia Vaquerano, a member of the Spanish-speaking congregation: 'For the parish community his death was devastating news. It was hard to believe as the night before we were all together celebrating his 50th birthday.'

> Difficult times are an inevitable part of life and can shake our faith and hope. However, in these circumstances it is that very faith and hope in God that are an ever-flowing fountain of support and consolation that can truly carry us to a sense of peace in these critical moments.

As she explains, the congregations went on a journey of listening, lamenting and discerning where God was calling them next:

> After [Fr Marco's] funeral, the community of St Martin's began to work on having one-to-one conversations with every member of the three congregations. The first round of one-to-ones focused on asking how people would like to commemorate Fr Marco and what they hoped for the future of the church. (Vaquerano, 2024)

This listening process led on to the construction of a memorial for Fr Marco in the church garden, a Requiem Mass on the first anniversary of his death, when the wider community in Newham made a posthumous award to recognize his work, and the whole congregation shaping the profile for the selection of a new vicar. 'In the midst of this we are resuming activities with the opening of the food bank, but this time in the form of a food pantry, new English classes, youth groups, Bible studies and a new listening campaign with asylum seekers' (Vaquerano, 2024).

Marla Largaespada joined the Spanish services at St Martin's church after Fr Marco's death. Originally from Nicaragua, she moved to London seeking asylum with her children. Marla first came to the church as a user of the food bank, established in response to the 2020 pandemic. That's when she experienced her first one-to-one meeting with a community organizer. Marla felt the organizer had an interest in knowing who she was and was attentively listening to what she wanted for herself and what she wanted from the church.

As a user from the food bank, Marla wanted to transform it into a place that was more relational and more welcoming; a place of real encounter where people could connect. Although she knew things needed to change and others seeking asylum needed to feel welcomed, she was worried about not having been at the church for very long.

During one of the one-to-one meetings the organizer told Marla that the church was there to inspire people, and that if she saw a need there was no one better than her to change things. This conversation led Marla to feel 'there is someone that hears me and supports me'.[4] As a result Marla is now a lead volunteer at the same food pantry where she had originally sought help. Reflecting on her experience, she explains that 'ultimate and total freedom is found in God and Jesus, and the Church reflects that' (Largaespada, 2024).

Alsácia Esperança worships in St Martin's Portuguese-speaking congregation. She is originally from São Tomé and lived in Portugal before moving to the UK seeking a better life for her eldest son. Alsácia is also a full-time carer for her two younger children.

Alsácia joined St Martin's after meeting Fr Marco in the streets of Newham. She was very impressed when he told her he was going to call her then kept his word. They met and he shared his hopes and dreams for St Martin's church. Fr Marco was full of enthusiasm. allowing Alsácia to be herself and bring her culture to the church, where she felt listened to and seen; as she says, St Martin's became her 'second home'.[5]

As a result of being able to express her faith and culture through the church, Alsácia founded a cultural and charitable group called Rosa da Fé (which means 'Rose of Faith') to bring people from São Tomé and the wider church community together. The group prays together, organizes events and supports the church as well as people in need in both London and São Tomé.

Drawing on the words of the Magnificat, Alsácia explains:

> This text says everything to me, it moves me, because it is a text I read every day at home. I am blessed because God has chosen me. The Holy Spirit is our guide and Mary is our intercessor. In such a short time we can see all we have done, and this can only be the work of the divine. 'The Lord has done wonders in me and holy is his name.' (Esperança, 2022)

Like Alsácia, Ju Lima is a member of St Martin's Portuguese-speaking congregation from São Tomé. Ju grew up singing in church choirs and her talent led her to write songs, and to record a CD in Portugal. She moved to London looking for a better life for herself and her children. Ju came to St Martin's church through Rosa da Fé and felt welcomed and listened to by Alsácia, explaining: 'She treats me like a daughter, she fought for me.' Alsácia saw Ju's love for music and invited her to support St Martin's choir.

For Ju, music's power comes from its impact on the emotions. Her faith has been lived through her love for music, which has inspired her to help with music during special services at St Martin's; to continue to write church music; and to build a church choir with other members of Rosa da Fé. In her latest song, 'A Ti eu louvo' (meaning 'To you I praise'), she writes:

> I am here I want to tell you about my great love,
> Hear my voice, oh Lord, Glory to you my God,
> Come and listen to me, I want to understand what I am for You.
> With my faith, I take your love, I act,
> How grateful am I, I am here to serve You, Lord of heaven, accept my praise.
> Glory to God, my Lord, I sing to You, My voice, oh Lord, I praise You,
> Glory to God, my Lord, hear my voice and accept my praise.[6]

The stories of these four women show how the words of 1 Corinthians 1 continue to become flesh today – and how community organizing has helped to form a local church in which they can grow from anonymity to agency, confidence and leadership. As Marla explained at a seminar for CTC interns: 'The Church is that place of hope for people. It provides a sense of certainty for the future, through the certainty of God that the state cannot provide' (Largaespada, 2024).

For St Paul's vision to be realized in the wider Church there must be a transformation in the pattern of its leadership. Clergy in particular must use the authority the wider Church has bestowed on them to identify and confront the ways those under their care are shaped by the patterns of the world. However, as we see in 2 Corinthians, the great challenge is to ensure that the manner of that confrontation does not simply reinforce the very patterns it is seeking to transform.

This question stands at the heart of Pope Francis's call for a 'Synodal church'. In one of his earliest homilies on the subject, Francis offered the 'inverted pyramid' as an image of hierarchical authority within the Church, where the action of the successors of the Apostles is designed to serve and not dominate the wider Body (Pope Francis, 2015). As that same homily made clear, the 'Synodal journey' is an ecumenical one, and our experience (as an Anglican priest and a Catholic researcher and community organizer working together in east London) is that each denomination and tradition has gifts that can enrich other parts of the Body. In this way we journey together to build a Church where the 'protagonism of the people' is more fully recognized – and in that process we experience more fully the 'protagonism of the Holy Spirit' (see Brittenden, França-Ferreira, Ritchie and Palmer, 2024).

One Body in Christ: organizing and relationships

In 1 Corinthians 11 and 12, St Paul turns to the theme of the Body of Christ. Appalled that some in the church are feasting while others go hungry, the Apostle writes that the manner in which they are celebrating the Eucharist is 'unworthy' owing to their failure to 'discern the Body' (1 Cor. 11.27, 29).

It is a revealing turn of phrase. St Paul's critique is not that the Corinthians have disobeyed a rule but that they are failing to discern a reality. John C. Haughey captures the logic of these verses. The Corinthians' attitudes towards one another showed 'that they had not grasped the fact, the intimacy or the import' of their union in Christ:

> The superficiality of their conversion was evident, not so much in their belief in Christ, which was unmistakable, as in their behavior toward one another. They did not believe that each of them was a member, an instance of the Christ reality. If they had, they would have seen that their behavior toward one another was sacrilegious. (Haughey, p. 111)

Here we see a holistic vision of 'being witness' that defies a neat division between right belief and right action.

Haughey's essay is a key text in the Recognizing the Stranger community organizing training developed by the Industrial Areas Foundation, under the leadership of Joe Rubio and Elizabeth Valdez. This programme equips congregations to recognize both the gifts new migrants bear and the injustices they endure.

St Paul's teaching on the Body of Christ implies that the treatment of refugees and migrants is a spiritual as well as an ethical question. To be indifferent to both the suffering and the gifts of those who have been baptized into Christ is every bit as much a failure to 'discern the Body' as it would be to receive the Eucharist in a manner that was irreverent or contemptuous.

As Leech writes, in the Eucharist:

> Human beings share in the life of the social God, the eucharistic God, the God of the common life. Here God becomes as small as a piece of bread, and little people taste the wonder of eternity. In this essentially social act, the mystical quest becomes one with the quest for community and equality among people. (1985, p. 293)

Community organizing offers a powerful method for the Church to live out the spiritual reality of the Body in its concrete relationships. The one-to-one relational meeting enables us to recognize the diverse gifts of the members of the Body of Christ. Through these one-to-ones the congregation also hears the stories of the injustices its members are enduring. In a community that truly 'discerns the Body' this will lead on to action to both bind these wounds and address their root causes.

Case study: St Barnabas' Church, Walthamstow

Many people seeking asylum in the UK have been forced to live in temporary hostels across the country. In the years it may take for their cases to be processed, many individuals and families have integrated into local congregations and communities.

St Barnabas Church in Walthamstow is a TELCO member in the east London borough of Waltham Forest. Its diverse congregation includes Afro-Caribbean members who moved to Walthamstow in the 1950s and 60s as part of the Windrush generation, as well as a large Filipino community who have come to east London over the last 50 years.

Like St Martin's, the congregation has used community organizing to develop a Warm Space and Food Pantry. In recent times these have welcomed asylum-seeking families living in nearby hostels. St Barnabas has provided a communal space to socialize, find support and even cook – something often impossible in their temporary accommodation. This has fostered deep bonds between the newly arrived families and the wider congregation and community.

In January 2024 the accommodation for people seeking asylum in Waltham Forest was scheduled to close, with only a few days' notice given to the residents. Both the asylum-seeking families and the wider community were devastated by this abrupt relocation – especially as they did not know where they were going to be sent.

The word 'anger' comes from an Old Norse word for 'grief'. The mixture of anger and lamentation among St Barnabas' congregation and the wider TELCO alliance swiftly led on to action. Over 90 people from member organizations across east London came together in solidarity with the families being displaced. They called on ClearSpring (the accommodation management company) to meet with the community and discuss how to improve the treatment of their residents.

This action brought together families being moved out and people who wanted to show support – both groups wanted to see change in how people seeking asylum are treated. It succeeded in halting the families' dispersal across the country; all the families were moved to other places within London – mostly in east London. In doing so it demonstrated the role community organizing can play in helping Christians discern and live out what it means to be part of the Body of Christ – and how slow, patient processes of prayer and relationship-building can bear fruit in swift and effective action when an urgent need arises.

Your labour is not in vain: organizing and resurrection faith

In 1 Corinthians 15, St Paul turns to the doctrine of the resurrection. Some in Corinth have denied the reality of the resurrection of the body, and the Apostle's response is to argue that it is precisely because Christ has been raised from the dead that they can be sure their 'labour is not in vain' (v. 15).

As with his earlier teaching on the Body, here again right action is an expression of our grasp of spiritual realities. Faithful witness does not flow from an anxious need for 'impact' or 'success'. The Corinthians can 'be steadfast, immovable, always excelling in the work of the Lord' (1 Cor. 15.58) because God has already granted them the victory (1 Cor. 15.57).

It is no coincidence that the New Testament word for witness (*martureō*) is the root of the English word 'martyr'. When the early Church faced the violence of the state, this was understood to be the last gasp of the 'principalities and powers'. At different points in history that confidence in the ultimate victory has given Christians the grace to endure injustices they could not change, and also to pray and organize for justice when the opportunity arose.

The same confidence is needed for faithful witness today; not an anxious desire to 'build the Kingdom' or 'grow the Church' in our own power. Precisely because 'being witness' goes beyond purely human agency, the Cycle of Prayer and Organizing is proving a central tool in renewing the life of east London parishes.

St Martin's and St Barnabas' were two of the six smaller, sacramental Anglican churches in east London that piloted a programme on Harnessing the Potential of Community Organizing for Congregational Growth. Rooting the community organizing work more deeply in 'people, patience and prayer' has helped six churches grow in number as well as depth and impact. They now have over 200 new worshippers, four in ten of them under 18 years of age (see Ritchie and Brittenden, 2024). Perhaps the most striking learning from the project is the extraordinary wealth of leadership contained within congregations who often feel overlooked and marginalized within the wider Body.

As Nuvia Vaquerano reminds us, resurrection faith has both a temporal and an eternal dimension. As the people of St Martin's know through experience, we can only overcome the 'adversities of life' by recalling God's promises and our experience of his providence – remembering that 'no matter the storm, we have a firm anchor in God's presence':

> When we feel that the world is shaking under our feet, we should remember these pillars and find support in them as they strengthen our faith, help us find peace and hope in order to continue forward. The peace and faithfulness of God is your shield and strength in adversity.
>
> Life does not end with death. It is then that true life begins for Christians because we are a wayfarer church walking towards our encounter with the Lord. (Vaquerano, 2024)

Conclusion

The stories of these east London churches echo the lessons we have drawn from St Paul's epistles. They speak of the need to move beyond worldly understandings of power and hierarchy; to reconnect our understanding of the sacramental and social body of the Church; and to act out of a confident faith in the victory of her crucified and risen Lord.

In her book *Tarry Awhile*, drawing on her own experience as a community organizer, Selina Stone argues that such faithful witness is only possible if we learn how to 'tarry'. To wait on God and to rest in his mercy and power is an essential prelude to faithful action.

That tarrying helps us to understand the true nature of the Kingdom. The witness of cleaners and carers on the minimum wage, and of refugees detained in hostels waiting for their applications to be processed, is an expression of their God-given dignity, not a means of securing it. These actions for justice, like the wider life of the Church, are a foretaste of the new creation, in which God, who has already won the victory, will at last be 'all in all' (1 Cor. 15.28, NIV).

> The scars we bear are not cause for shame, nor must they define us in our entirety. They remind us of the work of God which continues to be needed in the world and in each of us, as we tarry ever more for the reign of God to be made known among us in justice and peace. They speak to us, in a whisper or even in silence, of the life we have and the life being brought forth in us through the Spirit, even while we tarry for all things to be made new. And as we tarry we cry, 'Come, Lord Jesus!' (Stone, p. 179)

Notes

1 This is something the Catholic philosopher Jacques Maritain saw very clearly – see the discussion of the Alinsky–Maritain relationship in Bretherton, pp. 91–4.
2 This was initially developed by Revd Josh Harris.
3 Marco Lopes, interview with Miriam Brittenden, 12 October 2022.
4 Marla Largaespada, interview with Ana França-Ferreira, 7 June 2024.
5 Alsácia Esperança, interview with Ana França-Ferreira, 10 June 2024.
6 Translation by Ana França Ferreira.

References

Bretherton, Luke, 2010, *Christianity and Contemporary Politics: The Conditions and Possibilities of Faithful Witness*, Oxford: Wiley-Blackwell.
Brittenden, Miriam, Ana França-Ferreira, Daniele Palmer and Angus Ritchie, 2024, *Not only with Words: Synodality, Community Organising and Catholic Social Action*, London, Centre for Theology and Community.
Collins, Raymond F., 1999, *Sacra Pagina: 1 Corinthians*, Collegeville, MN: Michael Glazier.
Esperança, Alsácia, 2022, Address at the London Cleaners Carol Service, Guild Church of St Katharine Cree.
Pope Francis, 2015, Address to the ceremony commemorating the 50th anniversary of the institution of the Synod of Bishops.
Pope Francis, 2020, *Fratelli Tutti: Encyclical on fraternity and social friendship*, Vatican City: Libreria Editrice Vaticana, https://www.vatican.va/content/francesco/en/encyclicals/documents/papa-francesco_20201003_enciclica-fratelli-tutti.html (accessed 19.02.2025).
Furnish, Victor Paul, 2007, *Anchor Bible Commentary: 2 Corinthians*, New Haven, CT: Yale University Press.
Gordon, Mary, 1924, 'The Nationality of Slaves Under the Roman Empire', *Journal of Roman Studies* 14 (1924), pp. 93–111.
Haughey, John, 1980, 'Eucharist at Corinth: You Are the Christ', in Thomas E. Clarke (ed.), *Above Every Name: The Lordship of Christ and Social Systems*, Mahwah, NJ: Paulist Press.
Largaespada, Marla, 2024, 'Faith Without Works is Dead', talk given at Centre for Theology and Community Seminar.
Leech, Kenneth, 1985, *True God: An Exploration in Spiritual Theology*, London: Sheldon Press.
Leech, Kenneth, 2006, *We Preach Christ Crucified* (2nd edn), London: Darton, Longman & Todd.
Lopes, Marco and Francesca Webster, 2022, 'Springtime at St Martin's', The Centre for Theology and Community, http://www.theology-centre.org.uk/springtime-at-st-martins/ (accessed 8.06.2024).
Ritchie, Angus and Miriam Brittenden, 2024, *Organising for Growth: Growing Inner-city Churches in Number, Depth and Impact*, London: Centre for Theology and Community.
Stone, Selina, 2023, *Tarry Awhile: Wisdom from Black Spirituality for People of Faith*, London: SPCK.
Vaquerano, Nuvia, 2024, 'Encontrando paz y esperanza comunal en los tiempos difíciles', talk given at Diocese of Oxford Community Organizing Resource Hub Day in Milton Keynes, translated by Claire Moll Namas.
Young, Frances and David Ford, 1987, *Meaning and Truth in 2 Corinthians*, London: SPCK.

9

Being Witness to the Edges

JONNY BAKER

A turn to the Gospels

The church is Christ's body, a set of relations and connections made up of many parts and gifts. It's one global, universal, visible and invisible body held together in Christ. One Spirit is drunk by its members and animates its life. Its purpose in the world is to participate in the ongoing ministry and mission of Jesus Christ through God's Spirit as Christ's body in the world. It is missionary by nature. Mission is God's. To participate is to join in with what God is doing in the world; with the overflow of God's love for the whole world; with the healing, renewal or liberation of all creation; with the incoming shalom or Kingdom of God on earth as it is in heaven.

We are most likely to get at what that could be by immersing ourselves in the Gospels, in the life and ministry of Jesus Christ. That affords at least the possibility of developing our imagination, habits, reflexes, a repertoire of moves, of how to live in the way of Jesus Christ, as followers of the Way. This is not to say that we naively do what Jesus did. We don't live in first-century Palestine. It is rather to 'prolong the logic of the ministry of Jesus and the early church in an imaginative and creative way to our own time and context' (Bosch, p. 34). I am proposing a turn to the Gospels for an ecclesiology that resonates with today's challenges, especially being witness to the edges.

This can be skewed in a couple of ways at least. The first is that reading the Gospels can be very focused on the individual – in other words, we look at Jesus' life and think about being a disciple or a pioneer or a minister, and then we think about church from the book of Acts onwards. What we miss through that perhaps very Western response is that this is communal participation. My suggestion is that Jesus and the disciples afford a rich fund for our imagination and pattern for our life together. Stephen Bevans recently published a work on missionary ecclesiology that has been 50 years in the making. He landed on a title (and description of church): *Community of Missionary Disciples*. Graham Cray recently proposed understanding the church as a community of disciples 'On Mission With Jesus', which leans in this direction even more. This is as a result of his distilled wisdom through his participation in the Fresh Expressions movement in the Church of England.

One of the binds we are in is our imaginary around church. We are so used to thinking in a particular way when we hear 'church' that it is hard for us to see other possibilities. This is a second way things get skewed. Cray calls this our default setting (p. 10). We have a default of church as a gathering in a building for worship doing particular things. There is a very strong gravitational pull around that default coupled with rubrics and defenders of the realm that shore it up, so much so that we find it hard to imagine other possibilities. He ponders whether the church has an ecclesial arthritis (Cray, p. 12). As a result of this default, when we ponder the life of Jesus and the disciples, our response to it sits within the imaginary of gathered church we currently know regardless of the tradition, so it gets reduced or collapsed. The mixed ecology that ensues is really not that diverse and doesn't offer a rich biodiversity – it's more like a woodland with a variety of the same tree only. We need freedom of imagination about what the life of Jesus and the disciples affords.[1] There is a world of possibility.

Jesus and fringe dwelling

Jesus' ministry might be conceived of broadly speaking as having four spaces in which it took place. I noticed this when reading the first few chapters of Mark's Gospel. The first is in the synagogues, what we might think of as a gathered church space. Having called the disciples to follow him, Jesus goes to the synagogue in Capernaum and teaches (Mark 1.21). It becomes a confrontation with the powers as he heals a man possessed by an evil spirit. He proceeds to travel and teach at synagogues in other towns and villages (Mark 1.39). The second is people's homes. When they left the synagogue they went to Simon and Andrew's home, where Jesus heals Simon's mother-in-law (Mark 1.29–31). A crowd gathers with sick and possessed people and Jesus heals many. In chapter 2 of Mark, Jesus is at a house in Capernaum that gets very crowded and some visitors make a hole in the roof so they can get their friend to Jesus to be healed. The homes are many and varied and Jesus is more often the guest rather than the host. So much happens in and around homes and meals in Jesus' ministry. The third is in public spaces. In Mark 4, he sits in a boat to be able to address a crowd at the lakeside, telling the parable of the sower. Then, fourth, Jesus also ministers in spaces that are much more at the fringes. At the start of Mark he meets a man with leprosy. He meets Levi the tax collector, a disreputable sinner, and joins a party at his house of those the Pharisees consider to be scum (Mark 2.16, NLT). Mark records that 'There were many people of this kind among Jesus' followers' (Mark 2.15, NLT). After the parable of the sower he says to the disciples: 'Let's go to the other side of the lake.' That turns out to be in an area of tombs and therefore unclean, gentile, and with a man possessed by a legion of demons. Jesus was loved by people at the edges, outsiders, fringe dwellers (Baker and Ross, p. 13).

I'd like to take two stories by way of example of how I see this sort of contemplative practice informing what it means to participate in the ongoing ministry of Jesus as his body, as community of disciples at the edges. The two stories I have chosen are Jesus in Samaria and Jesus at Simon the Pharisee's house (there are many others that inform being witness to the edges, and of course there are many that inform being witness in the other kinds of spaces above). The encounter in Samaria belongs to the fourth kind of space, which perhaps is where we most expect being witness to the edges. The encounter in Simon's house is the second kind of space but it too opens up something about being witness to the edges. It is important to note, however, that Jesus bears witness to the edges in all four spaces whenever the opportunity arises.

Fringe dwelling encounter one – send us to Samaria

Jesus should not have met the woman at the well (see John 4.1–42). The world was set up so that kind of thing didn't happen.[2] Every society has its ways of keeping people in their place, subtly or otherwise. In Jesus' time there were plenty of religious and social outcasts, whether by virtue of being maimed, being Gentile, having disreputable jobs such as a tax collector or prostitute, or having been known to have visibly broken God's law in some way. Samaritans were certainly despised. They were viewed as a heretical sect. While they had been part of the family in the northern kingdom of Israel, they had fraternized with foreign gods of the five kingdoms surrounding Samaria after the exile. Most people took the long way round to get to Jerusalem so as to not go through Samaria. Even after being with Jesus in Samaria, the disciples are still quick to suggest raining down fire from heaven on a Samaritan village (Luke 9.51–56), which gives you some idea of the reframing they had to do. The Samaritan in this story is a woman and that too makes the encounter all the more surprising.

Jesus chooses his route intentionally. He finds a site of spiritual significance, Jacob's well, and he gets rid of the disciples for a period of time. The encounter would have been very unlikely to take place with a big group of men together at the well. Jesus asks the woman for a drink. He is vulnerable and not the one trying to be the provider. He is the one receiving rather than giving.

A conversation ensues that goes deep quite quickly. God is already at work in the woman, who says she is looking for the Messiah. She is thirsty for the living water Jesus talks about that is beyond the categories of religious difference. This is actually very common, to find that people at the edges are already spiritual, prayerful, and God is at work. That is often what pioneers bear witness to – God precedes our arrival. Good news is being seen, being known. Jesus has clearly done his thinking around Samaritans already and my own take is that when he refers to the five husbands, he is showing that he knows that there has been an ongoing shaming of Samaritans through the retelling of how they have prostituted themselves to the five pagan nations. Then the woman tells her story to her community. She becomes the apostle to the Samaritans. She is the gatekeeper, the leader in that community who opens the way for Jesus to be welcomed.

Jesus and the disciples stay for two days. Presumably they share stories, theology, prayer, friendship, food. We don't know much about what happens. We're invited to fill the gaps.

What doesn't happen is Jesus inviting them to come to Jerusalem to learn the Jewish way, religion, culture. Rather, he leaves them as a new group of followers of the Way inside the Samaritan religion. The disciples' default setting would not even remotely have entertained this possibility – they were on an extraordinary journey with Jesus. I imagine Jesus and the disciples came back that way at some point to revisit them. He has enabled the woman at the well to be the first apostle to the Samaritans. Before his ascension he tells the apostles that they will be witnesses in Jerusalem, Judea, Samaria and the ends of the earth, and we see the movement reach again into Samaria in Acts 8.

To indwell this story and allow it to inform how we might bear witness at the fringes is powerful. How does this story inform what it means to be a community of missionary disciples? By way of an oblique offering from my own contemplation, I wrote this liturgy/prayer to help me articulate and remember some of what I sense:

Disturbing Spirit of God
Lead us out of our comfort zones
From Jerusalem and Judea
To Samaria and the ends of the earth

Show us Samaria in our locale.
When we are tempted to walk round it
Give us courage to walk through
When we feel safety in a big group
Help us get away from the disciples
And like you
Choose vulnerability

Remind us that you are ahead of us
Help us to join in with what you are doing
Show us the wells in our community
Lead us to the woman at the well

Where others see sinners
May we see saints
Where others see heretics
May we see God seekers
Rather than play host
May we be guest
Rather than give
Help us receive

For those who are thirsty
Pour out living water
May we worship the Father
In Spirit and truth

When we are invited to stay in Samaria
Let's say yes

Surprise us when
You do it from the inside

The harvest is plentiful
But the labourers are few
Send us to Samaria
To find apostles like the woman at the well
The good Samaritan

Fringe dwelling encounter two – re-story the world that keeps people in their place

Jesus is guest rather than host. We often imagine him being hosted at the fringes but he says yes to being a guest in many spaces. That includes being hosted by religious leaders and the powers that be. This time round he is welcomed to dinner at Simon the Pharisee's house (Luke 7.36–50). There are several other Pharisees who are there who have come to meet and discuss with Jesus.

The meal is disrupted by a woman who is known as a sinner. As Jesus reclines, she weeps and pours expensive perfume on his feet and wipes his feet with her hair and kisses them. This is not the sort of thing that could possibly go unnoticed and the aroma of the perfume must have filled the air. In Jesus' first-century culture it would be common to welcome guests with foot-washing, anointing with olive oil, and a greeting with a kiss. The woman offers the welcome that has been neglected by the host. There is a polite veneer of niceness from the host but the real agenda is perhaps to question Jesus or even to set him straight. Simon mutters under his breath, presumably loud enough to be heard – Does Jesus not know what kind of woman is touching him? What he is really saying, of course, is that Jesus does know and shouldn't be allowing it. He judges her, he sees her as unclean, and it is clear he judges Jesus at the same time.

Jesus holds a very different posture. He creates a space of acceptance and non-judgement. Those who feel shame in other places are at ease around him. He sees their dignity, their humanity, their worth. He is secure enough in himself that he doesn't need to do what is expected, doesn't need to do 'the right thing'. He can rest with the disruption. Indeed, he is noticing God's presence in the disruption. He is of course fully aware of how this is going down with the Pharisees. He is also at ease receiving the loving friendship of women without it being turned into something sexual.

In the presumed order of things, the religious know God and the outcasts and fringe dwellers don't. But in this encounter as with many others, this is not true. The woman who is known to be a sinner is the one who seems to know God and expresses thanks and praise. She does so in a way that is visceral, honest, authentic and heartfelt. It's simple and direct. She is generous and lavish in her offering. There is so much to learn from those at the edge. She teaches us how to worship in a way that is in stark contrast to the formulaic and rehearsed prayers of the religious leaders.

Knowing when to speak and when to keep silent is not easy. For Jesus, defending himself is not the issue – let them judge! He is undefended. But when the judgement is on those at the edge, those who are broken, who have got used to being shamed, it's a different story. Jesus then speaks up and says to Simon that he has got something to say. I love the plot tension in this story. He speaks the truth. He sees and names what is hidden or unsaid so that it becomes visible. Jesus unmasks privilege and entitlement. He lays it bare. He does so artfully through a story but in no uncertain terms he contrasts the woman's welcome with the lack of welcome he has received from Simon. He pronounces that the woman's sins are forgiven and blesses her with peace in front of those who would do no such thing and presume she is not worthy of it. Ultimately this is the most important word spoken, a word of love, of forgiveness in God's name to the outcast woman. This is gospel. This is good news.

It's hard for the religious leaders to tolerate Jesus and his behaviour. He is doing what is obviously right and God's Kingdom surely comes in that place. But you sense a quiet rage brewing as the way things are ordered is disrupted. This is a reversal of the ordering of society, of its hierarchy and judgements, of place. Those normally kept in their place are no longer in their place. They are in the centre. Those in the place of privilege have been put in their place, which is to say they have been offered an invitation to a levelling up.

Jesus re-stories the world. Repentance is the ability to receive a new story, to be re-narrated. For those who are shamed, that new story is one where they stand tall, find a seat at the table and no longer have to remain in their place. For those in places of power and privilege, that story offers a level table where all are welcome, all are loved, without judgement. Can those in power see what is going on, be grateful, learn humility and repent of their superiority? Or will they remain in the false narrative they inhabit? The invitation is there. If they can embrace that story, God's Kingdom will surely be found.

Again, I offer a liturgical response that names what I sense the challenge of being witness to those at the edges might be – what the challenge of being re-storied might be. For many at the edges, they either feel that church is not for people like them or they feel that they are not good enough or both. They expect to be judged by the kinds of people who go to church. And therefore, why would they come?! Perhaps that whole model is simply the wrong approach. There is something really painful in this story – we are a lot more like Simon the Pharisee than we care to admit. How might we as a community of disciples indwell and participate in the ongoing mission and ministry of Jesus, friend of sinners, based on this story?

> Jesus, re-story the world
> **that keeps people in their place.**
>
> When we are host help us create a welcoming space
> **of acceptance and non-judgement.**
> When the meal is disturbed by someone not invited,
> **help me make room.**
> May those who experience shame elsewhere
> **be at ease here.**
>
> When we are guest,
> may we receive with grace the gifts offered
> **no matter the host.**
> Where there is power and privilege,
> superiority and entitlement,
> and people are looked down on,
> **help us be secure enough**
> **to defy expectations**
> **and name what is really going on.**
> When all the seats at the table are taken by men,
> **rearrange the furniture,**
> **make space for women.**
>
> Thank you for the crazy love of the outcast woman
> **poured out as perfume**

spontaneous,
unrehearsed,
heartfelt gift.
Let her teach us
to let go of the formulaic
and go with the flow.

May your Kingdom come,
where the shamed stand tall
and no longer have to remain in their place.
May your will be done,
where the powerful are brought low
and no longer have to remain in their place.

Jesus, re-story the world
that keeps people in their place.
Amen

Fringe dwelling in practice

I am proposing that being witness at the edges, being church at the edges might best be informed by contemplative practice that dwells on the life, ministry and mission of Jesus Christ. That then will resource our communal imagination for what it might mean to participate in the ongoing ministry of Jesus Christ as communities of followers of his Way. That is all. The imaginative possibilities for what that looks like are vast as it finds expression in many different contexts on the edge. That participation may be as a community, and it is equally plausible in twos or threes as the church scattered, present in the world like yeast and salt. Church is something we make in particular times and places; it's socially constructed in the sense that it can be unmade and remade in ways that suit local cultures. Those possibilities and makings will of course retain a family likeness – in other words they look like Jesus Christ when embodied faithfully, and they may have a denominational family likeness too. To do this we need to, temporarily at least, suspend what we already know when we hear the word 'church'. The two most dominant imaginings or defaults are either a building or a congregation gathered on a Sunday morning.

Leap over the wall or perish! That was John Taylor's encouragement to the church to become less focused on herself and her members (Baker and Ross, p. 3). To bear witness requires leaving the comfort and safety of what we know to go on a journey to the edges and see what we discover there, to sail off the edge of the map into the land of dragons (Passmore and Passmore). That journey might be geographical, like Jesus and the disciples going through and staying as guests in Samaria. It might also be cultural, theological, leaving the way we do things round here.

When that journey is made, invariably what people discover is that there is life at the edges, treasure to be found, and God is present and at work often in surprising and unexpected ways. In spite of the middle-class church telling herself a story of lost people and places in need of salvation and a church, what practitioners find is that 'rather than lost people, communities are full of people who bear God's image and in whom he is at work' (Ruddick, p. 140). This noticing comes through listening and being present.[3] Rather than focusing on what is wrong with communities at the edge or what the deficits are and how to fix them, those at the edges begin to see assets or strengths. Ash Barker describes the practice of joy detecting, focusing on what is strong in people and fanning their gifts into flame rather than focusing on what is wrong (Barker, p. 138).

Once that journey has been made and treasure is found, what next? The mission jargon around this is inculturation or contextualization, which is the practice of seeking to share the gospel in a way that can grow from the inside of a culture rather than in forms from the outsider's culture. In this process an essential spiritual practice of outsiders is letting go (Bevans and Schroeder, p. 90). We all have ways of doing things informed by our culture, upbringing, church experience and so on. It includes how we organize, plan, think, dress, speak, and what food, music, art we like, our values, our worship, our theology, and of course our imagination around what church is. There is nothing inherently wrong with any of that. But without some awareness and intention and deliberate practice of letting go, the temptation when we relocate will be to unwittingly impose our way of doing things on others rather than enabling something to develop that grows from the inside of a context, group or culture. This includes our framing of the gospel and church (Bevans and Schroeder, p. 92). This is bread and butter in the world of missiology, largely because of the painful awareness of how Western ways of doing things have been imposed on others. It is important because what is at stake is whether there is an at-homeness of

Christ or whether he is ultimately seen as foreign (Taylor, p. 185). It is much easier to have good theories than it is to embody them in practice.

Letting go also requires relinquishing our judgement. The story of Jesus at Simon the Pharisee's is a reminder of just how 'judgy' church people can be towards those at the edge. Whether it is to do with gender, sex, sexuality, race, class, neuro-divergence, disability, age or whatever other difference is perceived – let go of judgement. Natalie Williams and Paul Brown powerfully show in their book *Invisible Divides* how class divides are a huge factor in our churches. Those people experiencing poverty or coming from a working-class background variously describe their encounters with church as being bewildering, experiencing disdain or feeling that church is not for people like them (Williams and Brown, pp. 3, 125). Further, these authors suggest that the outreach and church-planting strategies of many churches have served to strengthen the dominant middle-class culture of the church, with resources going to 'the nicer parts of town' (Williams and Brown, p. 21).

The counterpoint to the practice of the outsider letting go is insiders speaking out (Bevans and Schroeder, p. 95). How might local leaders in edge contexts grow and be encouraged to voice and lead from within their own cultures? I have learnt so much from Ash and Anj Barker in this regard. Seedbeds, their ministry in Winson Green and elsewhere, has the enabling of local leadership at its core (Barker, p. 26). Language of centre and edges is complicated to navigate, and perhaps unhelpful. The church in the West is now at the edge and the centre is elsewhere. But Western ways of organizing, thinking, doing theology, being the people of God and so on have been and still are very dominant and central. It's time to shut up and listen to other voices and give space for speaking out. This can happen through the friendships we make, the books we read, the prayers and liturgies we use to worship and pray with.[4]

If it's messy, slow and complicated, you're probably doing something right (Ruddick, p. 77). This is one of the chapter headings in Anna Ruddick's book based on research she did with young Christians relocating to urban communities experiencing marginalization, and with urban community members they lived alongside. She highlights how the expectations of the sending churches are out of kilter with the reality of what happens. They come expecting people to quickly become Christians, join a church and see lives changed. The imagination around what that church looks like is a group meeting for worship, teaching and so on – in other words the sort of church those people have come from. It can feel like we want people to join our club. The reality is much more ordinary and slow. A few might join, which can be good. It can also be confusing and feel like disappointment. But if you look at what is happening in the spread-out community of disciples, what emerges over time is that a flourishing takes place and they themselves become changed by the experience as they find God present and at work in the lives of those they are among. Flourishing includes increasing awareness of a good God (Ruddick, p. 82). But how that is then lived out, what discipleship looks like and so on, is messy. This remains hidden and invisible if we are only looking to see a particular thing called 'church' grow in a particular way and counting success on the number of members who have joined the club. If on the other hand we look at Jesus' life and ministry with those at the edges and are looking for signs of the Kingdom of God, the picture looks significantly different.

It is long-term presence, patience, vulnerability, availability, being alongside and for people in neighbourhoods without judgement that leads to change in the long term. The focus is towards shalom in the neighbourhood, or good for the whole community. This is very different from a sole focus on planting and growing a church community. Nick Russell and Carlton Turner say that our imagined model of church hinders its ministry in these kinds of contexts (Barrett, p. 55). 'Jesus and his earliest disciples inhabited a movement that defied binary constructs of all types, particularly looking to social, political, cultural and even ecclesiastical margins as sites of renewal and transformation' (Barrett, p. 56). Perhaps this is where some of the difference between pioneering and church planting lies. Invariably people are involved in food poverty, jobs, practical things like form-filling or working to get a new school in the neighbourhood. Church is a community of disciples seeking the well-being of the city together as they follow Christ. Sometimes they gather but mostly they are church scattered, dispersed, present in the locale who collide as they participate in various things. This also requires rethinking how we resource ministry at the edges.

Over time, new worshipping communities that gather do emerge and grow at the edges and this is of course a good thing. I am a trustee of a local community project, Gurnell Grove. There is a worshipping community there that is emerging slowly but it has taken five years to get to that point. There is also a monthly 'bingo church', which is part of the wider whole. Ash and Anj Barker have seen two fresh expressions of church grow. They are a natural good that has come from the ministry there. Similarly, it took five years or so to get to that point. But it feels like a huge reduction to see those as what church is, or as the measure of success, at least on their own. Church is best seen as the whole and not collapsed into just the gathered expressions. Church is present with and among people who are in the social enterprises, meals, café, job clubs, band studio, pilgrimages, friendships, leadership training, fresh expressions and so on.

Being witness to the edges might best be informed by an imagination based on the Gospels to draw us into following and becoming the community that Jesus draws around him. To do so requires journeying to the edges, seeking treasure, outsiders letting go and insiders speaking out. That letting go includes letting go of our default setting of church as being church only when she is gathered. She is also being church when she is scattered, present in a community of disciples participating in the ongoing mission and ministry of Jesus Christ in the world, which is her milieu. Church, then, may be at her best when she is going to the edges and being joined by fringe dwellers, and she will most likely find herself renewed when she does.[5]

Notes

1 I make an attempt at this in the first chapter of *Imagining Mission with John V. Taylor*, where I begin each section with 'Imagine …'

2 See Nestor Miguez's chapter, 'Samaritans and Empires', 2021.

3 This is expressed well in the Fresh Expressions journey. Stage one is 'listening' and the overall process is described as underpinned by ongoing listening. See https://freshexpressions.org.uk/get-equipped/the-fresh-expressions-journey/.

4 I have reflected on reading the Bible from the edges and praying from the edges in these articles: 2024, 'Reading the Bible from the edges', *Jonny Baker blog*, 4 March, https://jonnybaker.blogs.com/jonnybaker/2024/03/reading-the-bible-from-the-edges.html (accessed 19.02.2025) and 2024, 'Praying from the edges', *Jonny Baker blog*, 8 April, https://jonnybaker.blogs.com/jonnybaker/2024/04/praying-from-the-edges.html (accessed 19.02.2025).

5 Rowan Williams, 2003, 'Archbishop's Presidential Address – General Synod, York, July 2003', http://rowanwilliams.archbishopofcanterbury.org/articles.php/1826/archbishops-presidential-address-general-synod-york-july-2003.html (accessed 19.02.2025).

References

Aisthorpe, Steve, 2016, *The Invisible Church: Learning from the Experiences of Churchless Christians*, Edinburgh: St Andrew Press.
Baker, Jonny and Cathy Ross, 2020, *Imagining Mission with John V. Taylor*, London: SCM Press.

Barker, Ash, 2023, *No Wastelands: How to Grow Seedbeds of Shalom in your Neighbourhood*, Birmingham: Seedbeds Communications.

Barrett, Al (ed.), 2023, *Finding the Treasure: Good News from the Estates*, London: SPCK.

Bevans, Stephen B., 2024, *Community of Missionary Disciples: The Continuing Creation of the Church*, Maryknoll, NY: Orbis Books.

Bevans, Stephen and Roger P. Schroeder, 2011, *Prophetic Dialogue: Reflections on Christian Mission Today*, Maryknoll, NY: Orbis Books.

Bosch, David, 1991, *Transforming Mission: Paradigm Shifts in Theology of Mission*, Maryknoll, NY: Orbis Books.

Cray, Graham, 2024, *On Mission With Jesus: Changing the Default Setting of the Church*, Norwich: Canterbury Press.

Jones, Simon (ed.), 2024, *Jesus & Justice*, Birmingham: Red Letter Christians.

Miguez, Nestor O., 2021, 'Samaritans and Empires', in Jione Havea and Monica Jyotsna Melanchthon (eds), *Bible Blindspots: Dispersion and Othering*, Eugene, OR: Pickwick Publications.

Passmore, Richard and Lorimer Passmore, 2013, *Here Be Dragons: Youthwork and Mission off the Map*, Porthouse: Frontier Youth Trust.

Ruddick, Anna, 2020, *Reimagining Mission From Urban Places: Missional Pastoral Care*, London: SCM Press.

Taylor, John V., 1975, *The Go-Between God*, London: SCM Press.

Ward, Pete, 1997, *Youthwork and the Mission of God: Frameworks for Relational Outreach*, London: SPCK.

Williams, Natalie and Paul Brown, 2022, *Invisible Divides: Class, Culture and Barriers to Belonging in the Church*, London: SPCK.

10

Being Witness at the End of Modernity: Paradigm Shifts in Mission for the English Parish Church

NIGEL ROOMS

How does the local church in England (and by extension the local church of whatever denomination in the wider UK and the rest of the Western world) take up an authentic public role as witness in its local community as the period of Modernity (c.1650–1950) fades from our societal life? This is the question I and many others before (and presumably after) me have wrestled with for decades. It is a question, as we shall see, that goes to the very heart of the future existence of the Church in the West.

I worked for most of the 1990s (the so-called 'Decade of Evangelism' in the Church of England) in Tanzania where the church was growing quickly under very different circumstances. When, in the early 2000s, I returned to the UK to work in a diocesan training role alongside researching for a professional Doctorate in missiology, I noticed that the language of mission was on everyone's lips in a way that it had not been when I left. It would not be long before the publication of *Mission-shaped Church* in 2004. I spent the next ten years or so investing in the formation and development or ordained and lay leaders in the local church to some effect. However, what I knew at the end of that time was that I had not been able to deeply affect the culture and behaviours of *whole churches* in relation to their wider communities, beyond particular individuals. I also knew that however well-trained and effective the clergy and lay leaders were, the members at the heart of the local church were the ones who held the long-term future of their Christian community in their hands – they only had to be patient! So it was that in 2010 I found myself attending a conference on mission in Western Europe to celebrate the hundred years since the Edinburgh 1910 World Mission Conference. One of the many presentations was from Revd

Prof Patrick Keifert and a colleague who had been working on the very question of how to effect change in the whole of the local church in its context for some 30 years in the USA, South Africa and elsewhere, using an action learning methodology. My ears pricked up at this; I made contact and we brought their wisdom and learning to the English parish church (and some Methodist ones too).

Thus, since 2011 over 150 churches in England have experienced the change available to them through the three-year process (Keifert, 2006) and spiritual practices (Rooms and Keifert, 2014) innovated via the spiritual journey called the Partnership for Missional Church (PMC). I was heavily involved in this development from 2011 onwards and even more so from within the Church Mission Society from 2016. In coming to write this chapter I realize I have published already much of what needs to be said and there is little point in rehearsing all of that material again here in detail. What follows then is rather more of a review of the existing literature, pointing the reader to these resources and bringing them together in some kind of synthesis, all in one place along with illustrative stories from example churches that will give some colour to the presentation. I will attempt this under six headings, which are all connected. They relate quite closely to the six 'paradigm shifts' that I described as necessary for the local church in mission in a book on liminality, or how change happens across thresholds (Carson et al., pp. 103–13), but to save myself from self-plagiarism I am offering them somewhat differently here.

Death is not inevitable *and* there is no magic bullet

At both ends of a spectrum it is easy to give up on a declining church dying a slow death (Church of England attendance statistics clearly show an overall 1% decline per year, seemingly irreversible over the past 50 or 60 years). 'I just need the church to still be here to bury me' is one end of the counsel of despair. At the other end are those who wish to bypass entirely what exists for the new, fresh and shiny initiative, which I am not against when it is offered alongside revealing the God-given life and vitality of existing churches.

As I shall note later on, the task of a local church is primarily a spiritual one and my experience of churches entering into the PMC process was that it was very difficult to tell at the start how they would fare on the long, slow journey of change we invited them into. Outwardly well-attended, active and attractional churches struggled with being invited to slow down and learn spiritual practices that would connect them with God's presence and activity in their local communities. Weak churches with high levels of internal dissatisfaction and conflict came alive when they took the time to notice what their wider community actually consisted of now (as opposed to their memory of what it looked like decades before) and engage across their boundary with that new reality.

A theological principle we work with is that God has gifted the local church with all the gifts and resources it needs to be and do what God is calling it to be and do. This is true but not enough people, it seems to me, believe it. If we were to take this principle seriously, no one would give up on a local church before a serious attempt had been made to engage its people in discerning God's preferred and promised future for their local Christian community and enabling them to embody that call in their life together alongside their wider parish. Such an approach requires *appreciation* of what already exists rather than a shaming problematizing of what is not happening. Thus, the theory and practice of *Appreciative Inquiry* (e.g. Lau Branson) are deeply embedded in what we attempt.

One church we worked with had been built in the late nineteenth century in a new part of town without pew-rents for those who could not afford to go to the existing churches. This foundational vision was recovered as a gift and given new vitality when today's congregation realized this was how God was *still* calling and sending them to be with the marginalized people of their town.

None of this is magic, just as emerging fruitfully from a process like PMC is not inevitable either. Everyone knows that there is no magic bullet that will fix the church, but that doesn't seem to stop people from inventing them and selling them! In fact those churches that did emerge fruitfully were the ones who had engaged with the reality of their decline and even the possibility of their death, which chimed very well with research a colleague and I did in churches where 'something was happening' in the north of England (Rooms and Wort) – they had all faced up to their own death or dying in different ways.

The church is simply not a machine that can be fixed with a technocratic solution. This is the imagination we inherit from Modernity where scientific rationalism reigned. What is required is *adaptive change*, following Ron Heifetz's work in business organizational change (Rooms and Keifert, 2014, p. 5). Adaptive challenge may mean addressing how a gentrified congregation can overcome the barriers it has set up between itself and its wider, predominantly working-class community. Doing this will bring real pain and real change since the adaptive change can only be addressed by *experimentation* and dealing with the concomitant failure that goes with trying out some new things, before a possible future emerges.

Change doesn't happen in a straight line from A to B – it is 'U' shaped

If the local church as a human organization is not a machine that requires a tool to fix it, it follows that change in a such an organization will not be in a straight line – it will be 'non-linear', since we can understand the organization as a 'complex adaptive system' (Rooms, 2019a). It is surprising therefore how much 'straight-line' thinking prevails in the Church of England, as demonstrated by the ubiquity of 'Vision–Strategy–Culture' language in how churches are planted (Foulger, p. 54). Here the general idea is that we define the current reality, create a vision of an ideal future at some point in that future (usually in the unrealistic short to medium term) and draw up a strategy for going from now to there in a straight line. Along the way the culture is expected to change. What Foulger's research shows, and what is obvious if one thinks seriously about it for a moment, is that such an approach ignores the possibility of resistance to both the vision and the strategy.

The PMC process isn't against vision and strategy but it reverses the movement by placing culture change at the beginning, middle and end of everything. Out of this emerges a vision and strategy that can be owned and embodied by enough of God's people that it can last and outlive a change of ordained leadership, since the vision now resides in the congregation and not just in the leader.

In PMC we generate culture change by introducing, over two years, six 'faithful disruptive missional practices' (see Rooms and Keifert, 2014). These are repetitive spiritual practices that we hope will become normal and habitual. They provoke the complex adaptive system to reorganize itself around them and they invite resistance as a positive effect. Each of them is faithful to the long Christian tradition but each also disrupts aspects of the culture and behaviours we inherit from the Modern period. The skill of the leader in introducing the practices is to notice and encourage those members they are 'diffusing' to, and staying in touch with those who are resisting them (Rooms and Keifert, 2019).

Two members of a certain PMC church rebelled at church council meetings against one of the practices two years after its inception, which occasioned a 'threshold', make-or-break conversation on the council. The two members shared their concerns, others spoke of the new life they had received through the practice, and a decision was taken to continue. Now a whole new vision and strategy could emerge (though the people wouldn't have called it that) since the Rubicon had been crossed. The leadership task here was to allow the possibility that this was the end of the road for missional movement across a paradigm shift in an undefended way. This work is the fine detail of the *craft* of creating a missional church, which involves *phronesis* and *poiesis* – that is, concrete, practical wisdom resulting in new creative being and action. The whole is much more the shape of the letter 'U' than a straight line – or repeated 'U's that form a wiggly line like the path of a tacking sailboat – an image we use a lot (Rooms and Keifert, 2014, p. 3).

Here is another connection with liminality, which I have discussed both in relation to spiritual direction (Chatfield and Rooms, p. 73) and the Paschal Mystery as exemplified in Philippians 2.5–11 (Carson et al., p. 57). The shape of discipleship for both the individual Christian and the whole body of Christ is that of dying to live – which is even more reason to embrace the deaths that the end of Modernity is gifting us, which I believe are also the work of the living God (Rooms and Wort, p. 109).

It's all gift – the sacramentality of life after Modernity

The foundational paradigm shift in the title of this chapter is found in David Bosch's magisterial work, where he establishes the fundamental importance of the *missio Dei* as it emerged in the twentieth century to become a proverbial 'game-changing' idea (Rooms and Keifert, 2014, pp. 10–12). Like all major theological concepts, it can be misused and driven in unhelpful directions (Rooms, 2022, p. 72), but at its best it releases the local church from ever more frenetic activity to prevent its own demise. The tangible relief among church members when they have embraced this paradigm shift through embodiment is very powerful (Rooms, 2022, pp. 13–14). Embracing the *missio Dei* releases faithful Christians from the guilt and shame of not *doing enough* into a spirit-filled energizing focus on God, God's presence and activity away from continual talk about (saving) the church.

Connected theological themes then quickly emerge from this starting point, of participation, partnership and communion. Andrew Davison, as a philosophical and systematic theologian, has written eruditely on how participation emerges as vital connective tissue in a Christian theistic and systematic understanding of God as Trinity. God creates and sustains all things *ex nihilo* and is therefore the efficient, formal and final cause of all things, but emphatically not the material cause. All reality is therefore about sharing in God's being and receiving the gifts of creation: perceiving all things in relation to God as their source and goal. God is the very act of being, thus God is much more of a verb than a noun – and every other creature is a being by *participation* in the prior being of God. In consequence we have partnership *in* God – or communion/*koinonia*. God becomes our primary partner in life and therefore mission.

We must be careful, as Alison Milbank and others have pointed out, not to think of how we participate or join in with the *missio Dei* as something we do outside of our creaturely being on the 'inside' of God and the flow of God in creation, sustaining and redeeming all things. Mission cannot be conceived of as an end in itself – it always flows from God and to God – thus our constant focus in PMC on seeking God's preferred (penultimate) and promised (ultimate) future for the local church.

A theology grounded in participation stands over and against the separation of sacred and secular, fact and value, private and public, subject and object that is such a destructive part of our inheritance from Modernity. Everything is gift and our task is spiritual discernment within that gift, asking always with a spirit of inquiry – What might God be up to here? It is hard to overestimate the power of the division between sacred and secular in the existing culture of local churches. This plays out most often in so-called 'business' meetings where prayers for God's blessing are said before and after, but the actual work rarely invokes God and God's desires for the community. Rather, the quickest, simplest and, more importantly, cheapest solution is sought. A kind of 'sanctified pragmatism' prevails. How the presence and activity of God can be woven into the life of congregations, and especially how they deal with divisive questions that cause real conflict, are issues we address head on in PMC with some of the spiritual practices we referred to earlier.

When God becomes the primary partner in mission another important outcome follows. An ability to discern and then focus on God's vision and desires for this community emerges away from what we call 'dissipation' – attempting to do too many good things to the detriment of all of them (the frenzied activity we mentioned earlier). When we introduced to a cluster of PMC churches the idea that it is good to say 'no' to good things in order to focus on what God is up to, a Church Council (PCC in Anglican terms) member who was present expressed shock and surprise, saying, 'I've just realized that on our PCC we've never said "no" to anything!'

Relationship, relationship, relationship – in public Christian witness

If participation in the gift of creation and redemption from God is the church's basic stance, this would suggest that seeking relationship in mission across boundaries is the key task of the local church. According to the *missio Dei*, God is missionary in God's being and the Church is also missionary by her very nature. Mission on earth therefore proceeds by one person relating to another within the presence and activity of God. However, once again the effects of Modernity provide serous barriers to how Western Christians are able to form relationships across the boundaries of the local church in public. First the Church has rather given in to the Enlightenment idea that religion is a private matter for the individual; we have serious evidence for this from research that our 150+ PMC churches undertook on themselves. Second, and according to Charles Taylor's monumental research, Western people are characterized by the 'buffered self' because we have largely rejected any porosity between this world and the next since the medieval period (Rooms, 2019a, pp. 14–15). The buffered self means that in the West the stranger is almost always imagined as a danger, rather than as blessing and gift (in Kiswahili, the language of Tanzania, there are no separate words for 'guest' and 'stranger'). Finally, it is clear to me from research I have conducted (Rooms, 2018) that Western 'post-Christians', as we might call them, are generally suspicious of the approach of Christians as they understand the Christians' need for recruitment in a declining Church.

A story might best illustrate this effect. In the second year of PMC, churches are invited to experiment with an adaptive challenge – as noted above, a challenge in their community they don't know the answer to. A church comprising of many professionals in a largely owner-occupier-populated parish knew one part of their community was different and had much more social housing present. They had never engaged with it and took the opportunity now through PMC to experiment and see if they could form meaningful public relationships there. The leader of the experimenting team had a highly professional day job but admitted to being terrified of making an approach in the name of the church to an individual they had never met from a list of potential such people the team had drawn up. The leader told us how they decided the best thing was to create a 'crib-sheet' of all the things that needed covering in the initial conversation, before a face-to-face meeting could happen. The phone call was made, the person answered (!) and the list was started upon. After around 30 seconds or so, it didn't seem to be going very well and so our experimenter got to the part where they admitted they came from the local church. 'Oh,' the person on the other end of the phone responded, 'I've been waiting for someone from your church to phone for 20 years!' This person ran a community centre on the social housing estate and knew the church might be able to help out, but had never been in touch. A 40-minute conversation ensued before the two people met together to make further plans. The local church's imagination about what was possible across their boundary entered a paradigm shift when this story became known among them.

Once churches begin acting in public in the name of their church, we have evidence from independent impact evaluation research[1] that what emerges among the membership is the possibility of 'public Christian witness', which is much more than individualized 'faith-sharing' though it definitely includes that (Rooms, 2019a, pp. 12–13). The new public action of the church creates a 'plausibility structure' for its members to take up their proper authority as people of faith in their community.

Community, community, community – fuzzy, porous boundaries

How does the local church form new Christian community around God's mission in the world? This is the next step on from learning how to form public relationships for their own sake. Again, from our internal research within existing PMC congregations we know that the current imagination about joining church is either through what we might call 'osmosis' and/or joining a catechetical course that inducts the novice into the tradition of the church they are joining. Osmosis is the belief that simply by joining and 'mucking in', somehow the new person will imbibe the faith from the existing members over time. In general this only works if the neophyte looks and talks like a majority of the existing people – if they are in any way different, they will be welcomed for a few weeks but they will find it difficult to fit in and will drift away. The congregation behaves unconsciously towards this stranger in freezing them out over time – what is happening is they are refusing to change or adapt to the presence and gifts of the newcomer. Just as they are terrified by crossing the boundary of the church into public, despite a physical Everyone Welcome sign outside the church, in truth only certain sorts of the public are actually welcome to cross into the church. There are more possibilities with the catechetical approach, if it is open to the stranger, but I suspect the same phenomenon may still operate in the longer term.

For new Christian community to form the church must be an 'Open System', fuzzy or porous at its boundary (Rooms and Keifert, 2019, pp. 8–9; Rooms, 2019a), such that the existing congregation is *open to being changed by those who are joining*. There is an inherent unresolvable tension in forming community between bonding/belonging and bridging/joining (Rooms and Keifert, 2019, pp. 23–4). The existing members, especially those who have been around a long time, 'belong': they positively hold the tradition and memory of the community and are faithful in the long term. Joiners are new, fresh in their faith and full of new ideas, but lack the depth and commitment of the long-term regulars. Holding all this together with the conflict that will inevitably arise is the task of the Christian leader. It is a complex and tricky task that requires great skill and judgement – and it is worth noting that this way of being the church is generally not taught in clergy training.

We have already referred to research in churches in the north of England where 'something was happening' – that is, new Christian community was forming, albeit in fragile and vulnerable ways (Rooms and Wort). In addition to having faced various kinds of dying, as we have already noted, all our research churches had also learnt how to create porous boundaries such that the people who were joining changed what pre-existed. I think of one ecumenically based new worshipping community that grew out of some local (relatively well-off) Christians starting a food bank and café. When the service users began to speak of the weekly event as church and ask for baptism, a whole new corporate reality emerged (for further examples see Rooms and Wort, pp. 80–3).

Spirituality (from the right hemisphere) trumps technique every time

All the tasks of the local church, whether upwardly in worship, inwardly in pastoral care or outwardly in mission, are, it goes without saying, rooted in spirituality. They begin and end in God. Focusing on creating spiritual capital is therefore the first task of the missional church, and will result in developing relational capital out of which economic capital will eventually emerge. This is a kind of waterfall or cascade, the source being in God and spirituality. The growth of the Church in the New Testament and throughout history follows this pattern, including renewal and reformation movements. What is curious therefore is the attempt in recent times in the Church of England to reverse this cascade; to apply enormous amounts of economic capital to create new relational capital through technocratic means in the hope that spiritual capital will result. In a final reflection on the deleterious effects of Modernity I turn to Iain McGilchrist's work on the right and left hemispheres of the brain, which I have explored more fully in a journal article (Rooms, 2022). What follows is a precis of how I introduce McGilchrist's thought in the article.

The human brain is divided into distinct left and right hemispheres. It is not that left and right hemispheres *do* different things, rather that they have distinct, different epistemic functions, different ways of attending to and seeing the world. There is, it seems, particularly in humans, an optimal relationship between the left and right hemisphere for flourishing that is constantly under threat because of the way the left hemisphere operates. The two different hemispheres offer different qualities of attention and McGilchrist demonstrates how the left hemisphere has tended over the course of Western history to dominate – resulting in its virtual hegemony in our current time. The differences in how the divided brain pays attention are key to understanding McGilchrist's argument. The left hemisphere *divides* and categorizes, it objectifies the world, sees things without relation to each other, only as separate entities; it reaches out to grasp the world, take power and rule; things have utility for the left hemisphere whether they are animate or inanimate. The right hemisphere on the other hand sees from the whole, understands all things as connected, allows things to simply be what they are and attends to the in-betweenness of the self and any Other with which it is in relationship.

Recovering the primacy of the right hemisphere (before and after the proper checks offered by the left hemisphere) is one of the most urgent tasks of Western society, on which human survival, according to McGilchrist, depends. The Church is also captured by the hegemony of the left hemisphere, as the above example of the reversal of the spiritual-relational-economic capital cascade shows. Spiritual practices that teach and train us how to pay attention especially through slowing down and silence reduce anxiety and enable us to dig deep wells of thirst-quenching water for a dry and broken world and church.

In PMC churches that engaged with the spiritual practices and stayed the course there was a distinct release of joy and even fun when the paradigm shifts required were made. A new freedom to be God's people with less anxiety and unfocused activity ensued and they became respected members of their wider communities, taking their place among the many others working for the good of all.

Conclusion

In this chapter I have attempted to answer the question we began with as to how local churches can 'be witness' in public to what God has done in Christ in our contemporary world. I hope readers can conclude with me that the answer to the question is not singular in any way. Three hundred years of a way of imagining how the world is, and the local church becoming embedded in that way of thinking and being, will not be shifted in six weeks or six months, though a lot can be achieved in six years, according to our data. There is not one thing that we can do, there are a multitude of complex interventions that are required and even then, resistance arising from the need for systemic equilibrium (or *autopoiesis* as it is known) in the church may win the day. Neither is there one person, a leader who alone can heroically lead God's people to the future. This work will be always one of community, embraced and supported by leaders, yes, but the task remains for the whole of the missionary people of God.

Several questions remain. Can we give ourselves, as national church bodies, the time we need away from anxious fixes that do not look more than ten years ahead? Could we allow culture change, experimenting and envisioning over a 30-year time frame, passing it on as a way of being beyond the end point of our current senior leaders? Can we look the death of the Church, as we have known and loved it in the West, in the face and believe in resurrection? Can we pay the price of all this when experiments fail, despair is a temptation and nothing seems to really change? Can we commit afresh to the God of mission always at work in the world, doing a new thing and calling us out beyond our safe horizons?

Note

1 We have conducted this research twice on the 150 or so PMC Churches in two batches, using the same methodology each time. The latest report is found here: https://churchmissionsociety.org/wp-content/uploads/2022/11/PMC_Review_Church_Mission_Society_2022.pdf (accessed 13.05.2024). The earlier report is embedded within it via a hyperlink on p. 2.

References

Bosch, David J., 1991, *Transforming Mission: Paradigm Shifts in Theology of Mission*, Maryknoll, NY: Orbis Books.
Carson, Timothy, Rosy Fairhurst, Nigel Rooms and Lisa R. Withrow, 2021, *Crossing Thresholds: A Practical Theology of Liminality*, Cambridge: Lutterworth Press.
Chatfield, Adrian and Nigel Rooms, 2019, *Soul Friendship: A Practical Theology of Spiritual Direction*, Norwich: Canterbury Press.
Davison, Andrew, 2019, *Participation in God: A Study in Christian Doctrine and Metaphysics*, Cambridge: Cambridge University Press.
Foulger, Will, 2024, 'New Things: A Theological Investigation into the Work of Starting New Churches across 11 Dioceses in the Church of England', Durham, UK: The Centre for Church Planting Theology and Research, Cranmer Hall, https://www.cranmerhall.com/wp-content/uploads/2024/03/New-Things-Final-1.pdf (accessed 1.05.2024).
Keifert, Patrick, 2006, *We are Here Now: A New Missional Era*, St Paul, MN: Church Innovations.
Lau Branson, Mark, 2004, *Memories, Hopes, and Conversations: Appreciative Inquiry and Congregational Change*, Lanham, MD: Rowman & Littlefield.
Milbank, Alison, 2020, 'The Gift of the Trinity in Mission', in Lucas, Susan (ed.), *God's Church in the World: The Gift of Catholic Mission*, Norwich: Canterbury Press, pp. 17–34.
Rooms, Nigel, 2018, 'Evangelism through Happiness? A Case-Study in Innovative "Pre-Evangelism" with Contemporary UK "Post-Christians"', *Mission Studies* 35.1, pp. 101–23.
Rooms, Nigel, 2019a, 'Understanding Local Church as Porous Living Systems: Insights from the Tavistock Tradition', *Ecclesial Practices* 6.2, pp. 182–97.
Rooms, Nigel, 2019b, *Missional Church: What Does Good Look Like?*, Cambridge: Grove Books.
Rooms, Nigel, 2022, 'Beholding: Recovering "Right Brain" Apophatic Spirituality for the Local Church in Mission', *Ecclesial Futures* 3.2, pp. 69–85.

Rooms, Nigel and Patrick Keifert, 2014, *Forming the Missional Church: Creating Deep Cultural Change in Congregations*, Cambridge: Grove Books.
Rooms, Nigel and Patrick Keifert, 2019, *Spiritual Leadership in the Missional Church: A Systems Approach to Leadership as Cultivation*, Cambridge: Grove Books.
Rooms, Nigel and Elli Wort, 2021, *Fuzzy Church: Gospel and Culture in the North of England*, Durham: Sacristy Press.

11

On the Ground: Pioneering a Fresh Expression of Church on an Outer Estate in Southampton

JON OLIVER

Monty's is a community hub, a grassroots charity and a fresh expression of church. It's a home from home, a family, a refuge. It's a place of hope and celebration, of tears and laughter. It's a full tummy and a happy heart. It's a place to connect to ourselves and to others, to creation and to the Creator. It's one of the best things I've ever been part of. And this is our story. (Or at least some of it.)

What would you like to see here?

My part in this story begins in 2013. At the time, I was a curate in Sholing – a large suburban parish on the eastern edge of Southampton – where I was released part-time to pioneer in the parish. Pioneering always begins with prayer, with listening deeply to God and to our context. So together with my wife Tammy I began prayer-walking around the parish, getting to know people, listening *with* them where possible, asking questions and being reminded that God often speaks from the most unexpected places. We explored lots of possibilities – engaging with schools and pubs, doing youth work and public art, reimagining our work with families, and loads more.

We were particularly on the lookout for a way to engage with a large estate on the outer edge of our parish; an area of significant and multiple deprivation, with minimal church engagement. In fact the parish had previously had a church building on the estate but it had closed down years before. Whenever we walked and prayed around the parish we always got a nagging sense that we needed to do something in this area, but had yet to find a way to connect.

Then one day the council announced the imminent closure of all the city's youth centres – including one based on this estate, in a shop unit within a small parade, right at the heart of the neighbourhood. We reached out and the local youth worker asked if the church could help, inviting us along to their youth club the very next day. I popped along, hung out with the kids and, as they prepared banners and petitions to save their youth centre, it dawned on me that this was the opportunity we'd been praying for; an opportunity to love, to serve and to join in with the local community. We arranged a meeting with the council, and a few weeks later I got a phone call telling me the centre was closing the next day – did we want the keys?

Obviously, yes!

We gathered together a handful of volunteers, got people praying and reopened the following week – starting off with just one weekly youth club. We were absolutely bursting with all sorts of ideas about what else we could do with this space, right slap-bang in the middle of this neighbourhood, but we knew this wasn't about us. We knew this wasn't about a bunch of well-meaning do-gooders from the other end of the parish coming in with our bright ideas. We were clear that we didn't want to do things 'for' people or 'to' people, rather we wanted to work 'with' our community. Therefore we took an 'asset-based' approach, which seeks to build on local gifts, skills, knowledge, capacities and other hidden resources, rather than simply trying to meet needs. In this way we hoped to create a culture of mutuality rather than dependency. As the saying goes, we wanted to use what's strong to address what's wrong.

One of the first things we did was to put up a massive sign in the window saying 'What would you like to see here?' and focused for months on getting to know our neighbours better; listening to their stories, their passions, their hopes. People told us they'd love another club for younger kids, a toddler group within toddling distance, and some homework support. In reply we told them we thought these were great ideas – and invited them to join in, to become volunteers and help make these ideas a reality. In this way, from the outset our team was drawn not only from the church but also the local community. Our nearest team members lived so close, they knew it was time to come over when they heard the clanking of our shutters opening!

We soon reimagined the centre as a community hub for people of all ages, and registered as a charity – both named Monty's Community Hub (after Montague Avenue, the main road through our estate). As we continued to listen to and work with our community, God always seemed to bring the right people along at the right time; bringing together our incredible volunteers, trustees, staff, friends and mentors, who helped make everything possible. Through this prayerful process of consultation, invitation and participation, we gradually grew into a thriving hub at the heart of our community – with well over 50 volunteers and hundreds of regulars, coming together to take positive action to improve their own and others' lives.

Fast-forward ten years and we've got a whole bunch of different youth clubs and activities, groups for parents and older people, health and well-being activities, community meals and a community pantry, educational and SEND support, training, mentoring, skills development, holiday activities and all sorts of other groups and activities. We've also developed Monty's Bike Hub – a bicycle-based social enterprise that teaches young people and adults how to fix their bikes, enables sustainable travel and healthy lifestyles, upcycles donated bikes to sell locally at affordable prices, offers alternative provision with kids at risk of exclusion from school, supports people to find routes into education and employment, employs half a dozen local residents and generates over half our annual budget.

Most importantly though, we've seen transformation in people's lives. We've seen young people growing in aspiration and achievement. We've seen local residents growing in confidence and capacity, working together to develop ideas for collective flourishing. We've seen people exploring faith for the very first time, and co-designing an expression of church that is both meaningful and accessible for our community.

Trusting the process

From the very beginning, from our very first youth club, we believed that all that we were doing was an expression of church in this particular place. Yet at the same time we were very intentional about our aspiration to see a distinctive ecclesial community emerge through this. We were church already, but not yet.

From the outset we had signposts to our church connection; not too in-your-face but obvious enough that people wouldn't feel tricked into getting unknowingly involved, and would feel able to ask questions if they wanted to know more. We installed a prayer box. We looked for opportunities to chat about Jesus. We regularly transformed the community hub into a 24-hour prayer room, full of fun and creative ways for people to explore prayer and the possibilities of God. We met fortnightly with a small group of local residents who were interested in exploring faith. We shared our lives and our faith with our volunteers and wider community. And through it all, we kept on praying, dreaming, scheming, hoping we'd see an ecclesial community emerge.

Throughout this journey we were clear that we wanted to nurture an expression of church that was meaningful and accessible within this particular community; we didn't want to crowbar in a Café Church, Messy Church or Sung Eucharist (or anything else) just because that's what we're familiar or comfortable with. Honestly though, after a few years I began to lose patience and started thinking about borrowing a model from elsewhere and simply plonking it in. Fortunately my team talked me out of it, reminded me that we were prayerfully following the fresh expressions journey and that as we continued to follow God's lead and respond to opportunities, eventually something authentic for this particular place would emerge. As Jürgen Moltmann suggests, it's not the church that has a mission to fulfil, it's the mission of God that creates a church along the way (Moltmann, p. 64).

Then one day, almost five years after we got the keys, I was chatting with one of my teammates, who had recently moved on to the estate. We talked about how exciting it was that more and more people were showing an interest in exploring faith. We also talked about how she and her husband had found it a bit hit-and-miss getting to know their neighbours, especially in terms of inviting them round for dinner, having found that loads of people preferred to watch TV while eating rather than chat around a table. However, they'd also found that there was something different, something special, about Sunday lunch – when people loved to get together over a roast and expected to eat and chat around a dinner table, often with their extended family and friends.

Something about this conversation felt special, holy, inspired. It wasn't complicated, but something clicked; loads of people wanted to explore faith and loads of people wanted to get together over a roast lunch. So we decided to give it a go.

A few weeks later, just after Easter, we invited people to join us for our very first Sunday Lunch Church. One of our volunteers cooked a giant roast lunch, and over 40 people turned up – to explore the Easter story and whether we'd like to meet regularly as a church. Everyone loved it (even those who loudly declared themselves atheists). They wanted to meet again soon, and to invite their friends. So we started meeting once a month – restricted in part by finding volunteers willing to cook a roast for this many people!

Our format isn't set in stone but when we meet we usually begin with a gathering prayer, before tucking into our huge roast lunch (with vegan options). We sit around a big table, often with conversation-starters on the theme of the day. After lunch we share a Bible story (using drama, video, godly play or simple storytelling) and then explore it in more depth, in groups or all together, through conversation and creative activities. We usually have crafts and games too, originally designed for the kids but often even more popular with adults. We sometimes sing songs. We often have space for people to share recent experiences of God and other good news. We usually end with a 'circle of gratitude' and our closing prayer. Then we have pudding, and finish the washing up.

Alongside this we've also developed a range of other gathering points – including a monthly 'wander and wonder' (where we explore God in nature, while walking, riding or paddling), various more liturgical or seasonal gatherings, and midweek groups for prayer, Bible study and young people.

Being/becoming church

The Church of England describes fresh expressions of church as being 'missional, formational, contextual and ecclesial', and I'd like to share a few reflections on our identity as an Anglican fresh expression of church, walking the unfolding path from the tradition of our past towards an uncertain future.

1) We are missional

We absolutely prioritize mission. When we talk about mission, of course we mean the *missio Dei*, God's own mission in and towards the world; healing, loving, forgiving, renewing. God was at work in our community and the lives of our neighbours long before we arrived, and God invited us to join in. And still does. Mission is not an optional extra, an add-on to the standard model church life – it's the core of who we are and what we do. As Emil Brunner suggests, 'The Church exists by mission, just as a fire exists by burning' (Brunner, p. 108).

We are focused on witnessing to the good news in our community, to making disciples, caring for creation, seeing people and place flourish. We are committed to the edges, to the margins, to the unchurched; especially those unable or unlikely to ever engage with mainstream church or show up to a Sunday service.

We are passionate about loving and serving with our community. I've sometimes described us as a serving community that gathers to worship, in contrast to a worshipping community that goes out to serve. On the one hand, this is a false distinction – because like the chicken and the egg, it's all cyclical (we gather to worship, we go out to serve, we gather, we go, we gather, we go), and because we worship God through our service, while serving God and others when we gather to worship. But on the other hand, I think this can be a helpful emphasis – because it reminds us of our identity as a people called to follow Jesus in his Way of love and service.

2) *We are formational*

We are all about discipleship. We are committed to journeying with people and seeing them grow in the Way of Jesus. We invite people to join us on this journey, regardless of whether or not they're interested in exploring faith. We're committed to seeing people flourish in themselves, in their relationships and in their faith. We've found that the distinction between evangelism and discipleship isn't always clear-cut, although authentic community is usually the best place for both.

From very early on, as we began to nurture a real sense of community, we found that loads of people started referring to this as their 'Monty's family' – a place where they're welcomed, loved, accepted; a place where they belong. As this sense of community grew, so too did our opportunities for discipleship. For many people this was an *inquisitive discipleship* – where we found or facilitated opportunities to ask questions about faith (such as at one of our prayer days, or simply over a cuppa) and were able to begin exploring the possibilities of God together. For many other people this was more of a *participative discipleship* – as they joined in, perhaps serving alongside us as volunteers, they found themselves being transformed by the way of life and love we shared together, long before they were able to give a name to this journey. Many others remain uninterested in finding out more about faith, yet continue to enjoy journeying together as we follow in the Way.

Several years ago, my wife Tammy asked Graham Cray for advice about doing discipleship in our contemporary context, and he suggested: 'The best way to do discipleship is to invite people to serve with you, to join in with you.' This is exactly what we found: the most effective discipleship happened while were serving alongside one another, often without words needing to be spoken. In fact we found that every single one of the people who joined our very first Sunday Lunch Church was one of our volunteers (or a member of their families).

3) *We are contextual*

We are rooted in our place, in our community. We take inspiration from the incarnation – in which Jesus moved into the neighbourhood, speaking our language and making his home among us (John 1.14, etc.). We seek to be truly rooted in our context, committed to listening deeply to people and to God in this place and to nurturing what emerges through this process.

And here's the hard part: to be truly contextual means that we need to *let go of the outcomes*. It means putting down all our own expectations, assumptions and agendas about what will emerge from this process. (Because if we think we know the answers before we even start, that's likely to be all we ever 'hear' when we attempt to listen to our community!) It means trusting in this process and trusting in the Holy Spirit to guide us into something more than we could ever think or imagine.

This is what we mean when we talk about being contextual, and in this way almost everything we've seen grow here has emerged from *within* our context, from within our community. This includes Sunday Lunch Church: as people gradually began to explore faith, we helped a new form of church take shape around them. We didn't follow an external blueprint as we explored what shape of church was appropriate for our context – instead, as we learnt about local rhythms (and tastebuds), and as we followed God's prompting, we were able to develop a pattern of church that is meaningful and accessible in this particular place.

4) *We are ecclesial*

From the very beginning we were clear that what we're doing here is an expression of church. First, this meant we didn't envisage Monty's as being some sort of missional or charitable enterprise apart from the church, but that everything we did was an expression of the church in this particular place. Second, this meant that we also hoped, prayed and planned from the outset that we would see a distinctive church community emerge within this.

Naturally there was the very real potential for this intention to conflict with our commitment to being contextual (to letting go of our assumptions and agendas). However, we found it possible to hold these two commitments in creative tension. On the one hand, we put down our assumption that an ecclesial community would definitely emerge, and let go of any agenda for what shape or format it might take if it did. On the other hand, we held on tight to our prayerful intention that we would see an ecclesial community emerge through our ministry here.

This intentionality is so important; we can't just idly hope a church will emerge while we're busy doing other things. Of course, Jesus promises to build his church (Matt. 16.18). However, he also invites us to join in the process (Matt. 28.16–20, etc.). And in my experience this requires deliberate intention, watchful waiting, hard work and divine guidance. It took five years before we gathered for our first Sunday Lunch Church, and throughout that time we were intentional about listening, growing community, making disciples, keeping our eyes open for opportunities and being ready to respond actively when the divinely appointed opportunity finally showed up. Throughout those years we didn't know for sure if an ecclesial community would ever emerge, and we didn't know what it would look like if it did. We knew it would include elements of mission, discipleship, community, giving, serving, teaching, Scripture, worship, baptism, communion and the expectation of transformation. But we didn't know what shape it would take or how it would all fit together. Instead we trusted in the process and the guidance of the Holy Spirit.

5) *We are Anglican*

Our gatherings may look unfamiliar but we're still Anglican. We gather around bread, wine and water. We have shaped something new in response to our context but really there's nothing new under the sun – after all, the church has been gathering around food since pretty much for ever. Among myriad definitions, I tend to agree with George Lings, who suggests that being Anglican isn't about whether we use centrally authorized worship texts or have a legal territory, but whether the bishop welcomes it as part of the diocesan family (Lings, p. 18).

My own bishop recently shared this gem from G. K. Chesterton: 'The more I considered Christianity, the more I found that while it had established a rule and order, the chief aim of that order was to give room for good things to run wild' (Chesterton, p. 113). This resonates deeply with our experience. The institution has established order and given us space. We have run wild. As we grow and mature, we are gradually becoming more ordered. Though hopefully not too much. And as we become more ordered, we too hope to make space to resource and release more good things, more fresh things. Doing so helps us to be renewed too. Unless we make space for fresh things to run wild we risk growing stale ourselves.

I believe the same goes for the wider Church of England. We need to make space for good things to run wild. If we're serious about becoming younger and more diverse, about prioritizing estates ministry and enabling access for all people, we need to be serious about making space for fresh things, for good things to run wild. We need to be serious about resourcing expressions of worship and witness that may feel completely unfamiliar, perhaps even uncomfortable. And as Graham Cray suggests, we need to ask ourselves over and over and over again: 'Who will never be reached if we only do what we're doing now?' (Cray, p. 29).

References

Brunner, Emil, 1931, *The Word and the World*, New York: Charles Scribner's Sons.
Chesterton, G. K., 1908, *Orthodoxy*, London: John Lane, The Bodley Head.
Cray, Graham, 2011, 'Youth Congregations: Right or Wrong?', *Youthwork* 2(4), pp. 28–30.
Lings, George, 2016, *The Day of Small Things*, Sheffield: Church Army Research Unit.
Moltmann, Jürgen, 1977, *The Church in the Power of the Spirit*, London: SCM Press.

12

On the Ground: Ecological Conversion and the Awakening from Earth Amnesia

JOHN WHITE

'When food, in the minds of eaters, is no longer associated with farming and with the land, then the eaters are suffering a kind of cultural amnesia that is misleading and dangerous.' (Berry, p. 145)

Earth amnesia

I awoke. Having spent my life sleepwalking through earth taking no notice of it. Benefiting from its life without ever concerning myself with it. My awakening happened in a city farm in Bristol. It was a beautiful warm day when I visited, I watched kids climbing trees and running around the allotments. I felt deep joy as I stood there, taking in the beautiful space that had been created. As the day progressed, I recognized that this city farm had many of the elements of a monastery. It is a hub for the community to gather around growing, food and education. My awakening was a beginning of seeing earth. Not just as something I notice in passing when it is too cold or hot, or when in a beautiful location on holiday. Rather it was the start of a journey seeing earth as the voice of God. Seeing in creation the glory of God and the blueprints of how to live. I have in time come to understand the language of St Francis of Assisi and the Canticle of Brother Sun and Sister Moon. Waking to discover earth is not separate from me. Rather I am part of the family of earth.

Another way of speaking of this awakening is what Pope Francis called an 'ecological conversion' (Francis, p. 220). This conversion opened my eyes to the fact that climate emergency is the biggest issue facing the world today and one that will need swift, radical and imaginative solutions (Alston, p. 1). And yet knowing all that we will face we continue to not make these changes. Why don't we make these radical and imaginative solutions? Norman Wirzba writes:

> Our growing separation from the land and our lack of understanding of the land's integrity result in a growing separation from people. Just as we view land abstractly – as a pile of natural resources – we also come to see people abstractly – as fodder for the growing economy. People cease to matter except if they contribute to a business plan. (Bahnson and Wirzba, p. 33)

We have distanced ourselves from land to the point that we have amnesia from the earth and only see it as a resource to be exploited. This is an issue of justice not just for land but for people – they are seen as resources to be exploited as well. Consideration must be given to the roots of earth amnesia and how we can wake from it.

Roots of earth amnesia

What is at the root of earth amnesia? Jürgen Moltmann offers a perspective:

> The crisis of the modern world is not due merely to the technologies for the exploitation of nature; nor can we put it down to the sciences which made human beings the lords of nature. It is based much more profoundly on the striving of human beings for power and dominion. (pp. 20–1)

This striving for power and dominion is the root of earth amnesia, the fruit of which is ecological breakdown/climate emergency. Earth is perceived as an asset that is meant to be exploited for our wants and desires. We add chemicals to the land to make it produce faster. We grow food and ship it across the world so that we can eat what we want whenever we want regardless of season. This creates a toxic consumerism as we can feel the effects of consuming what we want when we want, but the cost of this is abstract. We see the products of the earth without the cost to the earth; this toxic consumerism is the fruit of power and dominion. The earth continues to be an abstract concept that we are out of touch with. The result is that ecological breakdown is an abstract concept for much of the west. We cannot hear the groans of the earth.

Wirzba writes: 'Another way to describe our collective disorientation is to note that many people today do not know how to dwell in the places they are in' (2019, p. 83). The process of locating oneself in place and in land is the antidote for our land amnesia. Let us now consider the Christian response to the root of power and dominion and the need to awaken to place and land as an antidote in regards to the fifth mark of mission.

Fifth mark of mission

The Five Marks of Mission are a guide by the Church of England to help explain and guide mission in the church. For our purposes, we will consider the fifth mark of mission as it relates to caring for the earth. The fifth mark of mission is: 'To strive to safeguard the integrity of creation and sustain and renew the life of the earth' (Richards, p. 3). This mark of mission is meant to be a guide as to the direction the Church of England is heading in regard to creation. This mark of mission will be looked at critically through the lens of earth amnesia.

First, the fifth mark of mission assumes that humanity is the centre and it is our task to be care givers. This is a passive dominion theology. It is passive in that it is not explicitly stating our dominion over creation though it is assumed because it makes humanity the ones who safeguard, sustain and renew. This passive dominion means that we are muting creation and what it teaches us about Creator. We continue to live in earth amnesia believing that we can be the saviours of earth rather than learn from it. Earth is created by God to be our context, a context in which we are meant to be reminded of and to see the glory of God through it (Psalm 19.1). When we do not learn from the earth and see the glory of God in it, our answers to its problems tend not to involve the earth at all. For instance, in the Church of England the main focus has been on Net Zero. Net Zero has put carbon emissions from buildings at the centre of the conversation as well as all of its financial resources. This is an important piece of work but it ultimately places value on our created spaces (buildings) rather than engaging with the natural world that holds the fingerprints of Creator God. A church can fully subscribe to Net Zero while never engaging once with earth. Net Zero then is a manageable tickbox that enables us to continue to be in control, thus perpetuating a passive dominion theology.

Second, the fifth mark does not include a theology of earth or direct engagement with earth to be part of our spiritual practices. Wirzba critiques our spiritual practices:

> These spiritualities, though sometimes waxing eloquent about the beauties of this world, are fundamentally dualistic or gnostic. What I mean is that they assume materiality and embodiment to be deficient, and thus a lower order of reality that must ultimately be left behind, if not destroyed altogether. (2022, p. 3)

In the church today, earth is not nearly as important as spiritual realities. This allows the church to place earth in a category of mission rather than worship. It would be like saying it is important to safeguard the integrity of the Bible but not really engage deeply with it or listen to what it is saying. In the same way that we have a passive dominion theology so we have a passive Gnosticism. Though not directly stated, this edits out earth from our worship and seeks spiritual experiences that focus on spiritual practices that are disconnected from earth. We see earth as a place to save but not adding to our worship, thus creating a spiritual dualism. What is needed is a theology of creation that allows for listening and learning from earth. This repositions us, no longer as the centre but rather as part of a larger story of Creator and creation. This awakens us from a passive Gnosticism and dominion way of living and worshipping. I am not here claiming that at Hazelnut we have solved these issues. We are, however, trying to live differently and consider deeply these issues. I offer here the Hazelnut Community as an example of a practical way to encourage the church to awaken from earth amnesia and its effects.

Hazelnut Community

Remembering that day in the garden five years ago, we fast-forward to today. What has formed is Hazelnut Community, a church plant based around the rhythms of a community garden and the church calendar. It is also a network that aims to support churches in creating eco-congregations on their land in order to deepen worship, welcome their community and combat climate breakdown. This story is crucial because awakening from earth amnesia does not happen merely by reading a book or attending a lecture. These may help and aid the journey. However, the real work is done through putting hand in soil and engaging directly. Without this direct contact with land, awakening from our amnesia is not possible; it takes earth to see earth.

At Hazelnut the entire time is immersive and involved. We find the long road of waking up emerging from consistently linking Creator, creation and community. Birdsong as the backdrop for our prayers, unexpected conversations over a raised bed, standing around watching bees and counting their stripes, finding awe and wonder in God's creation. The entire garden is a sacred space. In fact it is our church, and we get to grow the walls of our church. This is a church that changes with the seasons, showing us the rhythms and patterns of life and thereby helping us to discover new ways of worshiping and living. Sharing from the produce of our worship, a sweet strawberry, a head of lettuce or a bouquet of sweet peas, makes worship tangible and bridges the gap between the hospitality of the altar and the hospitality of the dinner table. Gardening is not a hobby for our community though there is joy in it. What we have found is what Samuel Ewell so beautifully describes:

> Growing together is the art of creating and facilitating beneficial interactions in the ecology of relationships; I would argue that the same could be said about the relationship between ecological conversion and mission. We must value the edges in the local ecology of relationships, approaching them as privileged sites for reimagining mission and life together with neighbours in our shared garden. (Ewell, personal communication)

Lives lived together become diverse, like a shared garden, where those on the fringe become those at the centre. The gospel is propagated through caring for each other and visibly seeing life lived another way. Words of Pope Francis sum up the theology of holy biodiversity and capture the vision for Hazelnut Community as we begin our wonderful pilgrimage of waking from our earth amnesia:

> Everything is related, and we human beings are united as brothers and sisters on a wonderful pilgrimage, woven together by the love God has for each of his creatures and which also unites us in fond affection with brother sun, sister moon, brother river and mother earth. (Francis, p. 47)

We invite you to join with us as part of the family of earth. Created to encounter the glory of God in the heavens and earth through putting our hands in the soil. Awakening to the groan of the earth.

References

Alston, Philip, 2019, *Climate Change and Poverty: Report of the Special Rapporteur on Extreme Poverty and Human Rights*, United Nations Human Rights Council.
Bahnson, Fred and Norman Wirzba, 2012, *Making Peace with the Land: God's Call to Reconcile with Creation*, Resources for Reconciliation, Downers Grove, IL: IVP Books.
Berry, Wendell, 2018, *The World-Ending Fire: The Essential Wendell Berry*, ed. Paul Kingsnorth, London: Penguin Books.
Francis (Pope), 2015, *Laudato Si': On Care for Our Common Home*, Huntington, IN: Our Sunday Visitor.
Moltmann, Jürgen, 1993, *God in Creation: A New Theology of Creation and the Spirit of God*, The Gifford Lectures 1984–1985, Minneapolis, MN: Fortress Press.
Richards, Anne and Mission Theology Advisory Group, 2017, 'The Five Marks of Mission', London: Church House Publishing, 2.
Wirzba, Norman, 2019, *Food and Faith: A Theology of Eating*, 2nd edn, Cambridge: Cambridge University Press.
Wirzba, Norman, 2022, *Agrarian Spirit: Cultivating Faith, Community, and the Land*, Notre Dame, IN: University of Notre Dame Press.

13

Being Witness: Mission in a Changing Landscape

ANDY SMITH

The Church in England is navigating unprecedented change as it learns to minister in a postmodern, post-Christendom context. Where once it stood at the centre of community life, it now exists in a nation where the Christian story is just one voice among many. The chapters in Part II not only comment on the changes in wider society; they give practical testimony of what it means for the church to thrive and flourish in today's world. In doing so, they may offer us a glimpse of the future of the church in England and its participation in the mission of God as it serves the nation.

Each chapter offers theological reflection on diverse and unique contexts, and each offers differing methodologies reflecting their differing cultural setting. Yet there are common themes across them all: each provides an emerging vision of a church existing in a wider society that is increasingly sceptical of institutions and hierarchical power structures; and each reflects the changing nature of the Church of England's position in wider society. Across the contributors, four common themes emerge:

1. The postmodern and post-Christendom social context.
2. The movement from host to guest within wider society.
3. Shared theological lens, *missio Dei* and the Five Marks of Mission.
4. The challenge and necessity to retain a distinctly Christian witness amid continual societal change.

These chapters call for the church to remain rooted in the stories of Jesus yet flexible in how it engages within a rapidly and continually changing world, to be bold and yet humble.

1. Mission in postmodern and post-Christendom Europe

Each contributor in Part II acknowledges the significant societal shifts within contemporary Britain. Whether on an outer urban estate in Southampton, in the diverse, multicultural milieu of east London, with the Hazelnut farm community in Bristol, across the UK with pioneer ministers working with those on the fringe of society, or through the Partnership for Missional Church process, each author assumes with confidence that a significant cultural shift has taken place.

For each of the authors, postmodernity and post-Christendom are now simply a given of wider culture and unquestionably the dominant world view of contemporary Britain. If culture is 'the water we swim in', in that it is difficult to observe, but simply 'the ways things are', then often to comment well on the changes in our culture, we need those from outside. The Lutheran Archbishop of Estonia describes how secularism is now the dominant ideology of the European continent, such that it is 'close to becoming a religion in and of itself' (Viilma). As someone who was born and grew up in the former Soviet Union, in the midst of an oppressive political world view that included state atheism, Archbishop Viilma's observation of religion across contemporary Europe is particularly striking.

The context of each of our authors within the Church of England reflects this wider trend across Europe. That context is more than simply a decline of the church or fewer people expressing Christian faith, but that this world view is replaced with another world view altogether, and it is in this post-Christendom world view that each of the authors seeks to minister. Each author takes postmodernity and post-Christendom as a given of their cultural context. Each is also unequivocal that these changes demand that the church re-contextualize to be an effective Christian presence in contemporary society. There is consensus that to be an effective witness today requires a radical shift in missional practice.

2. From host to guest: a shift in posture

A key theme emerging is the change in how the church must relate to wider society; the shift can be described as from *host* to *guest*. Historically, the church acted as the *host*; not only was the church the institution within society that shaped social norms and values, it was also the convenor and arbitrator of such conversations – it set the agenda. This included education, healthcare, social cohesion and morality. Increasingly the church is no longer the most influential voice, and furthermore no longer sets the terms of debate or the agenda. This is a paradigm shift in how the church engages with the world.

The approach is far more profound than accepting that the church has less influence in the conversation. It requires a new orientation, a new posture, a new way of being. The church does not control or host the dialogue anymore. Instead it is called to humbly step into the places where these conversations are already happening, ready to listen and earn a right to speak with openness and generosity.

The change in posture, from *host* to *guest*, requires the church to embrace a vulnerability that differs from its usual way of operating. It necessitates giving up its need or desire to be in control of the narrative; instead it is called to listen deeply, including to those it profoundly disagrees with. This process may very well feel uncomfortable. Being a Christian witness in such an environment means watching for signs of the Kingdom in unexpected places, knowing that as we step out into the unknown, we discover that Jesus is ahead of us – he is already there.

Jonny Baker in Chapter 9 draws on these themes, focusing on listening to those on the edge of society and learning when to speak and when to keep silent – especially evident in his response prayer. Jon Oliver in Chapter 11 reflects this in a missional approach within an urban estate that sought to listen deeply *with* (rather than *for*) the wider community, discerning a need for a safe space for youth and responding to this social need in developing Monty's. Such an approach is also fundamental for the Partnership for Missional Church described by Nigel Rooms (Chapter 10) and for Ana França-Ferreira and Angus Ritchie's missional approach in East London (Chapter 8).

The Church of England has much to learn from the church in other parts of the world, where being a *guest* rather than a *host* has always been its modus operandi. In many global contexts, both where Christianity is a minority religion or where it is one of a plurality of faith traditions, the church is experienced and adept at such an approach. In these contexts the church is often marked by service and listening. It speaks to wider society, having earned a right to and been invited through the building of trust and influence. An example of this can be found in much of the church in Christian minority south-east Asia. In such contexts the church models a Christian witness not through power or control but through trust, relationship and service.

Ultimately the shift from *host* to *guest* is a reimagining of the church's place in and witness to society. It requires an acceptance that it is no longer the dominant institution, operating from a position of power and control, nor dominating the terms of the debate. It is called to witness God's redeeming life through genuine reciprocal relationship, through listening and loving service. This approach does not weaken the church but roots it more deeply in the lives and stories of those it encounters and the stories and mission of the Jesus we follow.

3. Shared theological lens: *missio Dei* and the Five Marks of Mission

During the theological symposium that laid the foundation for this book, there was extensive group work concerning the nature of mission in the contemporary world. The symposium hosted theologians and practitioners from across the theological and cultural diversity of the Church of England. We invited participants from theological colleges, cathedrals, parishes, pioneers, church plants, rural, estate, urban, universities, chaplaincy and mission agencies; it was intended to be diverse and representative. There was a significant commonality and unity from across this diversity during the discussions on the nature of mission. Underpinning this consensus was a shared language and theological framework; this allowed for creative conversations, for each other to be heard well without feeling threatened, and for each different theological viewpoint to sense it had a valued place in the wider dialogue. The significant differences were more about emphasis or practice, but people held to this lightly. In an era of polarized conversations, whether about human sexuality or parish vs pioneer vs plant, it was a welcome and joyous moment of shared unity. We really are one church. The areas of commonality were anchored first, in a common agreement of *missio Dei* being the source of mission and, second, in the Five Marks of Mission.

First, that mission is primarily understood as an identity of God rather than a task of the church, the *missio Dei*. Mission is who our God is, the triune God, who sends himself to the world to redeem creation; the task of the church is to join in with God's great plan to redeem his world. As Lesslie Newbigin argues, the church's mission is not a self-generated project; but a participation in the mission of God (Newbigin, pp. 118–19). Not only was this evident within the symposium, each of the chapters here has this as implicit throughout their theological approach, with Nigel Rooms, Jon Oliver and Jonny Baker discussing it explicitly.

Second, mission is broader than either of the typological theological defaults of a primary focus on social justice or evangelism. The Five Marks of Mission act as a focus for unity across the theological spectrum, and while different theological traditions may emphasize one of the marks more prominently than another, across all traditions there is an acceptance that each of the marks is of value and each is necessary. John White names the marks of mission in his chapter and focuses his theological reflection on the fifth mark of mission, to safeguard the integrity of creation. All the other chapters have a broad understanding of mission, encompassing the breadth the five marks demonstrate; each is clearly informed by them.

It seems significant, indeed, that the shared theological lenses that allowed for such unity coalesced around two theological approaches that, in the history of theology, are fairly recent. The concept of *missio Dei*, as we understand it today, originated only from theological discussion in the mid-twentieth century, developed by Karl Barth and Lesslie Newbigin and taken further by David Bosch. The Five Marks of Mission developed even later, only officially articulated by the Anglican Consultative Council in 1984.

Isabelle Hamley expresses in Chapter 7 that the conversations at the symposium relating to church and ecclesiology were far more fraught than those on mission. If these two lenses, developed only in the last 60 years, can provide such unity in the contemporary understanding of mission and witness, would such a theological development be possible in our ecclesiology? And what would that do to our visible unity? Perhaps it would be rooted in the ecclesiological lens of Sign, Instrument, Foretaste or some other yet to be developed proposal. What seems essential is that even if these conversations are fraught and challenging, they must continue to take place and that we all continue to pray and hope for a deeper unity in our shared life together.

4. A distinctly Christian witness amid continual societal change

Finally, observe within the contributions a striving to retain a prophetic and distinctive Christian voice as the church reimagines its role in society. There is an unhelpful caricature that missional approaches such as those in these chapters, in attempting to engage afresh with society, in revaluating power, in choosing to spend time with those on the edges, in listening before speaking, also compromise or somehow dilute the distinctiveness of the Christian story. This body of work challenges that. The contributions note that it is critical for the message to remain rooted in the life and teachings of Jesus, not in a way that isolates or judges but that points to a different vision of what it means to be human, demonstrating a love that is radical, for all, and unafraid to confront injustice.

John White in Chapter 12 notes the importance of integrating care for creation into God's mission, framing environmental stewardship as a core expression of living out the story of Jesus today. Ana França-Ferreira and Angus Ritchie in Chapter 8 highlight that the Centre for Theology and Community seeks to 'ground churches' organizing more deeply in the faith and worship'. Jonny Baker's proposition in Chapter 9 is to 'turn to the Gospels for an ecclesiology that resonates with today's challenges, especially being witness to the edges'.

Conclusion

The chapters in Part II portray a church dynamically engaged with the world around it and deeply rooted in its faith. They depict a church with a renewed focus on mission, actively participating in God's work in the world; a church that is learning to listen in fresh ways to God and his work in the world, to culture and society, to those on the margins, and to the needs of the earth. Together these contributions challenge the wider church to embrace its role as both a humble guest and a bold witness to a world that desperately needs hope.

References

Newbigin, L., 1989, *The Gospel in a Pluralist Society*, London: SPCK.
Viilma, Urmas, 2020, 'Archbishop Urmas Viilma's sermon in Haapsalu Cathedral, Baltic Bishops' Meeting', https://eelk.ee/uudised/archbishop-urmas-viilmas-sermon-in-haapsalu-cathedral-baltic-bishops-meeting/ (accessed 11.10.2024).

PART III

Being Pilgrim

14

Being Pilgrim, Being Parish

CHRIS HODDER

Introduction

One advent, zooming from an assembly to a funeral, I came off my bicycle, landing on my wrist. I dusted off, carried on to church, took some ibuprofen, conducted the funeral and then continued non-stop through other pre-Christmas events, a school run and tea, before heading out to PCC. At 10 p.m. I finally got to A&E, where they discovered a fractured scaphoid bone. What irony – here I was, maintaining the pastoral offices and rushing around civic events, while reminding my congregations to make space, slow down, prepare and reflect on the meaning behind the season.

Being a parish priest is a vocation to the best job in the world. It can be tough though. Recent discussions at General Synod and in the press include the Church of England's national strategy, finance, clergy numbers, buildings, minster churches, church planting, fresh expressions, ministerial identity, the need to 'save the parish', the increasing complexity of running voluntary organizations in the modern world and lament over growing centralization and managerialism within the church.[1]

It is not my intention to repeat well-covered debates.[2] Neither will I attempt a comprehensive missional theology for parishes acceptable to all within the Church of England. I will say something hopeful but realistic about what parish ministry can be when faithful to tradition and creatively missional; how we might approach leadership in that context; and how the wider church might mitigate some of the challenges of parish life. Where might we find God at work as we attempt 'being pilgrim, being parish', and how might we join with him?

Pilgrim communities who enjoy God

I'll begin by pointing out something obvious but sometimes overlooked in discussion about ministry – and that is, ministry is to do with God.

I remember, when exploring curacy options, reading the words of David Newman, my future training incumbent, about his hopes for the relationship between trainer and curate. They 'would be colleagues, albeit hopefully friends; professional in their attitudes towards ministry but without losing their simple faith and enjoyment of God'. David embodied that. As things turned out, the parish was a forgiving and special place to learn and grow as a young curate, but I would have happily been his curate anywhere, because the 'anywhere' would be shaped in a more forgiving and special direction by his ontology. Good spiritual leaders embody the message.

Remembering that ministry is to do with God is a vital safeguard in an increasingly secular age, as Andrew Root (2017, 2019, 2022a, 2022b, 2022c, 2023), building on Charles Taylor (2007), reminds us. His 'secular age' diagnosis of the twenty-first-century church is rooted in a North American context, and copious in volume. Nevertheless it is a corrective to some of the busyness, activism, obsession with programmes or latest ministry big ideas, and managerialism in the contemporary church leadership, critiqued by Davison and Milbank, by Martyn Percy and by Alison Milbank (2023a) among others. Root argues that attempts to find magic bullets that will arrest church decline demonstrate that the ideology of the secular age has taken deep root within the church itself. This ideology manifests in three symptoms.

Symptom one is connected to the division between the sacred and the secular. Despite our Christian roots, we now live in an age when the sacred no longer sets the agenda for all of society. Symptom two is a division between the public and the private sphere in terms of faith. If our society appears to function without its sacred foundation – murder is still murder, after all, whether or not we believe the Ten Commandments – then our motivation for attending church shifts from participation of faith in a public profession to participation of a private, more individual commitment.[3] Symptom three is connected to the division of the immanent and the transcendent, and the disenchantment of the world as we know it now.[4]

The danger is that church leaders become limited by the secular imagination. Proclaiming our faith, we betray our functional atheism by being trapped in the immanent frame, believing the church would grow if only we organized it better, bought into the latest programme, utilized the latest resources or led it into activism. God is a flat concept – a final contingent relation behind the curtain of other explanations – rather than an active or speaking agent in this world (Root, 2022b, p. 11). We say we believe in God – but we don't really believe he will turn up. The result can be what Root terms 'acceleration', busy people with a busy church that burns out, as opposed to the resonance that comes with real waiting. This is not to argue that innovation or programmes are, in and of themselves, unhelpful – discerning and communicating vision is a key part of effective church leadership – but it is a reminder that the task of parishes as pilgrim people is not to bring God to others but rather to discern where God is already at work in a given place and join in with him.

This notion is central to the concept of the *missio Dei*, part of Christian thought for centuries since Augustine (Poitras) but particularly significant since Karl Barth's address to the Brandenburg Missionary Conference in 1932. Barth's address reminded his hearers that understanding mission as an activity of God transforms one's view of the church and the world (Moltmann; Newbigin; Bosch). Mission is not something the church does or has but rather a movement of God to the world. Put succinctly, it is not that the church of God has a mission, but the God of mission has a church (Bosch, p. 390). This transforms our understanding of ministry and what it means to be a pilgrim people journeying with God in a parish.

Root (2022b, p. 16) reminds us that if we affirm that the church is the body of Christ we are affirming that the church's life is found in the resurrected body of Jesus himself. What gives the church life is participation in this body of Jesus by receiving the Holy Spirit, who is the Spirit of Life. This Spirit, who raised Jesus from the dead, is given at Pentecost, and the church lives because the Spirit lives within us, individually, in our gatherings and, crucially, in the world beyond.[5]

My curacy profile resonated because I knew instinctively that churches are richer when the vicar genuinely loves and enjoys the God whose love they are sharing with the parish(es) in which they serve. Of course, that is easy when life is going well; but as the psalmists attest, a fully dimensional relationship with God will also mean there is pain, anger, doubt as well as joy – the full spectrum of human experience. Part of the power of parishes is that they are pilgrim communities who have been through the ups and downs of the contexts in which they are set, including when people are dealing with life's wounds. That is the particular gift of occasional offices and the sharing together of life in the regular rhythm of weekly worship. As Root acknowledges, pedagogically it is helpful to show and not just tell people theological ideas (2022b, p. xi).

Pilgrim communities where people can belong and grow in the faith – from cradle to grave

Sherry and Jane had known each other for many years.[6] Contrasting but strong personalities, they were long-term church members who had supported and rubbed along together as their families had grown up. Jane, it was fair to say, was a bit of a 'me too, duck' with ailments. If you had a cold, she had had flu. If you banged your shin, she had broken her ankle before, and would tell you about it – at length. Sherry was more stoic and 'get on with it' in attitude, staying in the background. As an ongoing act of service to others Sherry always quietly moved out from her seat during the last hymn to start brewing the post-service teas and coffees for the church family – a ritual as familiar as the blessing I would pronounce as the hymn ended.

Now though, Sherry was in hospital. We had shared her long journey with cancer, and I had just finished reading Psalm 23 and offering prayers for grace, forgiveness and blessing while anointing her forehead with the sign of the cross. The words now finished, we sat silently together for a while. I held her hand. Internally I was wishing I could do more, and feeling the sadness that this might be our last time together in this life. Perhaps aware of what was going on inside me, Sherry looked kindly into my eyes and said, 'It is not all bad, Chris. At least I can say I have had something Jane has never had.'

In context, it was one of the funniest quips I have ever heard – summing up their relationship perfectly and demonstrating the link between tragedy and comedy. Sherry died the next morning, at the perfect time – as in life, so in death, she slipped out exactly while we were singing the final hymn.

It is hard to adequately express the beauty and tenderness present in end-of-life ministry. I don't want to romanticize it – not everyone goes gently into that good night, and the manner of death can leave wounds and trauma. But sometimes we do accompany someone on their way to a 'good' death. Parishes are pilgrim communities in concrete places where relationships grow, and the immanent, which is to say the presence of God in the world, as Root reminds us, can be witnessed – and witnessed to – over time. God is present in the mystery of life and death and the meaning of the gospel story is shared and lived together. Although, sadly, sometimes relationships in churches can be difficult, as they can in any community, at their best they are a means of growth and grace where we learn about ourselves and God.

Root contends that Taylor (2007) has taught us that the good life demands narrative (2022a, p. 184). You need a story about what makes life good to have an identity – a story that gives the different happenings in our life coherence. A parish is a spiritual, pilgrim community that enables this, and mediates people's experiences of God into a shared, embodied faith story. The Anglican tripos of Scripture, reason and tradition is a framework where our individual stories interact with the bigger stories of the local parish, the wider church and God's activity in the wider world, all of which enables coherence to be achieved by more than just an echo chamber.

This larger context is a crucial gift parish communities give that enables growth in a spiritually mature way. Although the nature of any geographic area will place limits on diversity, parishes are nevertheless communities who avoid some of the limitations caused by 'the homogenous unit principle' that, drawing on the legacy of McGavran, some argue are seen in fresh expressions. Fresh expressions have an important place within a mixed ecology – but parishes as pilgrim communities are a necessary and important counterbalance to them socially, missionally and ecclesiologically.[7]

In that regard, and before Root, Peterson's (1989) insights into the role both of pastoral ministry and geographically rooted church help us to understand the way they can enable the curing of souls – enabling spiritual direction in between, as well as on, Sundays. Healthy churches enable people to share their experiences of God and one another and become proficient in the language of personal intimacy and relationship, allowing us to experience resonance, as Root (2017 and later) would have it.[8]

Pilgrim communities with a vision that is faithful to tradition and relevant to culture

Parishes can have an integrating function, enabling God's pilgrim people to experience the resonance that comes through encountering God both individually and communally in a disconnected, accelerating world (Root, 2017). How then do we enable parish ministry as well as we can?

With Milbank (2023a), one answer is that simply by being connected to the ongoing inheritance of their tradition, parishes offer a witness to the gospel in their locality. Another is to do with specificity – arguably contra Milbank (2023a), there are ways to sharpen a church's connection with its culture, without necessarily losing its DNA or giving into managerialism or the spirit of the age. To say we must be careful with innovation is not to demonize it or call for inertia – the God of Israel is after all a God who moves (Root 2022b, p. 26). Given that Augustine's famous claim that 'all truth is God's truth' was enthusiastically picked up by the Reformation, there is something odd about arguing we have nothing to learn from the insights of the world, even if we do need to exercise discernment.

If the Holy Spirit is at work in culture (Bosch; Sherry), then although we need to be aware of the ultimate *telos* (Cavanaugh), there is nothing inherently wrong with a mixed-ecology church within which parishes have a prominent role; and within a parish, faith brands, programmes and theologically thought and prayed through vision/leadership processes can be a means of incarnating the gospel without becoming the end in themselves (Hodder; Einstein).[9]

Root and Bertrand's (pp. 101ff.) exercise for this discernment is for churches to prayerfully consider the needs of their communities and to develop a scripturally rooted 'watchword' that shapes their common purpose. Certainly a parish's vision needs to be connected to their prayerful discernment of the *missio Dei*. The minister, PCC and leadership team need to continually ask the 'God question' that I am arguing should be at the heart of all ministry – 'Where is God in all of this?'

In that regard I want to note three aspects of what I call a 'both-and' vision, before briefly considering some implications for dioceses and the national church.

Pilgrim parishes with 'both-and' vision

Pilgrim parishes should possess a both-and vision, faithful to what is good about their tradition, while connecting with the culture around them. Usually they are geographical places with a long history of celebrating and enacting Christian faith, so the people in their pews offer a rich resource to inform – without limiting – our discernment of where God has been and is at work in a local community. They neither need to be stuck in the past nor slaves to the now, but can navigate the task of what Wright (1991, 2011) calls 'faithful improvisation'.[10] Attending faithfully to both tradition and culture, pilgrim parishes are led by the Spirit to the fulfilment of their story in God's Kingdom, enabling their community to flourish as they navigate cultural changes in the world around. Hiestand and Wilson, and Vanhoozer and Strachan helpfully build on this in their argument for the primacy of being a theologian – viewing all life through a Christ-centred eschatological lens – in Christian leadership, as a counterweight to the danger of managerialism. As Percy (2022) notes, without theological vision, the people perish.

This both-and aspect is true not just of tradition and culture but also of the local and the national (or global); it is true of sharing the resources of faith and seeking justice; of word and sacrament; and of being Anglican, while being ecumenical. We may not be the only church in our locality and will learn from working with churches, as well as other faith or community groups. Both-and is also true of embracing diversity as well as challenging culture. Churches need to be places of grace, but inclusion in and of itself is not a gospel value, and (as Davison and Milbank rightly point out (pp. 78–9)), the gospel is not compatible with every aspect of a culture. We cannot proffer a thin incarnation that excludes the cross, resurrection, judgement and transformation.

Leading churches through change, with people's varying theological and cultural perspectives, differing liturgical tastes and temperamentally distinct attitudes to innovation, is a complex art requiring spiritual and pastoral sensitivity. David Newman joked that if the guns were silent either side of us, then we weren't in the right position! But discerning how to faithfully improvise, balancing the needs of growth, innovation, stability and faithfulness to tradition, is possible. As Peterson (1989) argues, it is not a distraction from the task of leadership. It is leadership, or at least a sizeable part of it.

A parish I led utilized its saint's day every year to gather as a whole church, pray, reflect and discern priorities for the coming year. We prepared through teaching/preaching, prayer and reflection over a number of weeks, and the day itself started and ended with prayer/worship. There was a mixture of input, group discussion and plenary facilitated by another, trusted church leader (embodying the connection between the wider church and our parish), as well as hospitality and eating together. Having reflected on the ideas discussed, we would each have three sticky notes to vote on the general priorities we felt God was leading us towards that year. This acted as a filter on the 'good ideas club' and managed our workload – there might be ten areas of a church's life that need developing, but sometimes less is more and you can't do it all at once. We also reflected on what we could stop doing to release energy for new growth.

It was remarkable how consensus emerged during these prayerful discussions. A part-elected, part-selected vision group then worked on the details of these general areas, reporting back to the PCC so their work could be overseen, authorized and communicated. The whole church community was on the journey but smaller groups were empowered to work out the detail and deliver. Curing souls and discerning vision were not separate, but a joint enterprise of working out how our church could join in with God's will for the local community.

Pilgrim parishes who attend to welcome and belonging

Pilgrim parishes also attend to welcome and belonging. Like Jesus in the Emmaus story, we sometimes walk alongside people who are heading in the wrong direction when we encounter them, as the disciples were. As we walk and share their story, Christ is gradually known. Sometimes this is slow, patient work; other times the penny decisively drops and they encounter him in the breaking of the bread, before then turning round and going to tell others about their meeting with the risen Lord.[11]

I recently dedicated a new altar cloth in one of the small village parishes in Lincolnshire in which I serve when RAF duties allow. It was being repurposed – once a 'best' tablecloth used for entertaining in the heart of a family home, now it was being offered for the table at the heart of the church family's food and drink celebration. The Eucharist is about the hospitality of God. We are the recipients of God's radical hospitality; and we, through a meal that is both encounter and witness, then offer his hospitality to others.[12] While Christian integrity necessitates that the church has a 'process of reception', it does not nevertheless own the sacrament. It is God's, and saints and sinners alike have stood in our parish churches, sometimes for centuries, each receiving the same grace. Nor is this task, even in the Eucharist, solely the role of the priest – the *Common Worship* ordination charge is explicit that '*With all God's people*, they [those about to be ordained priest] are to tell the story of God's love.'[13]

Most parish churches are accommodating, kind, welcoming and flexible communities, whose situatedness and long history of serving has given them strong integrity and clear ways of being. As someone now ministering in the armed forces, where short-termism and geographical instability can be the order of the day, I can tell you that you don't always appreciate something until it is gone.

Intentionality in fostering this community need not be contrived, and indeed is central to curing souls. Good administration, through clear intention, enables good pastoral care. Building collaborative teams to help ensure that pastoral needs are overseen, recognizing and releasing the gifts of all of the people of God and thinking constructively about how you enhance even simple areas of a church's life can help the whole church community reflect theologically about their *raison d'être*. One church I led considered how we did 'welcome' using *Everybody Welcome* by Jackson and Fisher. Talking about what a visit to our church looked like to newcomers, how to follow up visitors and what our pathways to inclusion within the church looked like released considerable energy. Suddenly the whole church was reflecting on wider questions – our patterns of worship, the role of welcomers, the pastoral team, our small groups and, more fundamentally, our shared sense of call and vocation within the local community. Why, under God, were we here at all? What (or who) were we welcoming them to? Attending to the human aspects of being church, thoughtfully and prayerfully, enhances local ministry without reducing it down to technique.

Pilgrim parishes who enable people to question and articulate faith

Is faith in Christ caught or taught? The answer, once again, is both-and. People have discernible points on their faith journey, but delineating believing and belonging too neatly becomes like the chicken and egg argument. There is a place for structured catechesis, whether through branded or locally created courses, and I have used several, in different ways and in different contexts. A particular strength of parishes is that they offer a natural space to blend thoughtful, focused opportunities to do evangelism with the natural rhythm of the liturgical, academic and civic calendars that provide shape to the lives of people in the local area. Churches of all traditions can grow, but they do need to be the kind of church that people are happy to invite their friends to. Most importantly, although programmes and courses have their place, they are sterile – and indeed could be counterproductive – if not accompanied by the walking alongside that enables the questioning and articulation of faith in a way that helps people to recognize God at work in their lives.[14]

This resonance can be seen in action (Root, 2017). You know you are being pilgrim, being parish, when:

- You see the baby you prayed for in the womb being baptized, and sense the trajectory of grace.
- You are shepherding people, some who feel change is coming too quickly and some who are frustrated it is not coming fast enough.
- You hear someone who was married in the church share the pain of how the relationship broke down, then see them walk not just through the valley of loss but into the joy of a new relationship being blessed and celebrated.
- The PCC is not simply about buildings and survival, but pregnant with the life of God, which is more than – but connected to – the finance reports, deanery news, pastoral care and vision/strategy items.
- A young person owns the faith of their baptism for themselves, having experienced the toddler group and church contact with their local school.
- Long-term members begin to catch the vision, serving in new ways and participating in the culture-making.
- You stand in the church lounge after your midweek Eucharist watching the older members delight in the life of the toddler group, eyes lighting up as they watch children exploring the toys, and one holding a baby so the mum can grab a mug of tea and a breather at the hatch.
- The church connects with the needs of the world around it, local, national or global, large or small, and members see the coherence of their faith with the Bible in one hand and their smartphone news app in the other.
- The school gate, post office, pub car park or dog walk routes are places of encounter.
- The communion rail has space for saints and sinners alike (we are both, after all); and where the spaces in the rail are noticed, prayed for and followed up that week.
- People walk together through their valleys, ordinary seasons and mountain tops, and share together in the life of the same Spirit who raised Jesus from the dead, enlivened the disciples at Pentecost and lives in the spaces of our gatherings, 'where two or three are gathered ...'.

A pilgrim church for pilgrim churches?

Embodying the enjoyment of God, enabling belonging, being faithful to tradition and relevant to culture – pilgrim churches walk as Christ's community through time and place. They connect tradition and history, while remembering their provisional nature in the space between their founding by and their fulfilment in Christ. What do such parishes need from their diocesan leadership or the national church?

Parishes vary hugely in their health and morale in different areas, parts of the country and dioceses. There are obvious debates about increasing clergy numbers, resourcing lay ministries, managing buildings and financial demands realistically, encouraging a culture of giving and making sure that incumbencies are 'doable' rather than marriages of convenience where clergy will rush around feeling dispirited as they manage decline. The gap between training posts and incumbencies can feel sizeable, and transition training or new incumbency support is helpful. Character and charism need to remain central to our understanding of ministry. When it comes to 'character', we need clergy to be collaborative team players, rejoicing in rather than feeling threatened by the gifts of others, and encouraging lay ministry.

Translating the vision and strategy of the national church locally needs careful communication and listening. Dioceses should not be imposing this from the top down, even if sometimes it is helpful for incumbents to be able to reference something external to challenge their congregations. Ministry is never complete, so special care is needed when it comes to data. Attendance and finances tell part of a parish's story, and sometimes difficult questions need to be asked, but we need to continue to ask the 'God question' and to be aware of the danger that sometimes in attempting to measure what we value we can end up valuing what we can measure. Nowhere is this more emotive than in relation to clergy numbers or buildings, where painful decisions need to be faced. Dioceses must help their clergy to find the best ministry-focused outcomes in different locales.

Different parish settings also bring different challenges in terms of the stressors, expectations and people – rural, urban, suburban, multi-parish and especially in socially disadvantaged areas, where clergy may need substantial support. One antidote to this, which would also combat perceived managerialism, is for senior diocesan staff to place a high priority on spending quality time with their clergy and church lay leadership teams – establishing learning/leadership communities, mentoring and walking alongside. What needs to happen to free senior staff up to do this? Bishops and archdeacons should be pastoral theologians who cure souls among parish leaders. Enjoyment of God should be modelled in every part of the church's life, and if ministry is to do with God, clergy and lay leaders need to be encouraged to maintain their inner life. A priest wrote to me recently:

> The church has asked me to serve in parish ministry, and I seek to follow Jesus as a disciple, while needing to attend to new believers, growing leaders, management, administration, safeguarding and a plethora of other things which mean we can pay the money into a common pot so ministry can happen beyond our door. Yet more than anything I need to be a person of prayer. Being a person of prayer is entirely unremarkable, and won't put you in the limelight, but it sustains the love for God and parishioners in the low days.

What else? A culture more open to calculated risk-taking might be helpful. There is always a need for proper oversight, training and safeguarding, but too often we are risk-averse to the point of stifling innovation. A bishop I respected often said he would rather people begged forgiveness than waiting to ask permission, and if dioceses can get the pendulum in the correct place in relation to creative risk-taking that would be a good place to start. Most parish clergy exercise sensible judgement when empowered to do so. The alternative is a culture where clergy feel they must control everything, which quite apart from being a recipe for burnout or anger is also the death of lay ministry and all the life that comes with it. Clergy can already feel overburdened or that things depend too much on them in the increased bureaucracy that characterizes all institutions in the modern age.

And yet. As I write, in one six-church rural benefice local to me, currently in vacancy and without a clear plan for succession, there are baptisms, weddings, funerals, a small weekly lay-led café church in the primary school and a weekly Eucharist that rotates around the churches. There is a weekly Bible study and other activities that continue. We celebrated the baptism and confirmation of two adult candidates at the cathedral this Easter. Everywhere I go, despite very real challenges – and they are very real challenges – God is still at work in parish ministry, spiritual communities who hold something of real value that some in the secular world are beginning to wake up to.

Writing in the *New Statesman* recently, albeit about the closure of a local Methodist rather than Anglican church, Robert Colls lamented:

> I am not calling for new chapels in every street. I am saying that their absence leaves a gap in who we are. If all history is contemporary history, all community is face-to-face. There are still coffee shops and cafés, and, of course, mosques and temples – and the pubs are clinging on. But, for the most part, a great deal of our society has been 'demutualised' (terrible word), and so-called social media is anything but social. Scanning a screen is not the same as belonging to anything as complex as a church. When we lose real contact (or should I say contact with the real?) we lose some part of what makes us human.
>
> St Paul told the Ephesians that we are all members of one another. What we have seen in little over a generation is the dismembering of one another. (Colls)

The acceleration that Root (2017) argues characterizes our modern world could hardly be more clearly described. The resources that parish churches can offer could hardly be more needed. And once again, we are reminded to look to God.

Rowan Williams, when Archbishop of Canterbury, once said to a group of us that when we look at the state of the church, we can either feel discouraged or be filled with wonder and gratitude. Discouraged because, frankly, it can be a divided, broken community, with practical and spiritual challenges. But encouraged because the God who brought it into existence and whose Spirit sustains its life must be even more wonderful than we thought to have not given up on us in over 2,000 years! Similarly, when I look at parishes, their futures can seem vastly different, with some thriving and some, seemingly, in dire need and hanging by a thread. We need to be realistic about the challenges facing them. But there is treasure in these jars of clay that, if they can be encouraged to be parochial in a proper sense – that is, concerned for their neighbours – can be a real resource of hope in our communities. I rejoice in new forms of ministry. But I rejoice too in the parish. It is tired and in need of renewal in places – but there is life in the old God yet.

Notes

1 Most recently as I write post-Easter 2024, and with his own particular political perspective, Peter Stanford.

2 See, e.g., Paul [online]; Orr-Ewing [online]; Percy (2022); Milbank (2023b).

3 The language of 'appearing' to function is deliberate – as MacIntyre (1981) rightly predicted, the removal of theology (and/or perhaps Aristotelian teleology) from ethics and moral philosophy has had profound effects on our ability to find agreement in public discourse, and the shift of emphasis on to the individual, the subjective and the emotive are evident in numerous contemporary debates. Taylor (2018) develops these themes further. Holland argues that although society appears doubtful of religion's claims, many of its instincts nevertheless remain Christian – a challenge and an opportunity for contemporary ministry, perhaps.

4 A helpful summary of these three 'symptoms' is found in Root (2023, pp. 9–12).

5 Related to all this, in my current role as an RAF Chaplain, our profession has to connect with the RAF's competency framework in ways that make sense to the service, listing and evidencing some of the core skills that chaplains need in ways that make sense to the service. There is no necessary problem with that, as long as we remain mindful of the danger that we might collapse ministry into being a technical discipline – the notion of calling, charism and our conviction about the *missio Dei* also need to form a part of our self-understanding as we engage in our mission of prayer, presence and proclamation. Chaplaincy, and ministry, is not simply about what we do, it is also about who we are and the God we serve.

6 Not their real names.

7 Having explored some of the well-known arguments for and against fresh expressions, my own PhD research into faith brands argues, drawing particularly on Padilla and also on Bosch (p. 427), that branding (as in Alpha) or closely contextualizing (as in fresh expressions) faith can be positive in reminding us of the contingent nature of all theology, but if contextualization goes too far it risks leading to an uncritical celebration of an infinite number of contextual and mutually exclusive theologies (relativism), the risk that suspicion of the biblical text by context could lead to a silencing of the text (and therefore the gospel), and the risk that pioneers might forget that the gospel often calls us to be 'out of step' with the world around. Bosch's remedy is that the catholicity of the church and interaction between different contexts can provide a counterbalance to over-contextualization (Hodder).

8 Peterson (1991) argues this, drawing particularly on the language of intimacy in the Psalms, which he contrasts with the language of information and motivation often found around us in the modern world. Although also important in the life of faith, he contends that this language becomes thin – informative talk reducing to list-making, and motivational talk reduced to crass manipulations – if not embedded in personal language, which enables us to share in life with God and one another; to enable us to experience the resonance that Root (2017 and later) argues is so essential.

9 Arguably, Winter's notion of modality and sodality, seen in historic forms,

such as church/chaplaincy or in the Mediaeval (Roman) church, with the contrast between the modality of the universal Catholic church and the sodality of orders, monasteries etc., applies today. Winter acknowledges that there could be rivalry or tensions between the structures (bishop vs abbot, diocese vs monastery etc.) but argues that for the most part the synthesis between modality and sodality was one of the great achievements of the Mediaeval period (p. 134). He laments the Reformation mistake that in seeking to curb excesses, the Protestant church became guilty of failing to exploit the power of sodality – a strategic error not corrected until the nineteenth century with the advent of mission organizations such as the Baptist Missionary Society or the Church Mission Society. Modern faith brands, fresh expressions and the like are arguably a continuation of this earlier model (Hodder).

10 Vanhoozer (2005, 2014), critiques these and similar ideas, which can also be seen in the approach to embodying Scripture/ethics found in Wells.

11 See Luke 24.13–35.

12 See 1 Corinthians 11.26.

13 https://www.churchofengland.org/prayer-and-worship/worship-texts-and-resources/common-worship/ministry/common-worship-ordination-0#mmo13; emphasis added.

14 Debates about this in relation to faith brands have been covered in depth in Hodder.

References

Bosch, D. J., 1991, *Transforming Mission: Paradigm Shifts in Theology of Mission*, Maryknoll, NY, Orbis Books.
Cavanaugh, W., 2008, *Being Consumed: Economics and Christian Desire*, Grand Rapids, MI: Eerdmans.
Colls, Robert, 2024, 'The Death of a Church', *New Stateman*, 20 March, https://www.newstatesman.com/politics/religion/2024/03/death-church-methodism-christianity-religion (accessed 7.10.2024).
Davison, A. and Alison Milbank, 2010, *For the Parish: A Critique of Fresh Expressions*, London: SCM Press.
Einstein, M., 2007, *Brands of Faith: Marketing Religion in a Commercial Age*, New York: Routledge.
Hiestand, G. and T. Wilson, 2015, *The Pastor as Theologian: Resurrecting an Ancient Vision*, Grand Rapids, MI: Zondervan.
Hodder, C. J., 2016, 'Are relationships with brands problematic or beneficial to Christian faith? An investigation into the role of faith brands in the faith development of members of some East Midlands Churches', PhD thesis, University of Derby.
Holland, T., 2019, *Dominion: The Making of the Western Mind*, London: Abacus Books.
Jackson, B. and G. Fisher, 2009, *Everybody Welcome*, London: Church House Publishing.

MacIntyre, Alasdair, 1981, *After Virtue: A Study in Moral Theory*, London: Bloomsbury.
McGavran, D. A., 1955, *The Bridges of God: A Study in the Strategy of Missions*, London: World Dominion Press.
Milbank, Alison, 2023a, *The Once and Future Parish*, London: SCM Press.
Milbank, Alison, 2023b, 'Management and Mission; The Church of England is not a Machine', *Church Times*, 27 October, https://www.churchtimes.co.uk/articles/2023/27-october/features/features/management-and-mission-the-church-of-england-is-not-a-machine (accessed 7.10.2024).
Moltmann, J., 1977, *The Church in the Power of the Spirit: A Contribution to Messianic Ecclesiology*, London: SCM Press.
Newbigin, L., 1996, *The Open Secret: An Introduction to the Theology of Mission*, London: Eerdmans.
Orr-Ewing, Frog, 2021, 'Do we need to "Save the Parish?"', *Psephizo*, 16 August, https://www.psephizo.com/life-ministry/do-we-need-to-save-the-parish/ (accessed 7.10.2024).
Padilla, C. R., 1982, 'The Unity of the Church and the Homogeneous Unit Principle', *International Bulletin of Missionary Research* 6(1), pp. 23–30.
Paul, Ian, 2020, 'What is the Vision and Strategy for the Church of England?', *Psephizo*, 11 December, https://www.psephizo.com/life-ministry/what-is-the-vision-and-strategy-of-the-church-of-england/ (accessed 7.10.2024).
Percy, Martyn, 2022, 'Some Critical Comments on the "Bishops and Ministry Fit for a New Context"', *Modern Church*, 17 February, https://modernchurch.org.uk/martyn-percy-some-critical-comment-on-bishops-and-ministry-fit-for-a-new-context (accessed 7.10.2024).
Peterson, Eugene H., 1989, *The Contemplative Pastor: Returning to the Art of Spiritual Direction*, Grand Rapids, MI: Eerdmans.
Peterson, Eugene H., 1991, *Answering God: The Psalms as Tools for Prayer*, New York: HarperCollins.
Poitras, E. W., 1999, 'St. Augustine and the *Missio Dei*: A Reflection on Mission at the Close of the Twentieth Century', *Mission Studies* 16(2), pp. 28–46.
Root, Andrew, 2017, *Faith Formation in a Secular Age: Responding to the Church's Obsession with Youthfulness*, Grand Rapids, MI: Baker Academic.
Root, Andrew, 2019, *The Pastor in a Secular Age: Ministry to People Who No Longer Need a God*, Grand Rapids, MI: Baker Academic.
Root, Andrew, 2022a, *The Congregation in a Secular Age: Keeping Sacred Time against the Speed of Modern Life*, Grand Rapids, MI: Baker Academic.
Root, Andrew, 2022b, *Churches and the Crisis of Decline: A Hopeful, Practical Ecclesiology for a Secular Age*, Grand Rapids, MI: Baker Academic.
Root, Andrew, 2022c, *The Church after Innovation: Questioning our Obsession with Work, Creativity, and Entrepreneurship*, Grand Rapids, MI: Baker Academic.
Root, Andrew, 2023, *The Church in an Age of Secular Mysticisms: Why Spiritualities without God fail to Transform us*, Grand Rapids, MI: Baker Academic.
Root, Andrew and Blair D. Bertrand, 2023, *When Church Stops Working: A Future for Your Congregation beyond More Money, Programs, and Innovation*, Grand Rapids, MI: Baker Academic.

Sherry, P., 2002, *Spirit and Beauty: An Introduction to Theological Aesthetics*, 2nd edn, London: SCM Press.
Stanford, Peter, 2024, 'How Britain lost Faith in the Church of England', *The Telegraph*, 31 March, https://www.telegraph.co.uk/news/2024/03/31/church-of-england-decline-slave-trade-reparations-welby/ (accessed 7.10.2024).
Taylor, Charles, 2007, *A Secular Age*, Cambridge, MA: Harvard University Press.
Taylor, Charles, 2018, *The Ethics of Authenticity*, Cambridge, MA: Harvard University Press.
Vanhoozer, K., 2005, *The Drama of Doctrine: A Canonical-Linguistic Approach to Theology*, Louisville, KY: Westminster John Knox Press.
Vanhoozer, K., 2014, *Faith Speaking Understanding: Performing the Drama of Doctrine*, Louisville, KY: Westminster John Knox Press.
Vanhoozer, K. and O. Strachan, 2015, *The Pastor as Public Theologian: Reclaiming a Lost Vision*, Grand Rapids, MI: Baker Academic.
Wells, S., 2018, *Improvisation: The Drama of Christian Ethics*, 2nd edn, Grand Rapids, MI: Baker Academic.
Winter, Ralph, 1974, 'The Two Redemptive Structures of God's Mission', *Missiology* 2(1), pp. 121–39.
Wright, N. T., 1991, 'How Can the Bible be Authoritative? (The Laing Lecture for 1989),' *Vox Evangelica* 21, pp. 7–32
Wright, N. T., 2011, *Scripture and the Authority of God: How to Read the Bible Today*, London: SPCK.

15

Being Pilgrim in the Cathedral

DAVID MONTEITH

Cathedrals have been reshaped by a new governance system, becoming regulated charities from 2021, partly as a result of significant failures in mission. It is also a recognition that the growth in the range of activity, worship, experimentation and contextual Christian mission within cathedrals has meant we have needed to be reshaped while remaining true to historic roles. The cathedral is now 'the seat of the bishop and a centre of worship and mission' as well as 'providing a focus for the life and work of the Church of England in the diocese' (Cathedral Measure 2021, Section 1:1). The previous 1999 Measure made no reference to mission.

Statistics about attendance in the Church of England have tended towards decline, while increasing in cathedrals (Church Commissioners, p. 21). Research has shown growth of 20% in attendance. Successive reports commissioned by the Association of English Cathedrals have pointed towards cathedrals having positive missional impact, in part through making a contribution to the spiritual life of a place, diocese and community. This has often included becoming the main public religious or spiritual focus with a wide range of activity, intentional missional, including music, the arts and culture, public debate, formal yet relaxed liturgical worship, community service and a focus on welcome. The outcome has been missional experimentation.

Research in 2012 undertaken by the think tank Theos and the Grubb Institute resulted in the report 'Spiritual Capital'. This showed that large numbers visited and had connections with cathedrals, including many younger people from a wide demographic spectrum, some with religious affiliation, others not. While this partly relates to those who visit these places as visitor attractions, this group recognized the wider spiritual role of cathedrals and their positive impact on wider society (Introduction, paras 6, 7). Nearly 60% of church non-attenders agreed that 'The cathedral gives me a greater sense of the sacred than I get elsewhere'

(Introduction, para. 5). What this showed was that cathedrals are good at providing bridging social capital that connects people and groups within communities and provides opportunities for Christian service and witness.

Finally, even in a post-Christian era, cathedrals are recognized as places that embody the history of Christianity rooted in communities. National events of significance give repeated opportunity to cathedrals to strengthen a widely held sense that we are worthy of trust. Though scandals and divisions over safeguarding, sex and gender undoubtedly undermine such trust, this is nevertheless fertile territory for mission, with both pilgrimage itself and ideas derived from it shaping the response. Cathedrals are, simply, 'signposts to God' (Cook, p. 13).

More than ten years on, this research is due to be repeated. Anecdotal evidence suggests it is likely we will discover similar patterns, while there has been further change in the missional poise of cathedral communities. For example, the role and reach of Canterbury Cathedral came to the fore during the Covid pandemic when the then Dean, Robert Willis, took to livestreaming traditional morning prayer with his reflections on the daily Scriptures aided by his cats and other animals. While parish churches understandably were faltering, cathedrals had resources enabling a quicker professional response. Thousands of people still participate in cathedral worship online so that cathedrals are providing worship for the diocese when local provision is faltering, enabling them to lean further into their calling as mother churches of their dioceses. This includes the offer of spiritual respite to local ordained and lay leaders overburdened by sustaining local churches. Pilgrimage has often had elements of rest and recuperation for well-being.

Such contemporary roles are not new and relate to the relationship between historic pilgrimage and greater churches and cathedrals. These places often contain shrines or stories of heroic Christians that are still viewed with intrigue and inspiration. The martyrdom of Thomas Becket in 1170 turned Canterbury from a special holy place into a global entity shaped by pilgrimage. The medieval miracle windows in Canterbury still recount the stories of healing and transformation that were wrought as people encountered God in new ways as a result of visiting as pilgrims.

Not all cathedrals are closely associated with a saint or a shrine. In particular, those that were created in the early twentieth century in the wake of industrialization may be minster or guild churches. However, even then pilgrimage to a place of significance, shaped by a community of prayer, creates its own gravity. We saw this in Leicester when, as

Dean, I found myself being responsible for the reburial of King Richard III. People made special journeys to connect with that ancient and modern history.

Feedback from visitors repeatedly showed that there was more going on than simply having a nice day out. This is borne out by empirical research at Canterbury – 'all who cross cathedral thresholds are on a life journey, with many keen to take the chance to reflect on it or spend time in quiet. Evidence shows a wide range of interaction with sacred places, past and present' (Dyas, p. 2). In Leicester we observed transformation at work in people's lives, including a deepening of explicit Christian faith and in others a reconnection with the Christian story. This is consistent with surveys which show that visiting cathedrals can engender a sense of pilgrimage whatever the reason for the visit. As far back as 1979 the English Tourist Board recognized that every visitor is a possible pilgrim, the cathedral's task being to draw the visitor into the spiritual dimension (Winter and Gasson, p. 1).

The British Pilgrimage Trust have recognized the growing popularity of pilgrimage. They provide accessible resources for pilgrim routes to a huge variety of places, explicitly recognizing that pilgrimage is a feature of most religious traditions and that many people these days do not walk as pilgrims for explicit religious reasons. Nevertheless, their website strapline affirms 'Walking is for the body, pilgrimage is for the soul'. They still see pilgrimage relating to spirituality. Simon Jenkins, not a person of faith, concedes that 'Just as Chaucer's travellers sought spiritual and physical renewal, modern pilgrims seek the same and certainly find it' (Mayhew-Smith and Hayward, p. 9).

There are well-established pilgrim routes to many cathedrals. New ones are being created. A number of pilgrims arrive in Canterbury every day having walked from Winchester, Southwark or Rochester on the old Pilgrims' Way. A number also set off to Rome on the Via Francigena asking for a pilgrim blessing. We offer pilgrimages to groups and individuals connecting the Anglican sites of the cathedral with that of St Augustine's Abbey and St Martin's church, where Augustine of Canterbury first worshipped. We frequently use the story of St Thomas Becket to offer candlelit pilgrimages with reflections at the different parts of the cathedral most associated with his story. We read Scripture, pray prayers and sing songs, and people often describe this as their most memorable moment with us.

The sense of being open places of faith with gravitas creates a perception of low thresholds even when admission charges apply. 'They are inevitably open to the fluid and changing traffic of the world as it passes by, and comes in and out' (Platten and Lewis, p. 155). This means the creation of cultures where there is movement, coming and going with a sense of permeability within the community. There are usually literally many doors in and out of cathedral buildings, an affirmation that this is also the mode in which these places operate.

As seat of the bishop, cathedrals are conscious that we are here to serve the whole church and the whole community. We have circles of connection deeply related to a place and a community. Deans and cathedral clergy usually have specific outward-facing roles in addition to anything internal. We expect encounter with the wider world. So while there may be a particular emphasis embodied in each cathedral, there is a commitment to remain open and permeable to Christians and people of all backgrounds. This has become a challenge when the divisions within the tribes of the church have become shriller, when some believe the welcome of some means the exclusion of others. Most cathedrals have tried to offer a 'both-and' approach wherein they may have opted for a particular stance towards divisive Christian matters while still making every effort to be inclusive of the diversity.

The architecture of cathedrals often self-consciously plays on the understanding that Christian faith is a journey. This may be true of other churches but it is highlighted by the scale and significance of cathedral buildings. It is heightened by art, lighting and decoration of key liturgical elements of font, lectern, pulpit and altar. This is clear in Canterbury as the building rises flight by flight of steps from the west end and the font (the place of faith beginnings) to high altar at the east end (the symbol of final heavenly destination). The building itself shouts that life is a journey and that faith is a pilgrimage. Cathedrals work with their architecture, letting it shape liturgy and mission. Even when cathedrals have been reordered it is often to reveal the underlying fundamental architectural language mapping out the spiritual journey.

Theology of the journey

There are many theological motifs that inform this idea of journey. The use of theology enables people to map their lives alongside God's story. It is the post-resurrection story of the journey of the disciples to Emmaus (Luke 24.13–35) that encompasses much that we also can discern in other accounts of the journey of faith. This becomes a key missional text in cathedrals, and leads one biblical scholar to speak of the 'pilgrim gospel' (Pederson, p. 1), noting that those most open to the gospel are those physically or emotionally on the move.

The story is set on the Sunday of the resurrection, following the women discovering with terror the stone rolled away from the tomb of Jesus. Later that day (verse 13) two of those witnesses in Jerusalem walk the seven-mile journey to the village called Emmaus. That name may have connection with the Hebrew word for 'hot springs', which may hint at a place of renewal. However, its significance is more that it is not Jerusalem, and the discussion on the road suggests that people may not have heard what had been going on over the previous days regarding Jesus of Nazareth (verse 18). As the story unfolds we observe that the news of the resurrection is already being announced outside Jerusalem. Something has changed, which means the stranger with whom these disciples walk remains hidden from them, yet he was present with them. Luke tells us that 'their eyes were kept from recognizing him' (verse 16) yet he walked with them. Starting with Moses, he told the stories of Scripture that have led to that moment. There is engagement with the Scriptures and the written word through dialogue and conversation. Just as Luke's Gospel began with a commitment to write 'an orderly account' (1.1), so here we see the need to travel together, to read the stories of faith in the presence of Jesus who has lived, died and risen again and is still present yet may not be visible to them.

Then, when they reach the village, the disciples have made a connection and relationship with this stranger. They have become people walking the road together. So they persuade their new friend to remain with them (verses 28, 29). The last thing Jesus does with his disciples before his death is to share a meal. Now in this fresh encounter, he again shares a meal. In the first meal there was wisdom shared about service. There was practice shared to give identity to the community so that through the sharing of bread and wine there would be remembrance of Jesus (22.7–27). In Emmaus, as he took bread, blessed it, broke it and shared it, 'their eyes were opened, and they recognized him' (verse 30). There is recognition of Jesus in their midst, which has transforming power. Their pilgrimage shifts from being about them to being about him.

Modern discipleship study courses used by cathedrals draw inspiration from this, married with a variety of pedagogical methods in adult education that recognize all that people already bring and which recognize the integrity and power of the adult. Of course, there are other scriptural accounts of more dramatic changes in life direction. Disciples immediately leave their nets to follow (Mark 1.18) or Saul on the Damascus Road (Acts 9.1–9) is dramatically converted to become Paul. Disciples down the ages can give similar accounts of dramatic conversions through direct encounter, and many Christians can identify significant moments of deepening commitment. However, it is the language of journey and pilgrimage that seems to be the more accurate description for most people. This does and can lead to conversion. For others it leads to the next step in faith. I have never met anyone who has been turned off faith through pilgrimage, unlike the stories that are shared about other dimensions of spiritual practice or courses that try to engineer response. In particular we see the importance of an 'evolving faith for our evolving self' (Hull, p. 149).

Journeys of discipleship with younger people

There has been a huge growth in discipleship courses in the Church of England in response to the need for evangelism and becoming a church of 'missionary disciples'. Many people do not have basic Christian grammar or encounter, so those coming to explore faith later need tools to undertake that journey. Much faith formation for children and young people is missing, hence the focus on doubling the number of young people in churches.

Cathedrals have continued to invest in children and young people through their education departments. They have grown in scale over the past decades, and thousands of predominantly primary school children visit cathedrals every year as part of their religious education curricula. Cross-curricular work has evolved, integrating everything from history to mathematics into encounter with a significant place of worship and Christian story. The insights of journey inform these educational methods with an emphasis on experience, movement, curiosity, meaning-making and the use of open questions to excite imagination. Children are invited to name experience that can be identified as spiritual and engage in wondering questions tied to the life of Christian discipleship and their relationship to that faith. This is available to children of all backgrounds and complements the aim of education provided through the Church of England schools as being both 'deeply Christian' and contributing to the building up of the 'common good'.

Some cathedrals have specifically shaped experiences for children by creating mini-pilgrimages. Leicester Cathedral developed one for school children. They walked along a watercourse from the edges of the city into the centre, stopping periodically for reflection and actions. This stational approach is akin to long pilgrimages, which stop at significant wells, shrines or markers. For example, the children stood on a bridge and were asked to reflect on what they needed to leave behind from their school experience. They then threw a stone into the water as a symbol of leaving that behind. This was accompanied by stories from the Bible, prayers and songs.

Or most movingly, the tradition of walking parts of or entire medieval pilgrimages in silence was used for the last half mile. Nearly always the children got it and became silent. They started noticing the rhythm of walking. Then arriving at the cathedral, open questions were asked on what they had noticed. This led to input on the use of silence within prayer where we can hear God's 'still small voice'. Stories such as that about Elijah in 1 Kings 19 were used when God was in 'a sound of sheer silence' (1 Kings 19.12).

Elements of experience, teaching and reflection combined to create the environment in which growth happened, including growth in faith. The children who engaged most with such experiences were then encouraged to lead class or whole-school acts of worship. A general exposure to faith became more personal for them. Additionally, positive transformations in behaviour were reported in children who responded to these more kinaesthetic experiences. Feedback included remarkable changes in some pupils from disruptive to more engaged behaviour.

Similar practices have evolved in cathedrals through both one-to-one encounters and also through study and discipleship courses as well as actual pilgrimages organized by cathedrals, including to other holy places. Such courses draw from Scripture and use a rich variety of other stories from witnesses to faith. They emphasize the importance of encounter, of dialogue, of curiosity into the riches of faith and with the complexities of life. They have periodic and sometimes repeated moments of arrival and departure marked by prayers or activities. These involve a review of the journey travelled and pauses to reflect and be nourished for the next stage of the journey. Ignatian and Celtic faith traditions inform these practices, such as use of the Examen. They avoid anything that treats faith as a product which can be delivered. Pilgrimages are context-based, shaped a great deal by participants. They are relational, utilizing mind and heart, sense and intellect to provide literal and metaphorical journeys in which faith flourishes.

Spiritual journeys with adults

The lived cathedral experience of pilgrimage influences the approaches to adult learning and faith formation. There is a scepticism towards approaches that see faith primarily as a body of teaching that has to be learnt. A former colleague likens this to the discipline of dance, where it is possible to train and to learn all the steps and still not really be able to dance. It is only when we truly hear the music and respond with our whole selves learning to use the steps we've learnt that we start to dance. The steps matter but they are not the dance.

So too with embodied experiences of discipleship through pilgrimage. Information may be shared and examined but in a dialogical way rather than in a didactic way. This kind of learning is more 'flexible, responsive and even biddable' and 'may be episodic and fragmented' (Craig, p. 5). Facts from history or resources from the Bible and tradition may be offered, but in order to deepen enquiry and to augment the experience. There has to be the freedom that in order to journey further these may be set aside for now as they may not connect or be of relevance to that person. Those who journey alongside pilgrims need confidence to see that 'God gave the growth' (1 Cor. 3.6). This is aided by the steadfastness of the buildings themselves. For example, Covid-19 was not the first plague to impact Canterbury Cathedral. Therefore we need not be overly anxious, defensive or aggressive about faith but rather with a sense of generous hospitality we can open it up, face the journey and grow. We operate from a sense of 'The one who calls you is faithful' (1 Thess. 5.24) rather than getting worried about making Christians or hitting targets for new disciples.

In cathedrals, the version par excellence of this open invitation of pilgrimage is to participate in the service of Choral Evensong. This service still uses the archaic beautiful language of the Book of Common Prayer (1662). Most of the service is sung, bar the Scripture readings and the prayers of the day. Much is offered to the participants and at some levels little is required of them. This means that those in very different places of discipleship can participate at different levels. This includes the intensely prayerful, to the enquiring, to the passer-by with little interest in faith. There is a happy mix of people reminding cathedrals daily that we are all on journeys, reinforcing the underlying discipleship model of pilgrimage.

Some see this as a 'set piece', the glory of it being the fact that it is mostly impervious to context and set apart from the humdrum of the world. However, increasingly cathedral clergy recognize that some pointers towards connection to wider life or more personal issues can be incorporated without losing the sense of flow of the sung service. Musicians have become more alert to the inherent liturgical seasonality of their music choices and therefore focus on context. They also respond through investment in the commissioning of new music, not least from female composers and those of global majority heritage, recognizing the wider commitments of the church to greater inclusivity and to addressing racial injustice as crucial elements of Christian mission. Such music, or additional words of introduction to Bible readings or prayer, can add a degree of disruption to the flow, which invites congregations towards engagement rather than a more passive experience of worship. At worst it grates but at best it builds connections. I note that people leaving speak of their encounter with beauty being an encounter with God, or that the words or intercessions that day touched their hearts to the point of tears.

Likewise, the way visitors are welcomed in and how cathedral spaces are interpreted both by people and by signage or digital interpretation are changing, becoming intentionally missional. Museums and galleries have moved to using interpretation to invite deeper engagement through a layered process, more detail being available for those who are more curious. This has sometimes led to interpretation where a particular approach to learning is chosen rather an attempt at simply providing information. Guides have been trained to pick up the interests of those who come rather than stand poised to deliver their set patter.

This approach has helped us recognize that history or story is rarely a non-partisan activity. It is usually told from a perspective, often with vested interests informing it. For example, in Canterbury we have few images, memorials or statues of women while having many of men. The building has been shaped by a view of the role of women in church and society over centuries. If we simply interpret it evenly, we will in fact continue to comply with a view that sees women as marginal, whereas an approach that wants to highlight the few women celebrated alongside the men begins to address the embedded assumptions. This alternative approach points towards a society and a church where both female and male disciples are valued and equal. It is therefore a theological stance.

This has a particular opportunity as cathedrals bear witness in our built environment to heritage that is contested, especially in relation to the transatlantic slave trade. Many cathedrals have benefited from funds emerging from that exploitative trade. Or they house memorials to slave-trading families and ecclesiastical figures embroiled in that trade. This has led cathedral communities to identify such heritage, to assess it often in partnership with local people and communities who are the direct or indirect ancestors of slaving communities, and to put in place strategies of engagement. No one believes that history can be undone but it can be understood afresh. Ongoing impact can be addressed and learning can reshape our sense of being global Christians. In Canterbury this has particular power as mother church of the Anglican Communion. The Cathedral Fabric Commission for England, which acts as the church planning system for cathedrals, has published specific guidance that ensures changes are addressed with wisdom. This also relates to how much imagery in cathedrals underpins a widely held Western view that Jesus and his community are white. This is so embedded that 'many believe in a man who never existed' (McDonald, p. 16).

This revisiting of heritage goes much further than slavery because other legacy stories impact our ability to shape disciples today. For example, in Canterbury we host memorials to the Anglo-Sikh wars from the mid-1840s. These wars are cast as examples of British colonial power in the Indian sub-continent quashing local rebellions. They do not recognize the valiant soldiery of the Sikhs nor do they recognize them as complex colonial conflicts. This now needs to be understood from both sides, not least since many British people are now Sikh, serving this nation in world wars and in the present time. Without interpretation these memorials can mislead, giving the idolatrous impression that God is partisan, inhibiting the Christian mission.

Or take Stephen Langton, a revered Archbishop of Canterbury from the twelfth and thirteenth century whose entombed feet still protrude from the cathedral walls. He positively influenced the process of Magna Carta and was the first biblical scholar to divide the Scriptures into manageable chapters. He also convened and heavily influenced the Oxford Conference, which fuelled medieval antisemitism, leading to the persecution of the Jews in England. The approach the cathedral takes to interpretation of this relates to local and international community cohesion or interfaith dialogue and so impacts what we say about God and the way we shape pilgrimage in the building.

So rather than simply allow the building to speak, we intervene to encourage genuine encounter in order to foster deeper engagement with the gifts of God and the complexity of human persons as understood today – even faithful disciples who are flawed. In some rare cases this has meant the removal of historic heritage that is so offensive that it cannot remain. Mostly the approach is to retain and interpret but often alongside a commitment to commissioning new works of art and memorials that offer other parts of the story. Occasionally a kind of psychological and spiritual disruption is introduced to encourage new engagement while avoiding new offence.

Third, cathedrals have been accused of being more like museums and galleries than places of Christian community and pilgrimage. They have experts in specific fields such as architecture or archives, with their own disciplines and norms. However, these potentially bring siloes or tensions between those most concerned with stewardship and heritage and those more concerned about spiritual life and discipleship. This has partly been exaggerated through the impact of external funders, many of whom do not have a religious commitment. Some have explicit secular agendas yet still see the value of cathedrals within society. However, this is now being addressed with new interpretation schemes.

I encountered this with a national funder who objected to the inclusion of Scripture verses on interpretation panels yet was quite content in a synagogue to allow Hebrew biblical script or in a historic mosque to permit Arabic Quranic script. This arose from a place of secular religious ignorance that saw one kind of text as artistic and of heritage value yet the same sort of text in English as religious propaganda. This was resolved but it was revealing of the need for cathedrals not to be unduly influenced by their funders, so as to avoid mission drift of a serious kind.

Cathedrals have begun to get better at being explicit about our mission, including sharing appropriate discipleship literature that seeks to connect the historic environment with the pilgrimage of faith. While secular guides and historic societies can interpret built heritage from that perspective, cathedrals are waking up to the need to offer interpretation informed by the insights of Christian pilgrimage.

So, for example, when we wrote the interpretation of Richard III for Leicester Cathedral associated with his reburial there in 2015, we sought to encourage curiosity around his life and to make connections with the timeless relevance of Scripture. This included reflections on the ethics of war, the interface of church and state, the morals of what it is to be good or evil, the vulnerability of grief, and the treachery and manipulations of public leadership. All this stood alongside reflections on the steadfastness and mercy of God as revealed in Richard's own prayer book held at Lambeth Palace Library. Interpretation of this kind for displays and websites led to training of guides who became comfortable working with these kinds of questions and issues. They then encouraged visitors to be more curious, while they also picked up some of the basic tenets of his story, and his rediscovery and reburial as they related to Christian ideas about life, death and salvation.

This kind of approach is also increasingly of interest to academic researchers who recognize the power and place of pilgrimage within the mission of the church. The best example of this is at the University of York. This has identified historic phenomena that have their modern-day equivalents, locating this approach as highly traditional and normative within Christianity as an ecclesial device to assist with evangelism and Christian formation.

The Centre for Christianity and Culture, University of York, has produced resources particularly aimed at inviting people to use the built environment as a stimulus to prayer. Cathedrals already provide prayer stations that provide implicit invitations to pray. However, we discovered that people often do not understand that invitation – it's too implicit. So the work of vergers and chaplains often includes assisting people to light candles, to voice prayers or use silence. Prayer-cards focusing on a wide range of human experiences (e.g. feeling sad, looking for God, being thankful, being accepted) have been produced. These seek to voice prayer from the perspective of the lived experience of the person, possibly enabling the taking of a step deeper in pilgrimage towards spiritual wisdom. They are well designed, using open language. They are all addressed to God rather than being 'self-help tools' but they deliberately not do not use complex developed Christian language. Such cards provide bridging resources for the many who now sit far away from the practices of faith.

Conclusion

British people regard cathedrals positively within their communities. As more and more of our community becomes disconnected from Christianity, cathedrals provide accessible and low-threshold entry opportunities to ignite or revisit a pilgrimage of faith. People expect to find beauty, history, faith grounded in an embedded place, inspirational music, thoughtful preaching and engagement with faith within cathedrals. Pilgrimage is a growing industry and it is popular, unlike the church at present.

In cathedrals there is less expectation to sign up for anything or to join anything there and then. Yet that openness is matched with the expectation that Christian faith matters and that cathedrals should embody Christianity in visible, intelligible, accessible ways. Visitors are intrigued by our daily pattern of prayer to sustain our Christian life and come to listen to it and to be changed by it. People express gratitude when we acknowledge we are all on spiritual journeys, thus closing the gap between them and us. We are not heavy-handed or aggressive with faith development yet we signpost all the time to the possibility of that journey.

Much of this stems from a deeply held set of values around hospitality that offers welcome but which, following the Benedictine tradition, sees the visitor also as already a bearer of God's image. St Benedict teaches in his Rule that the guest must be treated as if they were Christ. In chapter 53 he writes: 'Let all guests who arrive be received as Christ, because He will say: "I was a stranger and you took Me in" (Mt 25:35). And let due honor be shown to all, especially to those "of the household of the faith" (Gal. 6:10) and to wayfarers' (Benedict, p. 60). These guests are therefore those who can potentially reveal Christ or announce an aspect of the good news. A Benedictine monk reflects: 'What is asked of newcomers is that they enter into the life of the community' (Casey, p. 190). They are already fellow pilgrims on a journey; not opportunities to be exploited (fodder for evangelism) but gifts to be received. Cathedrals, while knowing they exist for the service of Christ as part of the mission of God, also realize that they are imperfect. They need continual repentance, conversion to Jesus. The gravitas and stability of cathedrals enables a profound sense of openness to others who continually remind us that we are for others not for ourselves.

However, as society has become more secular and postmodern, cathedrals have also realized that some things that were previously held to be implicit now need articulation. The basic Christian story from creation to incarnation, to cross and resurrection and ascension, addressed in so much cathedral art and architecture, is not so known. More clues or keys are needed to help people maximize their encounter in the place to interpret it. People also value prompts to make connection between their own journey and the possibility of a journey of Christian faith. So cathedrals are working hard on a public language of Christian faith that itself is as generous as the hospitality offered. Cathedrals are testing how challenging that language and approach need to be, how much can be assumed still as implicit and how much needs to be explicit.

Increasing numbers of opportunities for learning are being created for both children and adults. It is important that faith informs these innovations. This means that those we encounter have opportunity to connect with the heart of what makes a cathedral, the faith to which it witnesses in physical space and in the people who make these places communities.

To that end we are recognizing that we need elements of disruption in order to ensure that encounters at cathedrals do not avoid the questions posed by faith. Rachel Mann speaks of the 'missional necessity of interruption' (Barrett and Harley, p. xv). We can be so overstimulated by image and experience these days that we need something additional that gives us permission to engage and encounter more than the surface experience. A mode of challenging people to next steps of faith is being sought and offered through imaginative and fresh interpretation, through discipleship and spirituality courses based on the wisdom of pilgrimage, and through the practice of pilgrimage itself. The original pilgrims to Canterbury bore witness to what God did for them, and that remains our hope across cathedrals, that in our day we can bear the same witness, seeing lives transformed.

References

Barrett, Al and Ruth Harley, 2020, *Being Interrupted: Reimagining the Church's Mission from the Outside, In*, London: SCM Press.
Benedict, Saint, 1949, *The Holy Rule of St. Benedict*, trans. Boniface Verheyen, OSB, Grand Rapids, MI: Christian Classics Ethereal Library, https://www.documentacatholicaomnia.eu/03d/0480-0547,_Benedictus_Nursinus,_Regola,_EN.pdf, ch. 53.
Casey, Michael, 2013, *Strangers to the City: Reflections on the Beliefs and Values of the Rule of St Benedict*, Brewster, MA: Paraclete Press.
Church Commissioners, 2014, 'From Anecdote to Evidence: Findings from the Church Growth Research Programme 2011–2013', London: Church Commissioners for England, https://www.churchofengland.org/sites/default/files/2019-06/from_anecdote_to_evidence_-_the_report.pdf (accessed 7.10.2024).
Cook, Chris, 2010, *Finding God in a Holy Place: Explorations of Prayer in Durham Cathedral*, London: Mowbray.
Craig, Yvonne, 1994, *Learning for Life: A Handbook of Adult Religious Education*, London: Mowbray.
Dyas, Dee, 2014, *Pilgrimage and England's Cathedrals Past and Present*, Canterbury Cathedral, Centre for the Study of Christianity and Culture, University of York.
Hull, John M., 1991, *What Prevents Christian Adults from Learning?* Harrisburg, PA: Trinity Press International.

McDonald, Chine, 2021, *God is Not a White Man and Other Revelations*, London: Hodder & Stoughton.
Mayhew-Smith, Nick and Guy Hayward, 2020, *Britain's Pilgrim Places: The First Complete Guide to Every Spiritual Treasure*, Morden: Lifestyle Press.
Pederson, David J., 1999, 'The Pilgrim Gospel: The Old Testament as a Theology of the Journey', PhD thesis, Liberty University, Virginia.
Platten, Stephen and Christopher Lewis (eds), 1998, *Flagships of the Spirit: Cathedrals in Society*, London: Darton, Longman & Todd.
Theos and The Grubb Institute, 2012, 'Spiritual Capital: The Present and Future of English Cathedrals', London: Theos, https://www.theosthinktank.co.uk/cmsfiles/archive/files/Reports/Spiritual%20Capital%2064pp%20-%20FINAL.pdf (accessed 7.10.2024).
Winter, M. and R. Gasson, 1996, 'Pilgrimage and Tourism: Cathedral Visiting in Contemporary England', *International Journal of Heritage Studies* 2(3), pp. 172–82.

Useful websites

Archbishops' Anti-Racism Task Force, 2021, 'From Lament to Action', https://www.churchofengland.org/sites/default/files/2021-04/FromLamentToAction-report.pdf.
Association of English Cathedrals, https://www.englishcathedrals.co.uk/.
Canterbury-Becket Way, https://www.britishpilgrimage.org/portfolio/pilgrims-way-to-canterbury.
Cathedral Measure 2021, section 1a, https://www.legislation.gov.uk/ukcm/2021/2/contents.
Centre for the Study of Christianity and Culture, University of York, https://christianityandculture.org.uk/.
Church of England Vision for Education, https://www.churchofengland.org/about/education-and-schools/vision-education.
A Church of Missionary Disciples, https://www.churchofengland.org/about/vision-and-strategy.
Explore Project, Centre for the Study of Christianity and Culture, University of York, https://www.christianityandculture.org.uk/projects/explore-project.
Major Parish Churches, https://www.churchofengland.org/resources/diocesan-resources/strategic-planning-church-buildings/major-parish-churches.
Pilgrims and Pilgrimage, The Centre for the Study of Christianity and Culture, University of York, https://www.york.ac.uk/projects/pilgrimage/index.html.
St Augustine's Abbey, https://www.english-heritage.org.uk/visit/places/st-augustines-abbey/.
St Martin's Canterbury, https://www.martinpaul.org/.
Via Francigena, https://www.viefrancigene.org/en/.

16

Being Pilgrim in the Shadow of Empire

JAMES BUTLER AND CATHY ROSS

The shadow of empire

To think about the Church of England being pilgrim in the shadow of empire first requires some reflection on what we mean by 'shadow'.[1] We are understanding shadow in two ways. First, in the way all that happens in the Britain today takes place in the realities of a history of the British Empire. The reality of a small island nation ruling over an empire on which the sun never set. The reality which meant that people settled in the UK from across the globe, arriving from former British colonies. A reality which, as a country, Britain has to come to terms with: a reality of conquest, conversion, racism, enslavement, extraction and exploitation.

While the extent to which the British Empire was a good or bad thing continues to be debated, the fact is that we live in the shadow of such a history, even if it might be contested. The second way empire casts a shadow is more insidious: this shadow of empire is the way the imagination of Britain, and indeed the West, has been shaped by a particular logic, what we describe here as the 'logic of empire' (Butler and Ross, 2023). It is this shadow to which we pay more attention in this chapter.

We begin by exploring the logic of empire, first in British society but significantly within the life of the Church of England. The shadow of empire is not something that is outside of the Church of England; it is deeply woven into its life and fabric. Having outlined this logic, we focus in on three temptations that such a logic encourage: a concern for institutional reputation; an ethos of control from the centre; and an unwillingness to welcome diversity. To counter such a logic, we argue that the Church of England needs to be reimagined as pilgrim, and to do this reimagining we pay attention to witnesses from the 'edges' of the church, witnesses who call out the Church of England's complicity with empire and who witness to a different imagination of church: a pilgrim church.[2]

The logic of empire

Empire casts a long shadow. We in Britain are still living in the shadow of empire today, with all that it means for British society more generally and particularly for the church. Discourse on empire in the public arena ranges far and wide and considers such issues as land ownership and why certain people and institutions owned and continue to own so much land while others in our society do not (Hayes). The National Trust has had a high profile with its 2020 report investigating the colonial history of some of its properties. Writers such as Professor Corinne Fowler (2024) reveal how empire has shaped our landscape such as the Cotswolds with its ties to the East India Company or how historical links with Jamaican sugar and tobacco have shaped the whisky isles of Jura and Islay. Olivia Laing considers gardens funded by wealth from the slave trade, while Sathnam Sanghera (2021, 2024) is well known for his work into empire's lasting impact not only on Britain but also on the rest of the world. These are just a few examples of how the legacy and shadow of empire is firmly in the public discourse. These writers also reveal how the logic of empire, with its unquestioning assumptions around a particular kind of posture and world view, continue to the present day. The Church of England still operates within this logic of empire.

So what do we mean by the 'logic of empire' with respect to the Church of England? The Church of England has always been part of empire in its role as the established church. Its huge financial assets, many of which were obtained during the time of the British Empire, its honorific titles, its episcopal palaces and its hierarchical system of titles and preferments are all resonant of empire. It has behaved as such with its understanding of being a civilizing force throughout the world and has shaped its empire accordingly (Sanghera, 2021, p. 30). The history of mission is replete with ugly stories of forced conversion on unfortunate 'native' peoples. In the nineteenth century, Church Mission Society (CMS) strategy was to civilize the locals and once they had been civilized – in other words, become more like us – they were fit for conversion (Rountree; Langmore). The New Zealand historian Tanya Fitzgerald comments on the missionaries' attempts to Christianize Māori bringing an attitude of 'Englishness, progress, Christianity and civilisation'

(p. 16). Mission was carried out within the context and assumptions of empire with very little questioning of these underlying assumptions and attitudes.

The Church of England has learnt how to operate in the context of empire and has been and continues to be shaped by this. We do not think that anyone consciously wants to behave like empire but it colonizes our imaginations and world view to such an extent that the Church of England continues to perpetuate the logic of empire. As a church, we need to name this and work against this logic of empire. Empire offers particular temptations and there are three that we would like to explore. These are: a temptation to protect the institution's reputation and an instinct to cover up; the temptation to control the life of the Church of England from the centre; and the temptation to homogenize and not to embrace diversity. These temptations make it difficult for the Church of England to be a pilgrim church.

Temptations of empire

By their very nature, empires rule and exercise absolute sovereignty. There is a drive for expansion, conquest and universal rule. This is seen in empires throughout history whether it be the Roman Empire, the British Empire or the Ottoman Empire. The African American theologian Willie James Jennings, in his superb book *After Whiteness: An Education In Belonging*, introduces us to a figure who is behind much of Western theological education and who could also be behind much of empire and the self-understanding of the Church of England: a 'white self-sufficient man, his self-sufficiency defined by possession, control and mastery' (Jennings, p. 6). Jennings believes that this person is deeply lodged in the West's collective imaginations and that this world view is seductive. It can produce a desire for 'control of knowledge first, and of oneself second, and if possible of one's world' (p. 29). In his reflection on this description, Mike Higton, theology professor at Durham University, explains that: 'The same cognitive and affective structures that Jennings describes have certainly taken root in my imagination' (p. 14). Higton goes on to explore this within an academic context but there are resonances with the Church of England, where there is a seeming desire to control from the centre so that any other ways of imagining the world or questioning the centre are not welcome. The current Post Office scandal in the UK is an egregious example of this, where the centre refused to accept any challenge or any responsibility for a fault in its systems. There seemed to be a kind of 'wilful blindness' (Heffernan) or at the very least a lack of curiosity as to why so many sub-postmasters and sub-postmistresses all over the country were being prosecuted for alleged fraud. This unwillingness to dig deeper seemed to be to protect the institution and reputation of the Post Office. Such resistance at the centre has also been exemplified in the church over numerous sexual abuse scandals, most recently in the response to Soul Survivor and allegations about Mike Pilavachi that took far too long to be acknowledged and dealt with. As with the Post Office, there seems to be an initial instinct from the centre towards cover-up and minimizing reputational damage rather than a desire to walk in the light, to repent and to seek justice.

This control from the centre is damaging because it not only leads to this instinct to protect the institution but also means that the centre is and remains the most important thing. Therefore the centre often determines the flow of ideas, and the flow or direction is usually one-way. This means dioceses can end up controlling strategy and ministry from the centre rather than allowing a particular community or parish to respond to their own context.

For example, a particular diocesan team may be given the task of developing a mission strategy or a discipleship strategy. They may start with the question 'What do we want to see?' This is an excellent question but who exactly is the 'we'? Is it the wider diocese with its variety of congregations in many different contexts? Or is it the diocesan team at the centre, at the diocesan office, drawing on their own expertise with perhaps some memory of lived experience of former parish ministry? Perhaps there needs to be a wider consultation around the diocese. At CMS we believe that listening is vital and especially to those at the edges. The former CMS General Secretary John Taylor was well aware of this: 'If you are concerned with movement and growth in a Church or in a society, look to the fringes. Watch the things that are pushing out on the edge' (Taylor, 1965).

Another example is how money is distributed from the centre. In recent years there has been a growing emphasis on church planting with what seem quite fantastical numbers of churches to be planted given as targets from the centre. We have heard of dioceses aiming for numbers of more than 500 new congregations to be planted within a 5–10-year time frame and millions of pounds made available for this. The numbers and the amounts of money made available for this are enormous. Much of the funding is obtained by bidding in a competitive process to the Strategic Development Fund (SDF). Every year the SDF releases millions of pounds for church planting, pioneering and other such initiatives. This is money from the centre, released for a fixed term and with reporting forms that ask for specific numbers, attendance at specific activities such as Sunday services, food banks, Alpha or similar courses, family gatherings, home hubs, Bible study groups, prayer meetings, seasonal events, prayer walks, school visits, midweek services. Financial giving is also to be measured, along with the number of converts and de-churched.

None of these activities or indicators is necessarily bad or unhelpful, although the counting of heads week by week is surely anxiety-inducing and could potentially lead to some grade inflation to fulfil the expectations from the centre. It could be argued that this is robust accountability for the large amounts of money distributed by SDF. However, this model points to a universalized approach that is determined from the centre, where money or resources are allocated to certain areas and the model is expected to be followed in all contexts. It also assumes that money is a big part of the solution. Taylor firmly challenged this temptation:

> While we piously repeat the traditional assertion that without the Holy Spirit we can get nowhere in the Christian mission, we seem to press on notwithstanding with our man-made programmes. I have not heard recently of committee business adjourned because those present were still awaiting the arrival of the Spirit of God. I have known projects abandoned for lack of funds, but not for lack of the gifts of the Spirit. Provided the human resources are adequate we take the spiritual for granted. In fact we have only the haziest idea of what we mean by resources other than human wealth, human skill and human character. (1972, pp. 4–5)

Part of the logic of empire is that empires resist challenge and change and have a particular way of seeing the world. Jennings claims that this self-understanding of 'possession, control and mastery' promotes a kind of 'homogeneity that aims towards a cultural nationalism ... or cultural sovereignty' (p. 6). Writing about theological education, he asserts that in the West it was 'born in white hegemony and homogeneity', which leads to 'a control that aims for sameness and a sameness that imagines control' (pp. 6–7). Perhaps this is best seen in the Church of England's relative inability to embrace diversity. A good example of this is the recent Church of England report on racial justice, 'From Lament to Action' (2021). It identified 25 previous reports over 44 years calling for cultural and structural change within the Church of England that elicited little obvious interest, impact or response. The current report calls for action and highlights the 'urgency of now' because of the previous lack of any significant change.

Revd A. D. A. France-Williams offers a searing critique of institutional racism in the Church of England. He narrates a powerful story of tokenism: he was initially delighted to be invited to sit on a Bishop's Advisory Panel to select a new bishop, only to discover that he was there to represent 'BAME and younger clergy' (France-Williams, p. 178). He was upset by this and asserts: 'The cards are so stacked that the BAME card is often the only currency one has' (p. 179). He concludes, rather bleakly, that the Church of England, or the Cross and Crown Club as he calls it, was not designed for people of colour: 'If you are ignored for long enough, the social death, the isolation, and the futility of your efforts for change silence you and sentence you to a form of living exile' (p. 196).

The Church Commissioners have published a 45-page report into historic links to transatlantic chattel slavery,[3] and there has been a commitment to a £100 million fund to deliver a programme of investment, research and engagement. It is deliberately not called 'reparations' as it will not compensate individuals. Anthony Reddie, Professor of Black Theology at Regent's Park College, University of Oxford, criticized the amount as it was an arbitrary figure, but perhaps more importantly explains: 'For it to be reparations it needs to include a process of truth telling and a reappraisal of history so that we are cognisant of what is lost or damaged and how monetary support can be a part (not the sole basis) of a process of making repair.' He also calls for 'mutuality and dialogue'.[4] That is the crux of the issue. These top-down, hierarchical approaches seem to emerge from the logic of empire while a more Christian approach would surely be one of relationship and dialogue. France-Williams had suggested something similar – a Truth and Reparations Commission that could be 'a sharing of stories followed by recompense and maybe relationship' (France-Williams, p. 193). However, he wondered if that would be enough and what exactly that relationship would be based on.

So how does the Church of England resist these three temptations of empire: the desire to protect the institution and to cover up injustice; the seeming importance of the centre and its homogeneity; along with the inability to embrace diversity? We have found that it is in listening to voices from the edges that these temptations can begin to be resisted and a pilgrim church can begin to be imagined.

Witnessing from the edges

As 'From Lament to Action' has witnessed to, the Church of England has been able to recognize these shadows of empire – slavery, racism, colonialism, coercion – but recognizing and naming them through committees and reports has not resulted in significant action and change. Part of the problem is that the kind of change asked for is properly complex – the logic of empire is woven through the life of the Church of England in ways that defy individual action or simple solutions. Gregg Okesson draws on John Wesley's term 'complicated wickedness' to understand this. Wickedness is not about individuals being wicked but about how public life is complex: issues of injustice rarely have a single cause, nor simple solutions. The answer, Okesson argues, is not simple solutions but public witness (p. 20).

In Okesson's account this means the church witnessing to a different kind of public life – a different way of relating to God and to others, not in 'thin', simple ways but in 'thicker', complicated ways. However, here our critique is of a church whose life is woven into this complicated wickedness – these complex structures of injustice that are beyond individual action or simple solutions. As Pope Francis reminded us: 'The Church does not evangelize unless she constantly lets herself be evangelized' (Francis, para. 174). We see this witness coming from the edges and the margins; it is those who have experienced the negative consequences of the temptations of empire who can help us reimagine the Church of England in the shadow of empire.

By seeking witnesses from the edges we follow the instincts of John Taylor, who advocated watching the things 'that are pushing out from the edges' (1965). Rowan Williams had a similar instinct when he began the process of listening that resulted in Fresh Expressions, suggesting that the church is renewed from the edges (discussed in Steve Taylor, pp. 102–3). However, it is the WCC's affirmation on mission and evangelism, *Together Towards Life* (TTL), that offers the clearest rationale for how we wish to develop this ecclesiology, and it deserves attentive reading:

Jesus Christ relates to and embraces those who are most marginalized in society, in order to confront and transform all that denies life. This includes cultures and systems which generate and sustain massive poverty, discrimination, and dehumanization, and which exploit or destroy people and the earth. Mission from the margins calls for an understanding of the complexities of power dynamics, global systems and structures, and local contextual realities. Christian mission has at times been understood and practiced in ways which failed to recognize God's alignment with those consistently pushed to the margins. Therefore, mission from the margins invites the church to re-imagine mission as a vocation from God's Spirit who works for a world where the fullness of life is available for all. (Commission on World Mission and Evangelism, para. 37)

In this section we turn to the witness from the edges to ask how they reimagine church. Our focus here is on drawing on the voices we have heard in a series of research projects where we have paid careful attention to people who, in one sense of another, are witnessing to the Church of England from the edges.

The first thing to observe is that there is a suspicion of the church. In the Edgy Learning Project we heard from a number of people who would not immediately identify themselves as Christians.[5] It was interesting to hear their reflections in relation to Christian organizations and churches. And it was enlightening to hear the reflections from a number of participants who are part of a community centre in a deprived estate. When they were asked about the significance of the community centre's being Christian, they responded saying 'I don't think it's too relevant, because Graham (the leader) doesn't care what faith you are, he'll treat everyone the same' (Wendy); and 'It's never been forceful, like "I'm a Christian so you need to be like this"' (Amanda).[6] Similarly, in a Methodist Church that moved into a shop front in the centre of town, Irene commented: 'This doesn't look like a church ... they appear genuine people that aren't trying to force their religion down your throat ... genuinely anyone can come here with anything ... without the need to feel that you've got to be one of them, or you have to join them. There's no pressures.' All these comments, while positive about their particular engagement with church or Christianity, operate against a backdrop of suspicion. They suggest a perception of church and Christianity as discriminating against people who are not Christian, being judgemental and pressuring people to join or believe certain things.

Pioneers are another group of people who witness from the edges in a different way. According to the Church of England definition, 'Pioneers are people called by God who are the first to see and creatively respond to the Holy Spirit's initiatives with those outside the church' ('Vocations to Pioneer Ministry', 2018). The Church of England has named pioneering as a particular vocation within the church and yet the pioneers we spoke to in another research project identified how they felt marginalized and pressured to fit a particular mould.[7] Lydia described: 'I was experiencing being very much on the fringe, knowing that there was something I was really passionate about, but not seeing it prioritized at all within the mainstream church, and wondering if it would ever be.' For Donna in her pioneering: 'The rest of the church didn't get it at all', and she described how the church 'feels like this big ship that is going, where it's going and it is doing community stuff, but that's not what I want to do and you feel like you get on or you or you don't. There's not much flexibility.' Toby described how he wanted to be at the edge but others were wanting to 'drag people back to the centre', and Gary described the continual 'inward pull towards the middle of the institution'.

Some were frustrated by the Church of England's desire to 'resource and empower' people into mission, and felt, as Lydia responded, that 'the church needs to learn from these people'. Others like Kate were frustrated that the Church of England was not really listening. Through the relationships that she was developing with people 'at the edges', she was discovering that while many people would be very unlikely to walk through a church door, they were interested in having conversations about things that matter: life, spirituality and finding fulfilment. These pioneers witness to the Church of England, which has embraced the temptations of focusing on the centre but is increasingly peripheral to many people's lives. Many of the pioneers found that it was in making themselves more distant from the formal structures of the Church of England, from the institutional centre, and finding mutual support of other pioneers, that they were able to find the space to follow their sense of calling. Through building relationships in the community with individuals and organizations, 'church' still had a place, just not at the centre.

The fact that people perceive that a church will pressure them to believe certain things or try and 'shove their message down people's throats' demonstrates the importance of the gospel coming through a community of love and friendship. In the Edgy Learning Project, people who had joined the church or group did so because they found themselves cared for and supported. In particular in the Methodist congregation named above, it was not just a *friendly* welcome but the fact people became *friends*. We were reminded of how Jesus called his followers 'friends', not 'servants' (John 15.13–15), and how they would be known as his disciples by how they loved one another (John 13.35). We heard of people being drawn into the life of the community through that love and care, and discovering, or rediscovering, their own faith in Jesus. Kate, who ran an organization that had worked with the Methodist Church, said she was amazed 'how much these people love and care for one another. I haven't ever in my whole life seen anything like it.' She described how she had been on her 'own little journey' in relation to church and faith. This message of love was not primarily something communicated in a message but was discovered in friendship and conversation. In different research into fresh expressions, this was called chit-chat.[8] Sarah described how they come together for a sewing hub fresh expression of church:

> When we come together in the morning, you know, we get the kettle on as you do when you meet as friends, and God and whatever, we sit around for just a general chit-chat on how everybody is, if anybody's got any issues or so on and so on. And then we try and have a little bit of quiet time for prayer and reflection.

These conversations brought about a mutuality – support and sharing between each other. In contrast to the temptation of resourcing from the centre with a unidirectional flow, conversation, or chit-chat, emphasizes not only the multidirectional nature of support and learning but also the ways they take place in the midst of the ordinariness of everyday life, sitting around with the kettle on.

Back in the Edgy Learning Project we also worked with a group supporting prison leavers. The conversations there drew our attention to the way both 'discipleship' in church and 'going straight' after prison are very often framed around individual choice. The resonances with Jennings' critique of the self-sufficient man are unsurprising. What we discovered was that the agency of the ex-offenders, their ability to make choices to determine their future, was not something that they found within themselves but was realized through coming into a supportive and caring community, where they were given responsibility and encouraged to 'give back' through volunteering. We saw how becoming part of a recovery house community and connecting with their local church had enabled them to function as individuals, and how within a community of rules and norms they were able to exercise personal agency. This witnesses against the lies and the destructive nature of self-sufficiency and individuality, and to a reality of interdependency – one that is often occluded by wealth and privilege but seen starkly in these more edgy spaces.

The shadow of empire is not just about the way it has shaped imaginations but also the realities that it has left in the UK and in the Church of England. One of these realities is a multicultural Britain. Harvey Kwiyani, our colleague at CMS, points out that 'cultural diversity is fast becoming the new normal in British society' and challenges congregations to 'reflect the diversity in their membership' (Kwiyani, p. 110). In the research we carried out into being a multicultural learning community at CMS, we identified how it was in the relationships being built across diversity and difference that our students discovered new ways of thinking and being.[9] These kinds of cross-cultural conversations and relationships were not always easy – people had to navigate discomfort about colonial pasts and differing experience because of race, and confronting some of the logics we have discussed above.

Particularly focusing on the African diaspora voices, we heard how they were concerned to speak with care and not offend (Pedro) or wound (Gloria) those from a white British background, while having to challenge negative stereotypes of their African heritage (Francisco). This self-awareness witnessed to a dominant world view or logic, which they were careful when challenging due to past experience of negative responses. At the same time they witnessed to the ways they, as a diverse group of students, had learnt to 'honour each other's story' (Gloria) and to see people as gifts that God had brought into their life, making sure they were pausing long enough to listen and receive. Gloria described how they were building 'relationships for the future': their future ministries and the future church, which would be multicultural. The witness of these African diaspora voices was challenging to a church and culture dominated by particular ways of doing and seeing, but also witnessing to a new way of being a multicultural church, one that began to reveal the poverty of a homogenized Church of England and to look a little bit more like the new creation where all tribes and tongues would worship God together (Rev. 7.9).

A pilgrim church

These witnesses from the edges have further highlighted some of the logic and temptations of empire that the Church of England has inherited, and they have begun witnessing to a different imagination of church. Church is imagined as witness to the love of God through the love of one another. There is an interest and care for people in the ordinary and everyday. There is an openness to different views, different faiths, and an ability to engage with and learn from one another in normal conversations – the chit-chat of everyday life. They witness to the way faith is received in these contexts, where people go on their 'own little journeys', finding themselves drawn into the life of the church community. We hear the whisperings and the echoes of the Holy Spirit in much of what is witnessed, drawing people into friendship, into community and into the life of Jesus. This is not a church with the power of empire behind it, which has bought into a vision of the world around progress and homogenization, but a vision of a humbler church, a church on a journey, aware of its imperfections and fragile state and seeking to be faithful to God. It is a pilgrim church. Stephen Bevans draws on Pope Francis's identification of the pilgrim church as a 'community of missionary disciples', a church participating in God's mission to heal the whole created order. Bevans asserts that a pilgrim church involves itself in the contexts and cultures of the world and:

> journeys through the world in all its concreteness, in all its diversity, in all its beauty, in all its struggles and imperfections. As it makes its pilgrim way and proclaims the gospel message and witnesses to the reign of God, it does it by taking seriously the lands through which it journeys and the peoples among whom it witnesses, and embodies, demonstrates, and proclaims the gospel in ways that they can understand. (p. 206)

In a way that resonates with both the witnesses we have heard and from TTL, Bevans quotes the Roman Catholic theologian Rafael Luciani, who reminds us that 'the preferential sociocultural location of the Church' is among the poor, 'from which it will be able to generate processes for building the people-as-nation, but it will do so by journeying with the people-as-faithful, out of their beliefs and values, out of their faith and their struggles' (Bevans, p. 211).

The Church of England can be reimagined through the witness from the edges through the Spirit's work. Rather than following the temptation to reassert itself as the centre, and to think the answers come from the centre, the Church of England is being offered an invitation by those witnesses at the edges to rediscover itself as the pilgrim church, a church based on love and care, on friendship. These witnesses point to the fact that hope is not to be found in the centres of power but rather in the marginalized and often forgotten spaces; after all, in the Kingdom of God 'the last will be first, and the first will be last' (Matt. 20.16). It is a church that trusts and follows the work of the Spirit, a Spirit at home in the edgy spaces. This is not hope for a powerful church but hope for faithful witness in the shadow of empire to the realm of God.

Notes

1 Throughout the chapter 'we' is used to refer to us as authors.

2 Throughout this chapter we use the language of 'centres' and 'edges' while realizing that it is complicated. Whose edge and whose centre are obvious questions to ask. Our references to centres focus on organizational and institutional decision-making. By edges we are turning to those who have felt marginalized and distanced from those centres. Following Clare Watkins' reflections, the edges are best understood as fractures as a result of human finitude and sinfulness rather than inherent to church or society (Watkins). Witness from the edges is about listening to the accounts of those who have experienced the fractures – who have found themselves distanced due to a lack of justice.

3 Church Commissioners for England, 'Church Commissioners' Research into Historic Links to Transatlantic Chattel Slavery', London: Church House Publishing, https://www.churchofengland.org/sites/default/files/2023-01/church-commissioners-for-england-research-into-historic-links-to-transatlantic-chattel-slavery-report.pdf.

4 Private correspondence, 1 July 2024.

5 The Edgy Learning Project is a theological action research project developed by TARN at the University of Roehampton (https://theologyandactionresearch.net/), led by Professor Clare Watkins and funded by the St Peter's Saltley Trust (https://saltleytrust.org.uk) and the Susanna Wesley Foundation (https://susannawesleyfoundation.org/).

6 All names used are pseudonyms to protect identity.

7 James Butler carried out this research into the experience of lay pioneers. It is written up in *Lay Pioneering and Thriving in Mission* (Butler, 2023) and was funded by the Susanna Wesley Foundation.

8 A research project carried out by Cathy Ross and James Butler into the understanding of salvation in fresh expressions (Butler and Ross, 2025).

9 Research carried out by James Butler, Cathy Ross, Harvey Kwiyani and Joseph Ola into being a multicultural learning community as we brought together the pioneer and African diaspora MA pathways at CMS. This was funded by a

Common Awards Seedcorn Grant, and the report, 'Towards Multicultural Learning: "A Fellowship of the Unlike"', can be read here: https://www.durham.ac.uk/departments/academic/common-awards/research/previous-seedcorn-grants/.

References

Archbishops' Anti-Racism Task Force, 2021, 'From Lament to Action', https://www.churchofengland.org/sites/default/files/2021-04/FromLamentToAction report.pdf.

Bevans, Stephen, 2024, *Community of Missionary Disciples: The Continuing Creation of the Church*, Maryknoll, NY: Orbis Books.

Butler, James, 2023, *Lay Pioneering and Thriving in Mission*, Cambridge: Grove Books, https://scholar.google.com/citations?view_op=view_citation&hl=en&user=7mb8E9kAAAAJ&citation_for_view=7mb8E9kAAAAJ:YopCki6q_DkC.

Butler, James and Cathy Ross, 2023, 'Octavius Hadfield: Nineteenth-Century Goodie or Twenty-First-Century Baddie? Learnings from the Complexities of Mission and Empire', in Anthony Reddie and Carol Troupe (eds), *Deconstructing Whiteness, Empire and Mission*, London: SCM Press, pp. 75–90.

Butler, James and Cathy Ross, 2025, 'Who then can be Saved? Perspectives on a Lived Theology of Salvation among Fresh Expressions in the UK', in Hans Schaeffer, Jan Martijn Abrahamse, Karen Zwijze-Koning and Stefan Paas (eds), *Visions of the Good Life: Salvation, Church, and Mission in the Secular West*, Leiden: Brill.

Church of England, 2018, 'Vocations to Pioneer Ministry', https://web.archive.org/web/20181222141321/https://www.churchofengland.org/pioneering.

Commission on World Mission and Evangelism, 2013, *Together Towards Life: Mission and Evangelism in Changing Landscapes*, https://www.oikoumene.org/resources/documents/together-towards-life-mission-and-evangelism-in-changing-landscapes.

Fitzgerald, Tanya, 2001, 'Fences, Boundaries and Imagined Communities: Rethinking the Construction of Early Mission Schools and Communities in New Zealand 1823–1830', *History of Education Review* 30.2, pp. 14–25.

Fowler, Corinne, 2024, *Our Island Stories: Country Walks Through Colonial Britain*, London: Allen Lane.

France-Williams, A. D. A., 2020, *Ghost Ship: Institutional Racism and the Church of England*, London: SCM Press.

Francis (Pope), 2013, 'Apostolic Exhortation *Evangelii Gaudium* of the Holy Father Francis to the Bishops, Clergy, Consecrated Persons and the Lay Faithful on the Proclamation of the Gospel in Today's World', http://www.vatican.va/content/francesco/en/apost_exhortations/documents/papa-francesco_esortazione-ap_20131124_evangelii-gaudium.html.

Hayes, Nick, 2020, *The Book of Trespass: Crossing the Lines that Divide Us*, London: Bloomsbury.

Heffernan, Margaret, 2012, *Wilful Blindness: Why we Ignore the Obvious*, London: Simon & Schuster.

Higton, Mike, 2023, 'Beyond Theological Self-Possession', in Anthony Reddie and Carol Troupe (eds), *Deconstructing Whiteness, Empire and Mission*, London: SCM Press.

Jennings, Willie James, 2020, *After Whiteness: An Education in Belonging*, Grand Rapids, MI: Eerdmans.

Kwiyani, Harvey C., 2020, *Multicultural Kingdom: Ethnic Diversity, Mission and the Church*, London: SCM Press.

Laing, Olivia, 2024, *The Garden Against Time: In Search of a Common Paradise*, London: Picador.

Langmore, Diane, 1989, *Missionary Lives: Papua, 1874–1914*, chapter 'The Object Lesson of a Civilized Christian Home', Honolulu: University of Hawaii Press, pp. 65–88.

Okesson, Gregg, 2020, *A Public Missiology: How Local Churches Witness to a Complex World*, Grand Rapids, MI: Baker Academic.

Rountree, Kathryn, 2000, 'Re-making the Maori Female Body: Marianne Williams's Mission in the Bay of Islands', *The Journal of Pacific History* 35.1, pp. 49–66.

Sanghera, Sathnam, 2021, *Empireland: How Imperialism has Shaped Modern Britain*, London: Viking.

Sanghera, Sathnam, 2024, *Empireworld: How British Imperialism has Shaped the Globe*, London: Penguin.

Sechrest, Love L., Johnny Ramírez-Johnson and Amos Yong (eds), 2018, *Can 'White' People be Saved? Triangulating Race, Theology and Mission*, Downers Grove, IL: IVP Academic.

Taylor, Steve, 2019, *First Expressions: Innovation and the Mission of God*, London: SCM Press.

Taylor, John V., 1965, CMS Newsletter, No. 285, September.

Taylor, John V., 1972, *The Go-Between God: The Holy Spirit and Christian Mission*, London: SCM Press.

Watkins, Clare, 2024, 'Witness from the Church's Wounds: The Authority of Those Experiencing Marginalisation in the Church', in Stephen McKinney, Thomas McLoughlin and Beáta Tóth (eds), *Synodality and the Recovery of Vatican II: A New Way for Catholics*, Dublin: Messenger Publications, pp. 69–84.

17

Being Pilgrim into the Unknown

TINA HODGETT

Introduction

Pilgrimages are usually journeys to places of religious significance, historical sites of note. In this chapter, I will consider what it might be to undertake a journey towards a future destination of the imagination, a place in time and space that doesn't yet exist. This kind of journey can be individual or collective or a combination of both. It is, I believe, the journey we are on as the Church of England at this point in our history, and I understand my ordination as a call to be part of the network of individuals and groups enabling the church to adventure out into time.

Exploring the nature of my call to ordination in the early 2000s was an alienating experience. I visited vicars and churches of different traditions, looking for a model of priestly service that was an embodiment of the sense I held inside of what my future held. In some respects my call was clear and in others indistinct, but I didn't find an answer of recognition in anyone or anything I encountered. In the end I offered for ordination with a toolkit of three phrases I relied on for the early part of the journey: the verse in Isaiah that summarized my understanding of what God was up to in the world, 'Behold, I am doing a new thing'; a sense that I was called to be 'a voice calling in the wilderness, preparing the way of the Lord'; and the phrase that started to appear in my vocabulary involuntarily, 'the church of the future'. I wrote a poem about tandem jumping with Christ from a plane – this was how it felt to be saying 'Yes' to God under such circumstances. Like Brendan the Navigator launching himself on to the open sea in a coracle, allowing the winds of the Spirit to blow him to his destination, I was launching myself into a future life with no map or even a certainty that another land existed across the sea.

The roles I've held over the past 20 years have been presented in a just-in-time kind of way, each taking my learning and experience from the previous stage and allowing them to expand and extend into the next. I completed a pioneer curacy, was a team pioneer vicar, called the 'Team Pilgrim' recruited to minister chiefly outside the civic parish church, then co-authored and led an SDF-funded pioneer project in Bath and Wells. From there, via a rather unexpected route that felt like a bit of a shipwreck, I came to land where I am now, training lay pioneers through the Church Mission Society south-west hub and co-leading Pioneering Parishes, a small start-up training organization. Pioneering Parishes works with parish churches and their leaders to enable whole congregations to join in with God's mission in a similar way to individual pioneers, moving their energy out into the parish towards those who are yet unconnected. Both these roles and organizations are new; they have emerged, growing out of earlier conversations and connections, woven together by the slow, quiet, invisible agency of the Holy Spirit.

It has been a precarious, frightening pilgrimage at times, rich in human error and failure but also full of joy, awe and wonder at unexpected organic growth and the sense of God's hand making a way where previously there was no way. En route I have found few resources in the form of Christian literature to give me a sense of being accompanied on this unpredictable journey-without-a-destination until recently, when I was introduced to the extraordinary commentary on the Acts of the Apostles by Willie James Jennings, which I will draw on in the latter part of this chapter as I consider the playful agency of the Holy Spirit in the church today.

A rough map for this chapter

The Scriptures bear witness to other voyages into the unknown. I have chosen three contrasting stories of journeys into different 'unknowns' to explore what can be learnt for the post-Christendom church today. I begin with the paradigmatic story of the Exodus from Egypt; then consider Christ's incarnation as a journey from a purely spiritual mode of being to an embodied one; and third, look at the journey the apostles and early disciples made, under the compulsion of the Holy Spirit's agency, from the familiar territory of Judaism to the new world of early Christian communities.

Journey into the unknown 1: the journey from Egypt into the wilderness

At the Exodus the Hebrews leave a familiar world. For all their experience of exploitation and despair, Egypt has been home. The Hebrews have had children and also buried parents here. They are accustomed to the climate, landscape and diet. They have history here of salvation and sanctuary. However much they long for freedom from oppression, change will be hard because human beings are always culturally embedded in time and place (whether they are aware of it or not). Thus every permanent separation from familiar surroundings is disorientating even when it is necessary or deeply desired (Lyth, p. 26), as it was for the Hebrew slaves. The Hebrews left in such a hurry that they did not have time to grieve for what they were leaving behind. The mourning came later when they had time to reflect: they remembered, for example, the incredible fruits the fertile Nile land had provided (Num. 11.1–6). What else did they miss when they had time to process their departure? Did they find a way to lament their losses?

Today's church is faced with a similar journey into the future. Many congregations are embedded in their church culture and struggle to embrace the journey into newness. In our work with Pioneering Parishes my colleague Greg Bakker and I encounter many individuals and congregations who feel the loss of a familiar world of worship and congregational life. They list full churches, hearty singing, beloved hymns, the attention of a sole priest, children, young people, services from the Book of Common Prayer and much more as the things they miss. Increasingly they recognize the need to adapt to the changing world around but find it difficult to move forward. The cultural anthropologist Gerald Arbuckle argues powerfully that congregations need to be able to lament their losses in a way that acknowledges pain, grief and even anger towards God if there is to be any hope of making a new start:

> As long as we individually and as communities refuse to grieve over that which is lost or now apostolically irrelevant or unjust, we will not let go of the past. Thus we will be refusing to make room for much-needed apostolic resurrection, freshness, and innovation. (Arbuckle, p. 3)

Leading congregations on a journey into the unknown requires us to create liturgical spaces for lament according to the pattern of the Psalms, allowing people to come through disorientating liminal space into a place of trust in God's faithfulness. Without this they are not free to move forward. As the Old Testament scholar Walter Brueggemann states, 'Only grief permits newness' (p. 46).

Having moved house three times in the past five years under the compulsion of the Spirit, I know the challenge of rationalizing my belongings. The command of God is usually to travel light, which means leaving almost everything behind. Sending out the 72 disciples on their first mission assignment, Jesus tells them to take nothing for the journey (Luke 9.3). They were not to head out with everything they might possibly need, like the foolish missionary family in Barbara Kingsolver's novel *The Poisonwood Bible*, heading to Africa with pinking shears and cake mixes (pp. 15–17). Departures provide an opportunity to leave behind stuff that belongs to what is about to become a former way of life and take only what will be useful for the future. The Hebrews took flocks and herds, dough to make bread, and gold and silver donated by their Egyptian neighbours (Exod. 12.31–51), which were later used to build the wilderness tabernacle; most other things they seem to have left behind. The task of sorting can be an emotional one, as possessions and the rituals and memories they represent are hard to part with, even as letting them go allows a passage to open up ahead. The poet and philosopher David Whyte movingly portrays how his niece, a pilgrim, arrived at Finisterre Point from Santiago de Compostela. She decides what to take with her and what to leave behind as this land journey concludes. The tasks that face her are:

> To empty your bags; to sort this and to leave that;
> to promise what you needed to promise all along,
> and to abandon the shoes that had brought you here
> right at the water's edge, not because you had given up
> but because now, you would find a different way to tread,
> and because, through it all, part of you could still walk on,
> no matter how, over the waves. (Whyte, p. 24)

Many aspects of the Church of England are not wanted on voyage. These are, for example: abuses of power, along with ingrained postures of entitlement and clerical privilege, as came into glaring light in the case of Peter Ball, paedophile and bishop (IICSA); a culture of paternalism or maternalism; a presupposition the church as it is has a right to exist because of its history; a focus among church leaders on the exclusive growth of one's own church congregation(s) and reluctance to collaborate with others; prejudice still abiding in many places towards those who are not white, straight, well educated, middle class and male, and a lack of awareness and affirmation of the many axes of diversity in which people present themselves in the world (see, for example, France-Williams; Parker).

In terms of the breadth of church tradition, it is up to each tribe, as it were, to do the work of discernment of what to take and what to leave behind. In this it will be useful to bear in mind the whole arc of church history. Such a long view will give a sense of perspective that may aid the act of letting go, since the church across time and geography has taken many and varied forms, distinct from those today. According to the missiologist Andrew Walls, the principal unique continuous elements of tradition over 2,000 years of expressions of Christian community have been the person of Jesus Christ, the Scriptures, rituals of bread, wine and water, and the imperative to share the good news. These are the contents of the church's kitbag today, her essential travel items ready to be re-enculturated by the interpretative power of the Holy Spirit into the times and cultures through which she passes.

Setting out into the unknown involves letting go of accustomed security. The Hebrews step out of a world of oppression and exploitation, but equally out of the familiarity and certainty that the human psyche prefers, into a world where they are required to trust in God going ahead of them as a pillar of cloud by day and a pillar of cloud by night. They are given just enough revelation for the next 24 hours of their journey: this has to be enough. Their lenses have to be limited; they have to trust that this accumulation of daily revelations over time will reveal the land they have been promised. Our churches today, if they wish to venture into the unknown – and in some ways it is not a choice – will find themselves having to live in a similar way, trusting God for the revelation of each step forward, without the reassurance of knowing they are on course or being able to see the destination. We are unaccustomed to having to make do with enough revelation.

The Hebrews also have to learn to live in faith that there will be enough food and water for their needs in this wilderness environment. In fact the scarcity mindset of Pharaoh's Egypt, where the slaves were required to make bricks without straw, is replaced for the Hebrews by the reality of abundance in the desert. The people of God are provided with manna to eat each day. It may not be what they are used to or what they want, but it is more than enough, and is miraculously provided at their point of need.

In this new world the Hebrews have to change their understanding of what and how Jehovah will provide. This is something today's church will also need to learn as it journeys into the unknown and often suffers from a mindset of scarcity: a sense of not having enough people or money. In our current context, Parish Church Councils often ask how community initiatives and small new Christian communities – which are little forays into the unknown – will help pay the parish share. Finding ways to pay the share can be a real source of anxiety for clergy and PCCs, and this is a natural question to ask. It has been my experience, however, that abundant resources, human and financial, are often released for work in the community that would not be available purely for the running of the parish church. My pioneer colleagues often tell stories with this common thread, of abundant provision arriving miraculously from surprising places when the groups they are leading set out from the familiar safety of the church into the vulnerability of wilderness-living beyond church walls.

Resources of different kinds arrive via unforeseen routes to exclamations of joy and wonder at a God who can make water flow in a desert: gardening tools, shipping containers, volunteers, unsought donations of cash, pieces of wooden toy train-track, yurts and many other contextually necessary things have been supplied by the God who provides for those who trust him for what they need in building relationships with people in the wilderness places. For some churches this might need to be considered God's 'enough', even when – painfully – money is not being directed primarily towards the needs of the existing congregations. Experience, however, also shows that these are sometimes renewed via resources from the missional edges, again in ways that could not have been predicted.

The Hebrews, like the post-Christendom church, have to learn to live in provisionality. I have personally learnt through several short-term job roles, house moves and significant life changes that provisional living drives our faith in God deeper, refining our understanding of what is important in wilderness times. As the Benedictine nun and theologian Joan Chittister writes: 'What uncertainty brings us to is the security that comes with knowing that we finally developed in ourselves the ability to grow, adjust, to become' (p. 40).

Likewise, uncertainty has moved me towards a more contemplative mode of being. Contemplative prayer and practices of paying attention to the world around us, for both congregations and individuals, enable us to appreciate the gift of the now, where God is permanently present even when everything else is provisional. Contemplative practices have the potential to generate a sense of abundance and gratitude for what is:

The only life is Now, so let's cease this striving,
Driving, never arriving.
Let's rest in this imperfect, dappled now.
What if there's no longed-for future in tomorrow
And no perfect good old days.
The only life that's happening,
Is already here, it's now. (Sheehan, p. 173)

Journey into the unknown 2: the journey from heaven to earth

The journey into the unknown is a divine initiative. It is not simply something God leads us into, commands or facilitates, it is something God embodies in the incarnation. In the birth of the second person of the Trinity as a human baby, God journeys from heaven to earth, from spirit to matter, from infinite consciousness to finite creature. Trying to imagine this is like trying to imagine pouring the cosmos into a test tube. It is a concept so outrageous it cannot be captured by human minds. It defeats every logic and makes every ludicrous idea mundane.

The theologian Bernadette Roberts suggests that the incarnation is the hardest part of God's life on earth. Rather than crucifixion, death and resurrection, which were a means by which the Son of God returned to his eternal state, incarnation was the most sacrificial act: 'What was really hard for infinite consciousness was to come into this world in the first place' (Roberts, pp. 200–2). This is the predominant act of Christ's sacrificial self-emptying described in Philippians 2.5–8: regardless of the cost, God's son ventures into the state of humanity, journeying into the unknownness that is created and physical and material, a radically outward and downward journey in indescribable humility. It is a placing of self utterly at the service of God and humankind, motivated entirely by unconditional love.

The doctrine of the incarnation provides the precedent to be unorthodox, to divert from existing norms, to disrupt and shock, even be outrageous in order to move towards others in love. It gives permission to imagine, experiment, risk, cross boundaries and become like others in order to make God's love known.

Implicitly it advocates for the possibility of changes of state for the church as the Body of Christ. God's son, Jesus Christ, leaves the church on earth as his physical representation. His change of state for our sake in the incarnation mandates a change of state for his Body on earth if it is necessary for the sake of the world. If God himself is subject to change because of love, no institution can consider its form, traditions, culture or anything else beyond alteration if love so requires.

Theories abound as to what this new state might be towards which the church is journeying. It is perhaps the small, slow, simple communities described by Paul Bradbury (pp. 127–8), churches dispersed within the local neighbourhood developing in communities across the USA (Sparks et al., pp. 53–74) or online virtual reality churches for digital natives. A couple of towns in the south-west of England have recently seen a similar phenomenon developing independently of one another through the agency of local pioneers: a small number of separate but connected emerging communities have grown up, with participants flowing among them in a random but relational way. Some communities are faith-based and others not, some traditional and some not, some in church buildings and some not. One pioneer describes it like this:

> I use the metaphor of an artery with the idea of movement and flow of life pulsing from a central source which I see as God pumping round a community through different arteries and veins and capillaries bringing things to me I didn't know about and flowing out and round again … with a sense of momentum and vitality.[1]

The image offers an appropriately mystical metaphor for a state of being for the Body of Christ, representing as it does the separate but connected communities as internal bodily organs, places of exchange of the life of God in circulatory flow, like blood around a human system.

The incarnation of Christ makes a strong case for the organic cross-cultural pioneer work that grows slowly and relationally like a vulnerable human being. Other models of church planting may presume churches can avoid the journey into the unknown and the encounter with difference by repeating an established process of planting and reproducing a given form of church. Cross-cultural approaches are always journeys into an unknown future through which the missioner learns, deepens her understanding and is transformed as she tries to see the world through the lenses of the local people and the host context. Any church that grows out of an incarnational missional posture is likely to reflect the host culture in a glorious variety of ways. As Jones Ugochukwu Odili writes: 'Like the multicolored clothes of Joseph, the Church of God should be seen as exhibiting a mosaic of cultural responses, none superior to the other, but all seen as grateful and valid responses to God who calls' (p. 174).

Jesus' journey from pure spirit into the unknown of human physicality led him into the same cycle followed by every living creature: birth, maturity and eventually death. We may surmise, extending the idea a little further, that the church is the Body of Christ, that death is possible for the church as it imitates the journey Jesus took. Death of the church or of churches is rarely spoken of in Church of England circles today, just as taboo a subject as death in society generally, and it is another unknown after centuries of Christendom. But death, or 'creative destruction' as it is sometimes termed in the eco cycle, forms a natural stage in the life cycle of all created matter as well as in the life of organizations,[2] and it plays a critical role in the Christian story. Why should we fear contemplating the death of a particular church, given that according to the gospel, death offers the possibility of generating surprising newness that we call resurrection? It is likely that numerous churches will die in the sense of becoming financially unsustainable if they have been unable to adapt to meet the challenges of the day. It is painful and sad, as most deaths are, but resurrection in God's way and time is guaranteed by the arc of the gospel narrative and the faithfulness of God. There is, however, another form of death Jesus modelled – not the natural death of the body but the willingness to pour self out for the sake of others. What would it mean for the local church to give up its life so that others might live?

In Pioneering Parishes we invite churches to ask the question: 'Who do we aspire to be for God and our local community?' This question is asked in an open and honest conversation to which the community are invited to contribute, and their contribution often calls the church outwards. If the church has the resolve to embed and live out the proposed values elicited by the question, it can lead the congregation in new and sometimes surprising directions as the community responds to being included in the conversation. It is more willing to trust the church, which has humbly sought their views, and is more likely to look for and offer possibilities of partnership with the congregation in shared initiatives. The church chooses to put community before itself and in doing so has opportunities to give itself away. Sadly, however, it seems to be written into the cultural DNA of many churches that the majority of resources inevitably flow to the church's centre to secure its own survival. Agreeing who the church aspires to be for God and the community is the first step towards enabling the flow of energy to be reversed and new horizons to be opened up.

Journey into the unknown 3: from Israel to the early church

It is hard to take in that the apostles and early disciples after Pentecost did not have a map of any kind of the future. They did not know how the story unfolded, or how the church turned out. They held the responsibility for making each decision in the moment, which would lead to another moment and then another, and so on. The church of Jesus Christ was formed like a child's dot-to-dot image, with the dots joining one by one, gradually becoming more like a dense three-dimensional network. The individual apostles and groups of disciples, however, are not the central characters in the story. As Jennings puts it in his commentary on the Acts, the only central character in the Acts of the Apostles is the Holy Spirit (p. 2). The main task of the players charged with creating Israel's future out of the past is to yield to the Spirit in the present moment (pp. 11–12). This takes huge courage: some put their lives at risk, others break lifetime commitments to sacred traditions, others make radical choices without permission from the elders of the faith. Despite the high stakes, however, in this era of leading the apostles into the unknown, God is more than at work, God is at play. The book of Acts shows us the Holy Spirit and the apostles in a mutual responsive dance, improvising, experimenting, disrupting and rule-breaking, like children at play.

Jennings emphasizes the theme of improvisation (see, for example, pp. 69–70 and p. 76), which has been a theme of my own life and ministry. 'We're making it up as we go along' is a frequent refrain I have used to show we are in uncharted waters where there are no experts, no off-the-peg programmes and few right answers, and to encourage others to improvise. Improvisation honours intuition, experimentation and resourcefulness in the present moment; it creates space for exploring possibilities. Biological evolution and human progress of all kinds have relied on what the mathematician Stuart Kauffman calls 'jury-rigging': experimenting with familiar objects or processes used in a different way or brought together in a fresh combination to create an 'adjacent possible'. This is the sort of thing children do naturally: experiment with household objects and put them to an unconventional purpose or combine them in unusual ways. In Portishead my colleagues and I experimented with unusual combinations of things to create opportunities for spiritual encounters with passers-by: cocktails and gospel promises; car-washing and Good Friday; the Queen's Diamond Jubilee and an attempt to feed 5,000 people; ante-natal/post-natal classes and spirituality. Adjacent possibles are always potentially present alongside the actual, and according to Kauffman the potential has never been higher in human history for society and therefore also the church to find a pathway into a more fit-for-purpose unknown by exploring possibility.[3] The theme of improvisation is taken up by Ben Quash, who has developed a 'found theology' for the church, in which he proposes that the familiar known objects of the Christian tradition are 'given', as well as continually being 'found' in the light of fresh contexts; and new elements can be freshly 'found' as history develops. He cites the story of Cornelius in Acts 11 as an example of this, stating that 'a new theology had to be found then, and yet it is a story that continues to suggest the possibility of discoveries and surprises close at hand now' (Quash, p. 6). As ancient elements of the tradition are infused with contemporary factors they create the new; for example, neo-monasticism with its roots in early Christian monastic practice translated now into dispersed or local communities of lay people following a shared rhythm of life.

I believe the Holy Spirit is calling today's church to play. Play is usually considered to be a feature of the world of children and therefore trivial, but if we can see God at play – for example, opening the doors of the prison where Peter is incarcerated and allowing him to walk out past the guards thinking he is dreaming (Acts 12.1–16); or enabling people to speak in languages they had never learnt (Acts 2.1–12); or taking Peter by surprise by filling Cornelius and his family with the Holy Spirit before he has finished his gospel account (Acts 10.44–48) – it must also be of importance in the adult world. Serious play is an idea growing in importance in society as a means of increasing capacity for creativity.

According to the neuroscientist Beau Lotto, play is the answer evolution has provided to humanity's neurologically hard-wired preference for certainty, predictability and repetition, for in play the element of uncertainty is necessary and celebrated (pp. 285–6). A willingness to have a go at serious play is much needed if the church is to follow the call of the Holy Spirit to encounter new people in new places in new ways and thus create the church of the future. Creativity – closely aligned with the concept of play – is part of the nature of the Creator and reflected and expressed in human beings made in the image of God. In his online post 'A Cornish Call to Pioneer', Bishop Philip Mountstephen states: 'Our God is creative, and creativity is one of his greatest gifts to us. And mission is always a creative act' (Mountstephen).

A celebrated aspect of the experience of creativity involves the sense of being 'in flow', making progress with ease and focus and joy, just as the early disciples at times were caught up in the flow of divine intent and purposeful action. Even amid the aggressive interventions of the forces against them, and the shock and grief at lives and homes lost, the disciples' minds went through moments of being remarkably aligned with the divine mind in a way that is not common for much of the Christian life. Occasionally my colleagues and I share stories of being caught up in divine flow; such occasions are like the ladders on a snakes and ladders board or a wormhole in space that take you somewhere with delightful ease and remove the effort often involved in getting you to where you want to be. As one vicar described his experience of being caught up in divine flow in fostering a movement of Garden Churches, 'I'm seeing 90% wonder and 10% effort' (Bradbury, p. 104).

It is not always so easy; sometimes the experience of flow can be more dramatic and scary, like white-water rafting, and creative play can be disruptive. In the early years of the church, boundaries were breached, rules broken and walls pulled down in the Spirit's play. Body-boundaries were crossed when people's mouths were co-opted by the Spirit for urgent sharing of the incredible good news across linguistic barriers; food laws crumbled; walls of hostility between Jew and Gentile fell under the rumbunctious proactivity of divine agency. Jennings observes that:

> The deepest reality of life in the Spirit depicted in the book of Acts is that the disciples of Jesus rarely, if ever, go where they want to go or to whom they would want to go. Indeed the Spirit seems to always be pressing the disciples to go to those to whom they would in fact strongly prefer never to share space, or a meal, and definitely not life together. (p. 11)

The Spirit is like a child who challenges her parents' socially restricted thinking. As Jennings goes on to observe, the impetus to cross and dissolve former tightly preserved boundaries clearly marks the presence of the Spirit of Jesus who came to break down the walls of hostility between Jew and Gentile (Eph. 2.14). In the bringing together of previously separate peoples and cultures, adjacent possibles emerge. If the contemporary church seeks to chart a course through the unknown, it is likely to find it in following the Spirit towards the people it has until now wanted to avoid, either in or outside the church. The church only grows and changes through contact with difference; like the DNA of a family that has always intermarried, lack of diversity eventually weakens the family line. The voyage to the future church lands us among contexts and cultures that challenge us and cause us to question our current certainties. This is the way of Christ.

Conclusion

A chapter like this can have no conclusion. There is no tidy ending – only an openness to what is still to come. Like the women described at the original ending to the Gospel of Mark, we are still in the midst of fear, confusion and uncertainty. Like them we are invited to trust in the Holy Trinity's ability to provide, guide, empower, inspire, reveal, accompany, teach, play and co-create the future with us. Personally I do not know what I will be doing when my current temporary contract comes to an end in 18 months' time; I will still be metaphorically strapped to Christ's back, falling into the unknown, on this pilgrimage with many others to a place that may one day be a site of historical religious significance. As for the church, we move from dot to dot with the adjacent possibles slowly being revealed.

Notes

1 Gill Sakakini, personal communication, undated.
2 See, for example, https://www.innovation.wiki/en/method/ecocycle-planning-liberating-structure/.
3 https://www.ted.com/talks/stuart_kauffman_the_adjacent_possible_and_how_it_explains_human_innovation?subtitle=en.

References

Arbuckle, G. A., 1991, *Grieving for Change: A Spirituality for Re-Founding Gospel Communities*, London: Geoffrey Chapman.
Bourgeault, C., 2008, *The Wisdom Jesus: Transforming Heart and Mind – A New Perspective on Christ and his Message*, Boston, MA: Shambhala Publications.
Bradbury, P., 2024, *In the Fullness of Time: A Story from the Past and Future of the Church*, London: Canterbury Press.
Brueggemann, W., 1986, *Hopeful Imagination: Prophetic Voices in Exile*, Philadelphia, PA: Fortress Press.
Chittister, J., 2015, *Between the Dark and the Daylight: Embracing the Contradictions of Life*, New York: Image.

France-Williams, A., 2020, *Institutional Racism and The Church of England*, London: SCM Press.
Independent Inquiry Child Sexual Abuse (IICSA), 2022, 'Anglican Church Case Studies: Chichester/Peter Ball Investigation Report', https://www.iicsa.org.uk/reports-recommendations/publications/investigation/anglican-chichester-peter-ball/case-study-2-response-allegations-against-peter-ball/c1-introduction-peter-ball-case-study.html (accessed 20.02.2025).
Jennings, W. J., 2017, *Acts*, Louisville, KY: Westminster John Knox.
Kingsolver, B., 1998, *The Poisonwood Bible*, London: Faber & Faber.
Lotto, B., 2017, *Deviate: The Science of Seeing Differently*, London: Weidenfeld & Nicholson.
Lyth, Isabel Menzies, 1989, *The Dynamics of the Social: Selected Essays Vol. 2*, London: Free Association.
Mountstephen, P., 2020, 'A Cornish Call to Pioneer', 14 September, https://www.churchofengland.org/cornish-call-pioneer (accessed 20.02.2025).
Odili, Jones Ugochukwu, 2014, '"Shadows of the Good Things to Come": Confession and Repentance in the Interface between Christianity and Igbo Indigenous Religion', in Akuma-Kalu Njoku and Elochukwu Uzukwu (eds), *Interface between Igbo Theology and Christianity*, Newcastle: Cambridge Scholars Publishing, pp. 162–76.
Parker, E., 2022, *Trust in Theological Education: Deconstructing 'Trustworthiness' for a Pedagogy of Liberation*, London: SCM Press.
Quash, B., 2013, *Found Theology: History, Imagination and the Holy Spirit*, London: T&T Clark.
Roberts, B., 1989, *What is Self? A Study of the Spiritual Journey in Terms of Consciousness*, Austin, TX: Mary Goens.
Sheehan, M. L., 2020, *Trellis for the Soul: A Vision of Hope for Challenging Times*, Dublin: Veritas.
Sparks, P., T. Soerens and D. Friesen, 2014, *The New Parish: How Neighborhood Churches are Transforming Mission, Discipleship and Community*, Downers Grove, IL: IVP.
Whyte, D., 2014, *Pilgrim*, Washington: Many Rivers Press.

18

On the Ground: Garden Church, Norfolk

DAVID LLOYD

Introduction

Ten years of church planting had proved to be an intense ride. I'd had the privilege of ministering with an amazing team of vicars, volunteers, interns and paid staff, to partner and plant a resource church and help catalyse several offshoots, including repurposing a local pub, and several churches in and around Norwich. Seeing people come to faith, and churches come alive was and still is one of the most life-giving experiences. Honouring what has gone before while cultivating a seedbed of Kingdom innovation has, for me, always been stomach-churningly exciting. Too much of a good thing can, however, become a bad thing.

After many years there was much to celebrate and much to thank God for. Looking back, the first few years of revitalizing was like an amateur surfer being dropped on to the crest of a steep wave. At first it was possible to see the horizon. The whole venture teetered on the edge of momentum or moratorium, but then, as the tipping point came, so came a rush and surge of movement and we were soon simply trying to stay ahead of the curve.

Rebalancing Acts

Seven years later, one sad and surprising Saturday, my colleague, friend, co-planter and priest-in-charge was unable to work. Narrowly avoiding burnout, he rested for eight months and by the grace of God returned to leave well. He moved to a new parish and has led it into growth at a new pace. I continued, as interim priest-in-charge. The new year brought Covid-19 and 18 months later, out of the crucible, I embraced a new rhythm, of co-vocational ministry, and a different method, namely The Garden.

Leading up to all of this were a couple of significant pointers. In the wake of the increasing operational complexity of church life, my heart and soul had become conflicted and curious to know if the Lord of Luke 9 was still out there. I was thirsty to know if the Lord of 'Take nothing for your journey' (Luke 9.3) still applies today. The day-to-day script seemed heavily weighted towards the need for more money, better management models and missional initiatives. Was this really what stepping closer to the picture of the church in Acts looks like?

Coming across Alan Roxburgh's book, *Joining God in the Great Unraveling* was a sobering challenge. He laments: 'We have relocated God's presence inside ecclesiocentric systems directed by technocratic elites formed by a clergy industry and trained to focus on the inner life of congregations … The One made known to us in Jesus is wilder than these domestications' (p. 15). His call to release the 'wilder' Jesus points to an honest evaluation of our default settings. Roxburgh says: 'Churches default to religious forms of modernity's wager … that God has been made a useful element in our own agency' (p. 13). In other words, underneath everything, our habits and practices might *actually* tell the story of 'the primacy of human agency' (p. 13). Whether we are raising up great leaders, growing teams, delivering sermons, rebranding or refurbing, we may also inadvertently be domesticating God. Like preserving and pickling him into spectacular jam jars?

The nature of fruitfulness

In February 2019 my family embarked on an ecclesiological quest on a three-month sabbatical. Leaving Norwich with only hand luggage and a train ticket, we toured churches on the east and west coasts of America, sampling house churches to megachurches and following the scent of connections and conversations. We were invited to stay on the beautiful 'Garden Island' of Kauai, Hawaii. Somewhere on a mountaintop overlooking the serene green rainforest and turquoise waters of the Napali Coast, the complex layered symphony of nature, the absence of human industry and the euphony of bird song, I felt small, useless and joyful.

Alan Hirsch says of the rich supply of organic imagery in Scripture:

> These images are not just verbal metaphors that help us describe the theological nature of God's people but actually go to issues of essence. Therefore, they will need to be rediscovered, re-embraced, and relived

in order to position us as Jesus's people for the challenges and complexities facing us in the twenty-first century. (Ford, Wegner and Hirsch, p. 111)

The future promises in Scripture always look back to God's first and future garden, but perhaps, as Hirsch suggests, the imagery surrounding it all is here to help us navigate the present in fresh ways.

After Kauai we flew back to the UK, spending three weeks in the hills of rural Wales where again the dawn chorus did not seem to be in danger of folding for lack of leadership or financial resources. Ringing in my ears were the words from Francis Chan's Church Intensive, which I had attended in San Francisco: 'Sometimes leadership is about getting out of the way.' St Peter writes: 'His divine power has given us everything we need for a godly life through our knowledge of him who called us by his own glory and goodness' (2 Peter 1.3, NIV). God has given us his 'very great and precious promises' and through them we may participate in the divine nature (2 Peter 1.4, NIV). Our response to such a gift can be to listen and join in, to humbly add our voice to his.

Peter goes on to say: 'make every effort to add to your faith goodness; and to goodness, knowledge; and to knowledge, self-control; and to self-control, perseverance; and to perseverance, godliness; and to godliness, mutual affection; and to mutual affection, love' (2 Peter 1.5–8, NIV). St Peter's response to participating in God's divine nature seemed surprising. It was more about training my own ear and heart to sing in tune with God's divine initiative than to 'look busy'. What is more, St Peter says: 'if you possess these qualities in increasing measure, they will keep you from being ineffective and unproductive in your knowledge of our Lord Jesus Christ' (2 Peter 1.8, NIV). As Francis Chan succinctly put it at the Church Intensive: 'Godly character guarantees fruitfulness.'

Being church?

Returning home to Norwich, Norfolk, holding all we had learnt close to our hearts, the Garden Church began. There was no 'launch'. It gradually crept into our family life quietly and organically. We began meeting in our own home on Tuesday nights and invited anyone else who was around to join us whether of faith or none. This regular fixture in the diary was partly for our own nourishment and missional adventure, and partly because I wanted my children to grow up in a world where it would be normal for them to *be* church if there wasn't one in the area. It felt foolish back then – and sometimes, in the shade of the inherited church, does so today. I had to let go of the usual levers for growth. Hope came in a different way from how I had become used to expecting it. It came through the most surprising, impossible and random ways.

I began to notice church leavers in a different light. Were they the new apostles, planters and leaders? Authors such as Reggie McNeal, Steve Aisthorpe and Stuart Murray all write about the post-Christendom and post-congregational era in which we live (McNeal, p. 32; Aisthorpe, p. 18; Murray, p. 50). People are spiritually curious, hungry for relationship, and many are leaving church but not necessarily leaving God. It is interesting to see with hindsight that back in the fourth and fifth centuries, those on the margins, who headed to the desert and left the Christendom church, paved the way for the emergence of an enduring pattern of monasticism, the ensuing Benedictine rule that in turn laid the foundations for Western civilization and led thousands to be centred on the life of Christ. Is God calling us to extend a trellis, or flex our governance for the church in exile?

Norfolk is predominantly a rural county, and the diocese has the largest concentration of medieval church buildings in the world. The challenges facing clergy in leading multi-parish benefices are acute, not to mention the lack of resources. The phrase I felt God had given me on a Hawaiian beach on the other side of the world resonated deeply for this English landscape and context: 'Re-disciple the disciples for when the Church of England closes its doors.' I felt a call to cultivate a people who could navigate an uncertain future. A 'go anywhere' and 'do anything' sort of people. People who didn't need to wait for a vicar to turn up. It would require certain muscle groups to be reawakened and certain muscle memories to be unlearnt. We would need to become resilient and agile missionaries again. Perhaps in time these people would be in a position to repopulate and renew parts of the inherited church.

Little did I know that within six months every single 'church' door across the county would be closed because of a global pandemic, and that this process would be accelerated everywhere.

Layers of life

In Autumn 2021, I left my stipendiary role and the vicarage and began working part-time for the diocese in mission development as well as pursuing freelance music and other jobs in search of a new co-vocational rhythm. Today The Garden is a network of over 16 lay-led missional communities. Some are 'seeds' of two or three who are watching and waiting in the fallow ground (Hos. 10.12) of rural parish life in anticipation of a new season. Others are well-established groups with 20 to 40 members, scattering seeds in the workplace, in schools or local communities, enjoying being 'small enough to care but big enough to dare', seeking to understand how best to live out their faith together.

Each Garden seeks to be unique to its context. Across a range of expressions, I see eyes opening to the reality that *we are church*, wherever, whenever, with whoever and however. Whether this leads to walking the dog with more prayerful intent or forming a jazz and gospel collective to share faith stories in festival churches, we are more expectant of the possibility that a new crop of wild flowers might spring up in the gaps between the mosaic of ancient churches. It is, when you think about it, an amazing and intriguing reality that even without all of the inherited props of church, we are still God's temple and that God's Spirit dwells in our midst (1 Cor. 3.16).

For the Garden Church we have five values borrowed from Francis Chan's We Are Church movement. They act like liquid fertilizer poured into the soil of our lives and local villages. The values reassuringly abbreviated to 'Do Less' (D.L.E.S.S). They are taken from Acts 2.42–47 and serve to remind us that if we become Devoted Worshippers, Loving Families, Equipped Disciple Makers, Spirit Filled Missionaries, and are prepared to carry our cross (Suffering Sojourners), we can be expectant that Jesus, as the high priest of his church, will be at work. The Garden was adopted into a Church Planting and Revitalization programme by the diocese in 2021 to allow it the permission to pilot, and it was granted a Bishop's Mission Order in May 2024.

A healthy ecology

How does this fit with our heritage today? Howard Snyder says that three things were instituted through Moses in the Old Testament, namely 'sacrifice, priesthood and tabernacle', but these were fulfilled with the coming of Christ and the birth of the church as a body and not a building. As Snyder says: 'The great temptation of the organized church has been to reinstate these three elements among God's people; to turn community into an institution' (Snyder, p. 62). We perhaps serve as a reminder that the church is reformed and always reforming and that renewal over the centuries within the monastic traditions began with what was affectionately known as 'little churches within the church' (*ecclesiae in ecclesia*; Peters, p. 86). Nothing new is happening here. There is if anything simply a resurgence of some of the forgotten ways. In the Celtic monastics we saw a nomadic indigenous combination of movement and mission. In St Benedict we saw the development of a simple replicable rule to enable many people to practise the Christian faith. In Wesley we saw a liquid ecclesiology, the church going to the people rather than people going to the church. In nature a healthy ecology is always layered and complex. A healthy body relies on antagonistic muscles to stay upright and strong. In the same way, The Garden seeks to contribute to the ecology of church to strengthen, complement and not compete.

In the first few years, we have sought to avoid doing anything on Sundays, or ask for any funding, or use any church buildings or anything that might be a trigger. We only minister where we are welcomed and where something is clearly being kindled by God. We recognize that building on loving relationships is central to the story of God and central to a healthy mixed ecology today and the only way we want to work within the Anglican communion. However, five years on the Holy Spirit is leading us back to some of the ancient spaces to partner with the inherited church and explore the planting of new worshipping communities into fallow ground. It is an enormous joy to see the gifts of lay leaders released in initiatives such as the folk, gospel and jazz worship collectives as well as prison ministry, lay-leader training, creative storytelling. At the time of writing, an emergent Spanish-speaking missional initiative 'La Gran Mesa Familiar Colectivo de Salsa' (The Big Family Table Salsa Collective) is also under way. I'm full of hope and expectation for the season ahead.

References

Aisthorpe, Steve, 2016, *The Invisible Church: Learning from the Experiences of Churchless Christians*, Edinburgh: St Andrew Press.
Ford, Lance, Rob Wegner and Alan Hirsch, 2021, *The Starfish and The Spirit: Unleashing the Leadership Potential of Churches and Organizations* (Exponential Series), Grand Rapids, MI: Zondervan (Kindle edn).
McNeal, Reggie, 2011, *Missional Communities: The Rise of the Post-congregational Church* (Jossey-Bass Leadership Network Series Book 55), Hoboken, NJ: Wiley (Kindle edn).
Murray, Stuart, 2004, *Church after Christendom*, Milton Keynes: Paternoster Press.
Peters, Greg, 2015, *The Story of Monasticism: Retrieving an Ancient Tradition for Contemporary Spirituality*, Grand Rapids, MI: Baker Academic.
Roxburgh, Alan J., 2021, *Joining God in the Great Unraveling: Where We are and What I've Learned*, Eugene, OR: Cascade Books.
Snyder, Howard A., 2017, *The Problem of Wineskins: Church Structure in a Technological Age*, 40th Anniversary edn, Franklin, TN: Seedbed Publishing (Kindle edn).

19

On the Ground: Being Pilgrim on the Margins

FIONA GIBSON

Introduction

As an archdeacon living and ministering in the most rural diocese in the Church of England, I'm often asked when I knew I was called to rural ministry. The honest – and perhaps surprising – answer is that I've never felt a generic call to a generic ministry. Instead, like other clergy, God has called me to specific parishes and specific roles in specific places, and some of those places have been rural. The boundary lines, as the psalmist wrote, have fallen for me in pleasant places (Psalm 16.6). But the reality is that there's no such thing as generic rural ministry, and that's one of the first things those of us in rural churches would want those in other settings to understand.

'Rural' encompasses everything from tiny, isolated hamlets in the rugged hills, where determined sheep farmers battle the elements to raise their flocks, to affluent lowland 'commuter rural' areas. Some in rural areas offer hospitality to tourists, and many also pray that some of those tourists become pilgrims and discover God through the ministry of a country church. Rural livelihoods, and rural lives, are deeply shaped by place as well as by time. That may seem obvious, but like many obvious statements it's also true.

Rural life and ministry are also hard. There is no room or time for sentimentality in rural areas. If the weather changes, an entire year's income can be wiped out overnight. Images of rosy-cheeked men and maidens, and of gambolling lambs or fields of barley gently waving in the glorious sunshine, need to be replaced, or at the very least joined, by the reality of falling prices, few employment options and an exodus of the young because they cannot afford to live where their ancestors have lived. Levels of mental illness in rural areas are devastatingly high, and rural clergy regularly minister to the families of those who have taken their own lives because the pressure and the isolation have proved overwhelming.

For rural clergy and lay leaders it sometimes feels as though 'The Rural Church' is seen by the wider church as a problem to be solved rather than a gift to be celebrated. In the countryside, people live on the margins, sometimes metaphorically, sometimes literally.

Small, hidden and lonely

Rural clergy and congregations have been living with the weaknesses that the whole church is now coming to terms with for a long time. We know what it is to be small, hidden and lonely, and that is the charism we now offer to the wider church. If, in the coming decades, the whole church is going to have to come to terms with being a marginalized community, one that provokes both hostility and curiosity in those among whom we live, then those living, working and witnessing in rural contexts can lead the way. We have walked this way before and we have hard-won wisdom to share.

Throughout the pages of Scripture we see God's concern for the small, the hidden and the lonely. I wouldn't want to go as far as calling it a bias, because I don't believe that God has biases. I would want to say that God shows a particular concern for people and places that are overlooked by others.

In Deuteronomy, God reminds the people of Israel of the reality of how they came to be his people:

> It was not because you were more numerous than any other people that the LORD set his heart on you and chose you – for you were the fewest of all peoples. It was because the LORD loved you and kept the oath that he swore to your ancestors, that the LORD has brought you out with a mighty hand, and redeemed you from the house of slavery, from the hand of Pharaoh king of Egypt. (Deut. 7.7–8)

When it came to choosing a king to replace Saul, God did not choose the eldest, the strongest or the tallest of Jesse's sons. He chose David, the youngest, the weakest and the one his father apparently hadn't deemed important enough to have been included in the invitation to the sacrifice.

It was the same with the town where God's own incarnate Son would be born. Bethlehem was not a shining metropolis, that was Jerusalem. Bethlehem was, 'one of the little clans of Judah' (Micah 5.2).

Even more than that, Jesus' human family, though descended from David, was sufficiently poor in material terms to have to offer the smaller sacrifice when they brought him to the temple as a baby. This concern for the small, the hidden and the lonely is summed up in the writing of the apostle Paul. Writing to a church, some of whose members thought they were doomed in the face of a double attack from those who thought the gospel was foolish and others who thought it was weak, Paul stated:

> Brothers and sisters, think of what you were when you were called. Not many of you were wise by human standards; not many were influential; not many were of noble birth. But God chose the foolish things of the world to shame the wise; God chose the weak things of the world to shame the strong. God chose the lowly things of this world and the despised things – and the things that are not – to nullify the things that are, so that no one may boast before him. (1 Cor. 1.26–29, NIV)

In the rural church we can often feel as though we are weak and lowly. Sometimes we even feel despised. But God chooses the foolish to shame the wise, the weak to shame the strong and the lowly and despised to nullify the things that are, so that boasting is silenced and God alone is glorified.

The first lesson from the rural church to the wider church, then, is that being small, hidden, lonely, weak and even despised is a normal part of what it means to be the church. It's when we think we're strong and powerful that we need to be cautious, for then we are in danger of being self-sufficient, self-reliant and self-righteous.

As the church in England we shall need to learn to accept that, in the eyes of the world, the church and the gospel we have to share will frequently seem weak and foolish. That is a lesson to be neither denied nor feared. It's just a part of normal Christian life. Christ has promised to build his church and has promised that nothing will prevail against it, and in Christ we are strong. The church worldwide is growing, and growth matters, but growth matters just as much when it's measured in ones and twos as when it's measured in thousands. Being small is not in and of itself a sign of failure.

Treasures old and new

The second lesson from the margins is that doing the old things, and doing them well, can be just as effective as innovating. We need both. There's a tension there because the same God who says, 'Forget the former things; do not dwell on the past. See, I am doing a new thing! Now it springs up; do you not perceive it?' (Isa. 43.18–20, NIV) also inspires the writer of the letter to the Hebrews to say, 'Jesus Christ is the same yesterday and today and for ever' (Heb. 13.8). God's people are a pilgrim people, called ever forward into the new future that God is building, moving ever onwards towards the return of Christ and the renewal and restoration of all things in him.

What the rural church demonstrates is that there needn't be a dichotomy between old and new, because in our post-Christendom context the paradox is that the old *is* the new. We pivot between tradition and innovation, using the wifi in our buildings to livestream services of Compline in traditional language to reach the digital natives who love to find a connection with the deep past. Here in the Diocese of Hereford we have café churches alongside Book of Common Prayer Evensong. We have an online-only church and we have 'Hedgerow Communions' and pilgrim trails. We're pioneering a Youth 'Hub and Spoke' model for reaching 11s–18s and we also faithfully carry out occasional offices, collective worship in schools, the patient, long-term building of pastoral relationships, carol services, harvest, remembrance, Christmas, Easter and all the other 'ordinary' ways that parish churches and parish clergy live out their calling in a particular place over many years, which demonstrate faithfulness and obedience for the long haul.

Services using liturgy that embodies and enacts timeless truth can hold and shape our worship and our thinking to equip us for living out our faith in our frantic and changing world. All of that is often seen as 'ordinary' or 'business as usual', but it's our core ministry as a church. For generations of people in our society, hearing the old, old story of the love of God in Jesus Christ *is* new, and for many of them the first encounter they may have with that story is through the ordinary, hidden and often lonely ministry of their local vicar.

In the rural church we see and show that 'ordinary' ministry, done well, carried out in humility, dependent on God, bathed in prayer and offered with all the grace and energy we can give, bears fruit in season. It may never be seen as innovative and exciting, but it is humble, faithful, and God blesses it.

The 'old things' matter now as much as they ever did because, in a world suffering from spiritual amnesia, being grounded in the past can bring us back to ourselves so that we can plan for the future from a present place of unchanging certainty. Our watchwords are those of Christ: 'Therefore every scribe who has been trained for the kingdom of heaven is like the master of a household who brings out of his treasure what is new *and* what is old' (Matt. 13.52).

As Christians we are not called to be successful. Success can be a seductive trap. We are called to be obedient and faithful. We leave success and fruitfulness to God, who alone gives the growth.

The long-term perspective

Patience and planning within a long-term perspective are other things those who live and minister in rural areas know well. As a church in the coming years we are going to have to accept what a farmer I knew taught me: we make our plans for the future, all the while knowing we may not live to see those plans come to fruition.

If decades of decline in the church in England are to be turned around, and by God's grace they can be, it will take careful, prayerful, planning by those in leadership now. Part of that planning will be accepting that growth will neither be easy nor instant. There are no 'quick fixes'. It may well be those ministering decades in the future who will reap the harvest that we sow now. That takes wisdom and courage and even a willingness to be seen as unsuccessful in our own lifetimes. We need to think in the long term, fix the point on the horizon where we are aiming to go, knowing it may be reached long after our own time, and work backwards from there to draw up plans and take the first step.

In rural churches, where some of our buildings have stood for centuries, where our clergy still baptize babies in fonts crafted in Saxon times, preach from pulpits carved in the reign of the first King Charles with wood from trees planted before the Norman conquest, and bury our parishioners in ground where people have been buried since the great plague, we understand the long term. That long-term perspective is another gift we offer to the whole church. We shall need wisdom as we plan and pray, and patience as we go about our work of telling the old-yet-new story of the gospel.

Rural churches know their vulnerabilities, and their strengths. They are rooted in their communities and live interdependently with them.

Those on the PCC often also sit on the parish council, the WI, the Young Farmers and the village-hall committee. There is no sense in which the rural church 'stands apart' from its community.

As we face up to the future of our church which is both provisional and certain, rooted in the past and moving to God's future, extremely vulnerable and utterly secure, the message from the rural margins is that being weak is a key to strength, doing the old things well is a key to new growth and patient endurance is a key to a joyful completion of all things in Christ.

Further reading

Beaumont, Susan, 2019, *How to Lead when You Don't Know Where You're Going: Leading in a Liminal Season*, London: Rowman & Littlefield.

Paas, Stefan, 2019, *Pilgrims and Priests: Christian Mission in a Post-Christian Society*, London: SCM Press.

Rumsey, Andrew, 2017, *Parish: An Anglican Theology of Place*, London: SCM Press.

Vaters, Karl, 2012, *The Grasshopper Myth: Big Churches, Small Churches and the Small Thinking that Divides Us*, Fountain Valley, CA: NewSmallChurch.com

20

On the Ground: Navigating Faith and Identity – The Journey of Iranian Christian Converts in the UK

OMID MOLUDY

Introduction

The experience of a migrant is unique. A migrant carries their past with them: language, culture, customs and memories. These elements accompany them from place to place, as if they are living in their homeland while simultaneously striving to find their place in the new land and achieve their dreams and aspirations.

The subject of Iranian Christians in the UK is intertwined with the broader theme of migration. The topic of migrants' identity and their attachment to elements of identity in the host society or their society of origin is a significant sociological and psychological discussion in the contemporary era. From a sociological and psychological perspective, migration is not merely a change in geographical space but an immersion in an intermediary space of different cultures, allowing individuals to navigate the identity-forming elements of both destination and origin societies (Brown and Pehrson, p. 288). These elements can be similar or in conflict, revealing the shifting identities of individuals in the migration process.

Therefore, examining the subject of this chapter without delving into the roots of the identity of the Iranian Christian individual is unavoidable. Hence we will briefly review the past, even though this will encompass a significant portion of the chapter.

The role of the Apostles and the Persian Church

According to tradition, St Thomas is regarded as the founder of the Church of Persia (Alzog, p. 184; Edwards, p. 301). Before the arrival of Muslims in Iran in the seventh century, the Persian Church was strong, robust (Spuler et al., p. 198; Waterfield, 2011), and missionary-orientated. Numerous historical records mention the vitality, prestige and expansion of the Persian Church. During the Sassanian dynasty (AD 226–651), which spanned a vast geographical area from Mesopotamia to Transoxiana, the Caucasus to the southern shores of the Persian Gulf and Yemen, the Christian church flourished and expanded significantly across the region. Despite this growth and dynamism, the church also faced severe persecution from the Sassanian kings.

An example of the church's historical significance and spread is the Xi'an Stele, an inscription found in China, which explains the Christian faith in Syriac (the language of the Persian Church) and Chinese (Tejirian and Simon, p. 21). This indicates the church's expansion into the East before it was curtailed by the advent of Islam.

The introduction of Islam

The arrival of Islam in Persia subjected Christians to the laws of *dhimma* ܕܡܐ, which granted non-Muslims protection and security under specific conditions (Minnerop, Wolfrum and Lachenmann, p. 534). Under this treaty, Jews, Christians and Zoroastrians could participate and enjoy relative security throughout the Islamic realm based on the conditions and commitments of the *dhimma* contract (Emon, pp. 69–72).[1] After the advent of Islam, the relationship between Christians and Muslims oscillated between tolerance and strict measures. According to the majority of Shi'ite and Sunni jurists, apostasy from Islam is considered a severe offence, potentially punishable by death (Peters, p. 65). At times the strictness of Muslim jurists towards Christians increased, causing crises within the Christian community, while at other times Christians experienced leniency.

From the Safavid dynasty (1501–1736) onwards

From the Safavid period, political relations between Western societies and Iran led to the presence of Christian missionaries in Iranian society (Thomas and Chesworth, pp. 15–19). During the Qajar dynasty (1794–1925), under the influence of Western colonial powers and the weakness of the Iranian government, there was a formal and serious presence of churches and Christian organizations, such as the Anglican Church. This period saw significant figures, including the Prime Minister Qa'im Maqam (1834–35), strongly criticizing Henry Martyn's presence in Iran and his debates with Muslim scholars (Farahani, p. 222), leading to the writing of many books refuting *Padori* پادری (Haeri, pp. 516–25). This movement, which began during the Qajar dynasty, continued into the Pahlavi dynasty (1925–79), which allowed religious freedoms. Despite this the movement led to the establishment of numerous churches, including the Roman Catholic Church and the Anglican Church, resulting in the formation of the Anglican Diocese of Iran in 1912. Bishop Hassan Dehqani-Tafti (1960–90), the first Iranian bishop of the Anglican Church in Iran who converted from Islam to Christianity (Van Gorder, p. 134), played a significant role.

The Islamic Revolution of Iran plunged the country into political, social, economic and religious crises, bringing Iran to the brink of civil war. Another crisis ensued with Saddam Hussein's invasion of Iran in 1980, leading to an eight-year war with hundreds of thousands of casualties (Montgomery, p. 10). The Islamic Revolution intensified religious strictures, causing all missionaries who had come to Iran from various countries to leave or be expelled. From the early days of the Islamic Revolution, severe incidents occurred, such as the beheading of Revd Aristos Sayah of the Episcopal Church of Iran in his office. There was also an assassination attempt on Bishop Dehqani-Tafti, and on 6 May 1980 his son was murdered. These killings continued for a long time, targeting several key and influential ministers from the Iranian Church, such as Mikaelian of the Evangelical Church, Haik Hovsepian of the Assemblies of God Church, and several others (Ross, Jeyaraj and Johnson, pp. 86–8).

The Iranian Revolution and subsequent waves of migration

The Iranian Revolution triggered several waves of migration, with estimates suggesting that about four million Iranians left the country following the Islamic Revolution (Esfandiari; Secretariat of the High Council of Iranian Affairs Abroad). These migrants encompassed various groups and periods. Initially, many associated with the former regime, including nobles and major capitalists, fled due to the legitimate fear of political retribution. Additionally, members of opposition groups and parties, and political intellectuals, left to escape persecution. Others fled due to insecurity caused by war, to safeguard their assets or to escape religious persecution. Many skilled professionals also left in search of a better life.

The encounter with radical Islam led to the suppression of various groups, disillusioning society regarding religion. Islam, which had held a high place among Iranians, became a source of disappointment. The clergy, historically seen as protectors against tyranny, became oppressors after coming to power. Consequently, people gradually became disillusioned with religion as a whole, particularly the post-revolution young generation. This led to a growing interest in mysticism and various religions as spiritual alternatives to Islam. During this time the era of communications and satellite networks introduced Christianity, with its tolerance, leniency and spirituality resonating with Iranian culture, leading to remarkable growth in interest.

During the relatively liberal era of President Khatami, there was a surge of enthusiasm and hope among Iranian youth (Dabashi, p. 63). However, with the advent of the radical government of Ahmadinejad, the suppression of various political, social, cultural and religious groups intensified. This increase in repression, coupled with political issues and serious economic corruption, plunged Iran into a crisis, a trend that continues to this day.

Over the past 20 years there has been a significant wave of new migrations and asylum seekers. This included wealthy, educated and entrepreneurial individuals who mostly moved to countries like the USA and Canada, with fewer settling in Europe. However, a large segment of asylum seekers, driven by political, religious, social and economic pressures, headed west. This group included young families and individuals from all social classes, even rural and unskilled workers, fleeing to free countries.

The majority of those who now attend churches outside Iran, especially in England, belong to this diverse and often desperate group of migrants. Many groups of asylum seekers come to the UK, for various reasons, including political, social and economic asylum. Additionally, there are those who converted from Islam to Christianity, practising their faith in secret or in 'house churches' in Iran (Landinfo, 2018). Among these converts many naturally seek out the church. At the same time numerous other groups are attracted to the church and convert to Christianity due to the love, support and outreach they experience from the local Christian community. Therefore the role of the church is not only to provide spiritual guidance but also to offer a tangible expression of the inclusive and hospitable nature of the body of Christ, providing a safe haven for these distressed individuals.

Cultural integration

Iranian converts to Christianity face significant challenges in cultural integration, both in Iran and in England. Transitioning from an Islamic to a Christian cultural context is daunting and involves changes in religious practices, social norms and values. This shift can lead to feelings of alienation and isolation, especially when converts encounter scepticism or rejection from both their former and new communities.

Language barriers, different social norms and the loss of familiar cultural practices further exacerbate these feelings of alienation (Saghafi, 2009). The stigma associated with changing one's religion often leads to rejection by family members in Iran and within the Iranian community in Britain. Converts may find themselves caught between two worlds, struggling to gain acceptance in both the Iranian diaspora and the broader British society. This can create a severe crisis, as migration and seeking asylum are already isolating experiences.

Many Iranian converts leave behind family and friends who may not understand or support their decision, intensifying their sense of isolation. Building new social networks in a foreign country is challenging, and without a strong community of fellow believers or understanding friends, converts may struggle to find a sense of belonging and purpose. This lack of a supportive community can significantly impact their mental health and well-being. Additionally, converting from Islam to Christianity can be seen as a betrayal of national and social identity, leading to a profound crisis of identity. This loss of identity and cultural integration can severely impact one's sense of self, causing deep psychological distress.

The role of the church

The church plays a crucial role in supporting Iranian Muslims who convert to Christianity. This support can be multifaceted, addressing both spiritual and practical needs.

One of the primary responsibilities of the church is to provide spiritual guidance and education. Many Iranian converts are new to Christianity and require comprehensive discipleship to understand their new faith. Churches can offer Bible studies, catechism classes and mentorship programmes to help converts deepen their understanding and grow in their faith. Additionally, worship services and prayer groups provide opportunities for communal worship and spiritual encouragement. These gatherings can be sources of strength and inspiration, helping converts connect with a larger religious community.

Churches must be culturally sensitive and inclusive to effectively support Iranian converts. This entails understanding the unique cultural backgrounds of Iranian believers and creating a welcoming environment that respects and values their heritage. Churches can offer services in Persian or provide translation services to make worship more accessible. Inclusivity also means acknowledging the trauma and challenges that converts may have faced. Churches should be prepared to offer pastoral care and counselling to address the emotional and psychological needs of converts, many of whom may have experienced persecution and displacement.

Practical assistance is another critical area where churches can make a significant impact. This can include helping converts navigate the asylum process, providing language classes and assisting with finding housing and employment. Churches can also facilitate connections to local resources and services. Building community is essential to help converts overcome feelings of isolation and loneliness. Churches can organize social events, support groups and communal activities to foster a sense of belonging. By creating a strong and supportive community, churches can help converts feel more integrated and valued.

The growth and legacy of St Aphrahat: the Iranian Church in Manchester

The journey of Iranian Christians navigating faith and identity in the UK finds a particularly poignant example in the story of the Iranian Church in Manchester, which began its mission in 2004 with the founding of St Aphrahat, the Persian Sage Church. This church has not only served as a place of worship but has also become a sanctuary for Iranian migrants, providing a vital sense of community amid the challenges of migration. From its inception, St Aphrahat aimed to create a space where Iranian Christians could find spiritual refuge and cultural solidarity.

In 2007, as the church congregation grew, it became clear that a larger venue was necessary to accommodate the increasing number attending and the expanding scope of the church's activities. A turning point came when Revd Marcus Maxwell, from the Church of England, offered the congregation a permanent home at St John the Baptist Church in south Manchester. Revd Maxwell's support and hospitality created a safe environment where the Iranian Church could thrive, allowing it to focus on its activities during the transition to the Church of England. His empathy and provision of a secure space were instrumental in helping the congregation establish itself. The church offered Bible study and catechism classes, conducted in Persian, to deepen the congregation's understanding of their newfound faith.

As the church matured, its influence grew, both in numbers and in the richness of its activities. However, the leadership recognized that for the community to sustain its mission long term, a formal ecclesiastical affiliation was necessary. In 2011, St Aphrahat officially became part of the Anglican Church, joining the Diocese of Manchester. This affiliation provided the Iranian Church with both legal status and spiritual support, ensuring its integration into the broader Anglican communion.

The role of the Diocese of Manchester leadership and its leadership team was instrumental in facilitating this transition. Their commitment to the growth of the Iranian Church extended beyond mere affiliation: they focused on leadership training and spiritual education, laying the foundation for a robust future. Over the years, eight members of the Iranian congregation were ordained as priests in the Diocese of Manchester, with another, who had spent their formative years at St Aphrahat, ordained in the Diocese of Durham. Notably, five of these new priests were women, a groundbreaking achievement for the Iranian

Church, both in the UK and historically within Iran, symbolizing a significant step forward for gender equality in church leadership.

Despite these advances, St Aphrahat faced significant challenges, particularly in establishing a clear legal and strategic framework for independent churches wishing to join the Anglican Church. This issue became more pronounced after the retirement of Revd Marcus Maxwell, whose leadership had been a stabilizing force. In the wake of his departure, the church encountered difficulties in defining its legal identity and governance structure. Yet the support of the Diocese of Manchester leadership during this critical period proved invaluable. They guided the church through the complexities of ecclesiastical governance, helping to establish sustainable managerial and legal foundations.

Today, St Aphrahat Church in Manchester stands as a vibrant centre for the Iranian Christian community. With the continuous support of the Diocese of Manchester the church has evolved into a crucial spiritual and social hub for Iranian migrants. It serves not only to strengthen the Christian faith of its members but also to foster a sense of community and cultural identity. Through its educational, spiritual and social programmes, St Aphrahat offers Iranian migrants a place of belonging, bridging the gap between their past in Iran and their present in the UK. The church's role in shaping both the religious and cultural lives of its members exemplifies the enduring resilience of Iranian Christians as they navigate faith and identity in a new land.

Conclusion

The journey of Iranians who convert to Christianity in Britain is fraught with challenges, from navigating the asylum process to overcoming cultural and social barriers. However, it also offers significant opportunities for personal and spiritual growth, community building and the exercise of religious freedom. The church plays a vital role in this journey. By providing spiritual guidance, practical assistance and a welcoming community, churches can help Iranian converts overcome the challenges they face and fully embrace their new faith. Through their support and advocacy, churches can also contribute to a fairer and more compassionate asylum process.

Notes

1 The conditions imposed on *dhimmīs* under the *dhimma* contract included several specific regulations aimed at delineating their rights and responsibilities within Islamic societies. Some of these conditions were as follows:
- Non-Muslims will not build new places of worship.
- Non-Muslims will not replace dilapidated places of worship in areas where Muslims live.
- Muslims can take refuge in non-Muslim places of worship and should be treated hospitably for three days.
- Non-Muslims will not teach their children the Quran.
- Non-Muslims will not prevent relatives from converting to Islam.
- Non-Muslims will not ride upon saddles or carry weapons.

References

Alzog, J., 1874, *Manual of Universal Church History, Volume 1*, Cincinnati, OH: Robert Clarke & Co..

Brown, R. and S. Pehrson, 2019, *Group Processes: Dynamics Within and Between Groups*, 3rd edn, Hoboken, NJ: Wiley-Blackwell.

Dabashi, H., 2008, *Islamic Liberation Theology: Resisting the Empire*, Abingdon and New York: Routledge.

Edwards, J. C., 2022, *Early New Testament Apocrypha: 9 (Ancient Literature for New Testament Studies)*, Grand Rapids, MI: Zondervan Academic.

Emon, Anver M., 2012, *Religious Pluralism and Islamic Law: Dhimmis and Others in the Empire of Law*, New York: Oxford University Press.

Esfandiari, G., 2004, 'Iran: Coping with the World's Highest Rate of Brain Drain', *Radio Free Europe/Radio Liberty*, https://www.rferl.org/a/1051803.html (accessed 14.05.2024).

Farahani, Q. M., 1969, *The Collected Writings of Qaim Maqam Farahani*, compiled by Farhad Mirza, Tehran: Aristotle-Apadana.

Haeri, A., 1993, *The First Encounters of Iranian Thinkers with the Two Facets of Western Bourgeois Civilization*, Tehran: Amir Kabir Publishing.

Landinfo, 2018, 'Iran: Christian Converts and House Churches (1)', translation provided by the Office of the Commissioner General for Refugees and Stateless Persons, Belgium, https://landinfo.no/wp-content/uploads/2018/04/Iran-Christian-converts-and-house-churches-1-prevalence-and-conditions-for-religious-practice.pdf (accessed 14.05.2024).

Minnerop, P., R. Wolfrum and F. Lachenmann (eds), 2019, *International Development Law: The Max Planck Encyclopedia of Public International Law (Thematic, 3)*, Oxford: Oxford University Press.

Montgomery, B. P., 2019, *The Seizure of Saddam Hussein's Archive of Atrocity*, Lanham, MD: Lexington Books.

Peters, R., 2006, *Crime and Punishment in Islamic Law: Theory and Practice from the Sixteenth to the Twenty-first Ccentury: 2 (Themes in Islamic Law, Series Number 2)*, Cambridge: Cambridge University Press.

Ross, K., D. Jeyaraj and T. Johnson (eds), 2019, *Christianity in South and Central Asia (Edinburgh Companions to Global Christianity)*, illustrated edn, Edinburgh: Edinburgh University Press.

Saghafi, N., 2009, 'The Relationship of Religious Self-Identification to Cultural Adaptation Among Iranian Immigrants and First Generation Iranians', PhD thesis, Pepperdine University, https://digitalcommons.pepperdine.edu/cgi/viewcontent.cgi?article=1034&context=etd (accessed 14.05.2024).

Secretariat of the High Council of Iranian Affairs Abroad, n.d., 'Statistics on the Distribution of Iranians Residing Abroad', https://iranian.mfa.ir/files/mfairanian/Amar.pdf (accessed 14.05.2024).

Spuler, B., R. G. Hoyland, G. Goldbloom and B. Walburg (eds), 2014, *Iran in the Early Islamic Period: Politics, Culture, Administration and Public Life between the Arab and the Seljuk Conquests, 633–1055: 12 (Iran Studies)*, bilingual edn, Leiden: Brill.

Tejirian, E. and R. S. Simon, 2012, *Conflict, Conquest, and Conversion: Two Thousand Years of Christian Missions in the Middle East*, New York: Columbia University Press.

Thomas, D. R. and J. A. Chesworth (eds), 2017, *Christian–Muslim Relations: A Bibliographical History, Volume 10. Ottoman and Safavid Empires (1600–1700)*, Leiden: Brill.

Van Gorder, C. A., 2010, *Christianity in Persia and the Status of Non-Muslims in Modern Iran*, Lanham, MD: Lexington Books.

Waterfield, R., 2011, *Christians in Persia (RLE Iran C): Assyrians, Armenians, Roman Catholics and Protestants (Routledge Library Editions: Iran)*, London: Routledge.

21

Being Pilgrim: The Church in the Movement of the Spirit

PAUL BRADBURY

At the symposium from which the framework for this book emerged, I offered the reflection that the church might want to think of itself more as verb than noun. In other words, to think of itself more as a pilgrim community with a constant sense of movement and becoming, rather than a 'fixed star' that might somehow be named and thoroughly defined. In some of the feedback from the subsequent discussion it was interesting to sense pushback against this idea of the church as verb. The concern was voiced that in attending to the church as verb we would lose essential elements of its nature as noun.

Setting up a binary may well have been unhelpful though, for the nature of the church is surely in the dynamic between its settled and nomadic natures. Nevertheless, the cultural climate of modernism continues to tempt us into what the Māori philosopher Carl Mika calls 'wording the world', referring to the kind of attention to the world that wishes to name, define, index, examine and understand, the better to manage, manipulate and seek to keep control of the future. In response Mika offers instead an invitation to a language that *'worlds* the world'. To 'world the world' is to offer the kind of attention and description of the world that opens up possibility, inspires imagination and which, in the midst of uncertainty, can help transform people and communities as they journey into the future. Story is the main medium of worlding the world – stories that reflect on deep traditions and myths in the light of new experience (Machado de Olivera). In many ways in the contributions in Part III, each author is worlding the world, narrating stories, biblical, personal, as well as of church communities, in order to invite us to new thinking, new imaginings of what the church might become.

Perhaps the felt resistance we noted to the church as a verb suggests the tendency to 'word the world' is very much alive in our ecclesial life. Such a tendency may well explain our preference for what Nicholas Healy called 'blueprint ecclesiologies': ecclesiologies that model the church but in doing so tend to abstract it from the complexity of the world in which it is set. The contributions in Part III have all sought to attend to the verbal nature, the becoming nature of the church, as it exists in time within the givens of place, heritage and tradition. Chris Hodder in Chapter 14 reflects on the parish as a dynamic between tradition and culture, a 'both-and' church that values the constancy of tradition in conversation with the unfolding human stories of its community. James Butler and Cathy Ross in Chapter 16 argue for an attention to the edges and margins where new stories of church are being formed, as a way of helping the church relinquish 'the logic of empire'. David Monteith (Chapter 15) describes the way pilgrimage itself is both practical reality and metaphor for the life of cathedrals as they explore their particular dynamic between faith, heritage and culture. Tina Hodgett's attention in Chapter 17 to the movement of the people of God leads to a theological grounding for the church as verb, what we might summarize as a 'pneumatology of play'.

In that sense the longer chapters in Part III are offerings that open up possibility and invite the church to consider giving attention to lived experience, experiments and stories that might help us 'world the world'. They invite us to a kind of discernment of how the church might be becoming in this new post-Christendom, post-Christian, secular, post/metamodern age we are journeying into. In that sense we are asked not to better define or systemize the church through these reflections but to discern her, find her in the conversation between her traditions, heritage, Scriptures and her evolving context.

As I read these contributions I discerned two themes in particular emerging that are worth exploring briefly. First, posture. The word 'posture' signifies a way of gathering descriptions and understandings of how the church sees its own presence and agency in the public space, local and national. This internal collective perspective on the world is one that deeply shapes the church's own action in the world. Butler and Ross's chapter on the church in the shadow of empire argues that the church has to a great extent taken on the 'logic of empire'. That logic itself is ultimately a posture and a world view, shaped by dominant values of uniformity and control. For Butler and Ross, the way to challenge this posture, and to disrupt its deeply held logic, is to listen to the voices 'from the edges'. Monteith's reflection of cathedrals as places of pilgrimage likewise tells a story of a transition in posture for cathedrals.

He explores how heritage, liturgy and art are opening up more shared spaces of conversation between the cathedral as a place of pilgrimage and the experience and perspective of the pilgrim. Hodgett recognizes in the metaphor of play a posture of openness to happenstance made possible by play's non-utilitarian nature. The creative fusion between unlikely artefacts or themes invites 'the adjacent possible', an emergent option that could not have been predicted. Each of these chapters explores practices and modes of attention that recognize the need for the church to relinquish postures hardened by the certainties of modernity, empire and Christendom and explore a posture open to marginal voices, interruptions and the unpredictable. We are discerning what kind of posture is required of pilgrim church, a church on the move, but also the kind of practices and forms of attention it needs to inhabit such a posture fully.

Second, God. You might expect a book on ecclesiology to have God as a central theme. Yet in much of the conversation about the future of the church there is often a strongly pragmatic attitude, a sense in which the answer to our problems lies fundamentally within the orbit of our own actions. This pragmatic leaning is rendered in various versions of the search for a magic bullet to fix the decline of the church in terms of numbers and financial viability – 'If only we organized ourselves and did x or y all would be well!' What very often strikes me about this trait in our ecclesiology is its lack of transcendence, the loss of God's action, or the movement of the Spirit, or the leading of the *missio Dei* in much of this talk. In the chapters offered here, however, there is consistent appeal, not to the latest technique or ecclesial intervention but to the presence of God. Butler and Ross's appeal to attend to the edges draws on John V. Taylor's assertion that it is at the fringes of institutional life that we find an organic life 'pushing out from the edges'. Taylor's conviction, however, was not primarily a pragmatic but a theological one, more specifically a pneumatological one. Where the normative structures and practices of the church meet the foundness of the world, the Spirit is so often creatively at work, opening up the church to newness and reimagination (Taylor, 1972). This divine dynamic is likewise at the heart of Hodgett's theology of play, drawing on the pattern of Acts and the action of the Spirit who invites the church across established boundaries and towards others. Monteith points to the Emmaus road as a theological basis for the pilgrimage ministry of cathedrals, where God is at work unseen, in between, as people travel together. Hodder points to Andrew Root's theology, whose work has consistently warned against the idolization of innovation or the technical fix, and invited the church to rediscover 'the God who is God' (Root, 2022).

These contributions reinforce the importance of Root's appeal to 'resonance' (Root, 2021), a concept borrowed from the German social philosopher Hartmut Rosa. Rosa has argued that organizations in late-modernity are working within a logic of 'dynamic stabilization' where the only way to create stability is to grow. Within this logic, growth becomes a higher good, innovative programmes and interventions, and those who can deliver them, hugely valued commodities within organizations. It is in this context that our conversations as a church gather around pragmatic concerns to reverse decline. As a sociologist, Rosa invites societies to create spaces of 'resonance', non-instrumentalized places of connection and conversation that offer the possibility of generative, humane life. For Root, writing as an ecclesiologist, such spaces invite a connection with the transcendent, with the 'God who is God'. Resonance is a metaphor with an emergent quality. Resonance is generated by a coming together, and from within the space in-between people, conversations and relationships. It cannot be forced or manipulated. Resonance invites us to listen and to reflect, to ask what we are learning for the future from what has been experienced. The chapters in Part III invite us to attend to such resonances as a way of attending to the Spirit at work.

In the light of these themes we might ask what we notice and learn from the On the Ground reflections from three practitioners offered in Part III, as these provide particular, and very different, windows on the present experience of the Church of England. Fiona Gibson offers an appeal towards 'doing old things well' and to 'patient endurance'. She recognizes the dynamic inherent in being certain but provisional, traditional yet future orientated, small and vulnerable yet secure in identity. The lack of appeal to the new or the innovative in Gibson's piece is interesting in itself. Instead there is an appeal for patience, not so much perhaps as a trust in the ultimate efficacy of the 'old things' themselves but in the faithfulness of God within a far broader framework of time than our institutional anxieties often afford us. David Lloyd's experience, on the other hand, tells a narrative of rapid growth as 16 new lay-led communities developed within a matter of a few years. Yet fundamental to this story of growth is a deep reflection on the place of human agency in the mission of God. Responding personally to the demands of strategies of renewal, and recognizing in those drifting away from many of our churches a desire for something less busy, Lloyd's story in Chapter 18 invites a wider reflection on how we discern our participation in the *missio Dei* alongside our own considerable power, resource and agency as an institution. Omid Moludy's important story and reflection in Chapter 20 on the growing community of Iranian refugee Christians and converts finding a home within the Church of England provides a different insight into the becoming of the church. Who could have predicted such a movement following the Islamic Revolution in 1979 and the near eradication of the Anglican Church in Iran? The welcoming in of such a move of the Spirit is another way the church embraces its nature as a pilgrim people.

It was Daniel Hardy who argued that the church must be a church that walks: 'The Anglican Church must become a wandering ecclesia. Such an ecclesia has inner and outer order but on the move, a mobile order. Its order is measured and guided by Scripture, by the Eucharist and by Jesus' steps' (Hardy et al., p. 85). Despite the often heavy-seeming nature of its architecture (not just the built reality of its cathedrals and parish churches but also its organizational structures and the architecture of its own logic), the church must yet seek to be a moving ecclesia. Such movement, however, is not careless or random but quite the opposite: care*ful*, deeply attentive and reflective to the ways God might be inviting her to move and change in the midst of the flow of history. Scripture, tradition and discipleship in the Way of Jesus act as measures and guides, therefore, in an ongoing process of discernment on the nature and form of a pilgrim church.

This, then, is a 'moving ecclesiology', and one that requires a high regard for theological reflection whereby 'theologians of a walking Church wander first and then think theologically and practically in response to what they have found' (Hardy et al., p. 86). The discussions and practical reflections in Part III might be read in the light of this assertion, and also as an invitation to do the same ourselves, so that the church might walk more attentively in the present towards the future coming to meet us.

References

Hardy, D. et al., 2010, *Wording a Radiance: Parting Conversations on God and the Church*, London: SCM Press.
Healy, N., 2000, *Church, World and the Christian Life: Practical-Prophetic Ecclesiology*, Cambridge: Cambridge University Press.

Machado de Olivera, V., 2021, *Hospicing Modernity: Facing Humanity's Wrongs and the Implications for Social Activism*, Berkeley, CA: North Atlantic Books.

Root, A., 2021, *The Congregation in a Secular Age: Keeping Sacred Time against the Speed of Modern Life*, Grand Rapids, MI: Baker Books.

Root, A., 2022, *Churches and the Crisis of Decline: A Hopeful, Practical Ecclesiology for a Secular Age*, Grand Rapids, MI: Baker Books.

Rosa, H., 2017, 'Two versions of the Good Life and Two Forms of Fear: Dynamic Stabilization and the Resonance Conception of the Good Life – Presented to the Yale Center for Faith and Culture/"Joy, Security, and Fear"/November 8–9, 2017', https://faith.yale.edu/media/two-versions-of-the-good-life-two-forms-of-fear (accessed 18.10.2024).

Taylor, J. V., 1972, *The Go-Between God: The Holy Spirit and Christian Mission*, London: SCM Press.

In Place of a Conclusion

MIKE HARRISON

The past decades have seen a dramatically changed context challenging the church to examine afresh its very identity/nature and what it is to be a missional church. We have, in the language of some of the authors of this volume, moved 'beyond modernity' (Nigel Rooms), moving into a missional era 'beyond' Christendom (Hannah Steele), and need to revisit the shape of the church and how the gospel is to be heard in the culture(s) of today. The 2004 *Mission-Shaped Church* report addressed precisely this challenge in its time, and it remains the best-selling report of the Church of England. The report, in addressing changing cultural and ecclesial contexts, commended new models and ways of being church, including fresh expressions, church plants and 'traditional' church, and argued for ways of understanding these models that could fit with Anglican ecclesiology and practice. The report's generally positive reception owed much to the support of the then Archbishop of Canterbury, Rowan Williams, whose own breathtakingly broad description of the church helped pave the way. Williams wrote:

> If 'church' is what happens when people encounter the Risen Jesus and commit themselves to sustaining and deepening that encounter in their encounter with each other, there is plenty of theological room for diversity of rhythm and style, so long as we have ways of identifying the same living Christ at the heart of every expression of Christian life in common. (Church of England, Foreword, p. vii)

Critiques were quick to follow, however, with Professor John Hull writing scathingly (and somewhat unfairly) that in the report 'We looked for a mission-shaped Church, but what we found was a church-shaped mission', Hull suggesting the report was preoccupied with generating more churches in self-serving fashion rather than being concerned with serving the poor, actualizing the Kingdom and discerning God at work in the world and joining in with that work. Others critiqued the report for suggesting that some so-called examples of 'church' were ecclesially wanting in terms of particular definitions of the church, such as 'the Body of Christ, in time, united with him through word, sacrament and the recognition of the threefold orders of ministry' (Tilby, p. 81). Some critics, such as Angela Tilby, would see fresh expressions of church, for example, as at best bridges to true church and better described as mission initiatives rather than church per se.

One of the pushbacks on such critiques is that these descriptions of church seemed to lack any sense that mission is an essential element within ecclesiology – that there appeared to be no goal for the church beyond the church itself, an omission Karl Barth had previously described as the 'yawning gap' in Reformation theology and practice (Scott, pp. 22–3). Part of the background conversation out of which some of these chapters arose is precisely around how we are to understand the church and its life and what that entails about appropriate ways of being and doing church. (And if space allowed it would be useful to explore how we understand church in terms of a form of sociality rather than some kind of 'stuff' – so Graham Ward's prescient comments on 'ecclesiality' as being in some ways preferable to 'ecclesiology' (Ward, pp. 202–3).

Part of what has given impetus to the missional ecclesiology that we see sketched in a number of these chapters is its practical adaptability to our present context(s). While statistics vary estimating the percentage of our population with no previous engagement with church or the Christian faith, most would agree it is 90%+ and most would agree that while 'traditional' church can be wonderfully uplifting, inspiring and nurturing of the faith for some (and can reach some of that 90%+ – see Alison Milbank in Chapter 3), nevertheless the vast majority of the population are not engaged. As such we are challenged to consider how the church might order its life both for its own well-being and flourishing and for the sake of its engagement in God's mission.

And what gives further impetus to a missional ecclesiology is a particular understanding of the church's genesis and *raison d'être* rooted in the doctrine of God.

Drawing on insights from this volume, four steps in this missional ecclesiology might be outlined. **First**, missional ecclesiology begins with a focus on God, on God's activity and attentiveness to that activity. *Mission-Shaped Church* contained the seeds of this focus on God's activity – so 'God is on the move and the Church is always catching up with him. We join his mission. We should not invite him to join ours' (p. 85). Such a focus is taken further by Al Barrett in Chapter 2 and Nigel Rooms in Chapter 10. The pull towards a focus on human agency in mission is ever-present, where missional ecclesiology quickly reduces to the mission of the church. Critically, what matters is whether one begins with the identity/nature of the church (as called to participate in God's life, including being sent to participate in God's mission) or with the purpose/mission of the church. If the latter is the case, there is a diminishment of the sense of God's agency and in particular of pneumatological ecclesiology, the sense of the church as the creation of the Spirit, or of the Spirit as the leader of mission. The church represents that participation in the life and mission of the Trinity, which means it is a community of promise for the wider world. On this account, as Graham Cray puts it: 'mission is not so much a task to be accomplished as an identity to be fulfilled, and a relationship with God to be enjoyed' (Cray, p. 99).

Fulfilling this relationship is about being caught up into worship *and* into God's dynamic outward movement of ecstatic love in our relationships and witness – again the emphasis needs to be primarily on God's activity. Here we can see how mission and worship are both elements of this participation, Isabelle Hamley (Chapter 7) and Hannah Steele (Chapter 1) underlining their interconnectedness while authors such as Alison Milbank (Chapter 3) and Jonny Baker (Chapter 9) stress different ways this participation might be ordered. In a culture where wedges are driven (see Chris Hodder in Chapter 14) between sacred and secular, immanent and transcendent, faith and knowledge and much else besides, it becomes all the more important to provide ways of breaking through such naive polarizations, for example in providing settings where 'signposting' God enables us to hear the divine music and dance to its tune (David Monteith in Chapter 15).

The **second** step in this missional ecclesiology is to emphasize that the foundation of all mission is that God is a sending God. The *Mission-Shaped Church* report understands the mission of God (*missio Dei*) to express God's relational nature, noting that: 'The communion of the persons of the Trinity is not to be understood as closed in on itself, but rather open in an outgoing movement of generosity. Creation and redemption are the overflow of God's triune life' (p. 85). This sending can be differently emphasized but it is of the essence that this is God's initiative directed towards the world God loves. One danger of 'sending' terminology is that God's sending is one way and so is ours – losing the profound openness and reciprocity of God's inner Trinitarian life and interactive relationship with the world. So in using this language we need to ensure we are focused on our participating in the life and mission of Trinity and being caught up in that dynamic. That is why the language of 'participation' peppered across the contributions to this volume is so welcome – it keeps the focus on God's activity, begs the question of discernment and what God is up to (Van Gelder and Zscheile, p. 113), shows that our relationships matter, keeps us focused on salvation in, of and for world, not out of it, and invites kenotic, passionate, reconciling participation in the life of the world. This participation has a profoundly contextual nature, whether it finds expression in Chapter 8, Ana França-Ferreira's and Angus Ritchie's faithful witness in community organizing, or in the pioneering sketched by Jon Oliver (Chapter 11) or the ecological creation care underlined by John White (Chapter 12).

A **third** step in this missional ecclesiology is understanding that the church is called into being and sent to participate in this sending love. God's pattern throughout Scripture is to choose the one for the sake of the many, be it Abraham and Sarah, the people of Israel or now the church; blessed to be a blessing in God's words to Abraham in Genesis 12 (Van Gelder and Zscheile, p. 38). It is not the church that sends but God that sends the church. The *Mission-Shaped Church* report points out that it is of the 'essence' of the church to be a missionary community and that 'There is Church because there is mission, not vice versa'; 'It is not the Church of God that has a mission in the world, but the God of mission who has a Church in the world' and 'Mission comes from the Father, through the Son in the power of the Spirit' (p. 85). The nature of sharing in this sending love is differently illustrated in the foregoing chapters, for example in tender-hearted interrelationships enabling mutual flourishing (Sharon Prentis, Chapter 4), in friendship and conversation with one another (Ross and Butler, Chapter 16), in mutual responsive dance with the Holy Spirit, 'improvising, experimenting, disrupting and rule-breaking, like children at play' (so Tina Hodgett in Chapter 17), or in embodying the Garden Church's values of D.L.E.S.S (David Lloyd, Chapter 18).

The **fourth** step is understanding how the church participates in God's mission – and perhaps the description of sign, witness, foretaste and instrument remains as good as any other at present (Andy Smith, Chapter 5). So, for example, the Church participates as sign in signalling by its way of being that the redemptive reign of God is fully present: 'The Church is a sign and disclosure of the kingdom of God' (*Mission-Shaped Church*, p. 94). It participates as witness not only in proclaiming that reign which is here and which future consummation God is creating, but by living out of that reign in its communal life (with-ness). The church participates as foretaste in living out of its future citizenship of heaven in the here and now, living out of the identity coming to us from the future and which eschatological future has already begun. Finally (though not exhaustively) the church participates as instrument under the leadership and prevenient activity of the Spirit, bringing that redemptive reign to bear on every dimension of life (Newbigin, p. 124).

This is a simplification and of course there are further steps, such as sketching how the local church's participation in the life of God and God's sending love will exhibit certain characteristics. Some such characteristics include particular postures in specific contexts (Paul Bradbury, Chapter 21), oft-times marginal by worldly appearances (Fiona Gibson, Chapter 19), and perennially seeking to reach the unreached (Omid Moludy in Chapter 20 and Sarah McDonald Haden in Chapter 6).

All of the contributions here point to ways of inviting unreached individuals and groups to share in the life of God, from sacrament to service, postures to play, creation care to community-organizing, and are exploring, in contexts previously largely uninhabited, what it is to be those who are caught up in the dynamic at the heart of the Trinity. Inevitably this exploration involves trial and error, investigation and slow learning. However, in situations of decline, loss of influence, prestige and popularity, institutions are classically tempted to alleviate anxiety and fear by imagining there are straightforward solutions, quick fixes and technical answers to what are adaptive and complex challenges. Resisting such temptations while placing God's agency (in Christ through the Holy Spirit) centre-stage, listening carefully and experimenting widely through 'excellent failure', deep attentiveness and being interrupted, are just some of the key qualities called for at a time such as this. So come Holy Spirit, come.

References

Church of England, 2004, *Mission-Shaped Church: Church Planting and Fresh Expressions of Church in a Changing Context*, London: Church House Publishing.
Cray, Graham, 2011, 'Discernment: The Key to Sharing in the Mission of God',

in Jane Williams (ed.), *The Holy Spirit in the World Today*, London: Alpha International.
Hull, John, 2006, *Mission-Shaped Church: A Theological Response*, London: SCM Press.
Newbigin, Lesslie, *The Open Secret: An Introduction to the Theology of Mission*, London: SPCK.
Scott, Waldron, 1978, *Karl Barth's Theology of Mission*, London: InterVarsity Press.
Tilby, Angela, 2008, 'What Questions does Catholic Ecclesiology Pose for Contemporary Mission and Fresh Expressions', in Steven Croft (ed.), *Mission-Shaped Questions: Defining Issues for Today's Church*, London: Church House Publishing.
Van Gelder, Craig and Dwight Zscheile, 2011, *The Missional Church in Perspective: Mapping Trends and Shaping the Conversation*, Grand Rapids, MI: Baker Academic.
Ward, Graham, 2009, *The Politics of Discipleship: Becoming Postmaterial Citizens*, London: SCM Press.

Index of Names and Subjects

Abraham 11
adaptive challenge 118
adaptive change 114–15
After Whiteness: An Education in Belonging (Jennings) 183
Albrech, Glenn 24–5, 28, 35
Alinsky, Saul 84
Alpha course 47
Ancient Future Evangelism (Webber) 19
Anglo-Sikh wars 175
apocalypticism 25, 26
Apostolic Constitutions 41
Appreciative Inquiry 114
Aquinas, Thomas 42
Arbuckle, Gerald 198
Ascension (Southampton) 66–9
attendance, church 65, 67
attentiveness 52–3

Bakker, Greg 198
Barker, Anj 108, 109–10
Barker, Ash 107, 108, 109–10
Barth, Karl 151, 240
Becket, St Thomas 168
Benedict, St 178, 215
Benedict XVI 45
Berry, Wendell 134
Bertrand, D. 154
Bevans, Stephen 192
  Community of Missionary Disciples 99

Bible
  Acts
    and community 12
    and disciples 17
    edges 101
    Eucharist 39
    and the Garden Church 214
    Holy Spirit 205
    pilgrimage into the unknown 205, 206
    pilgrims and the cathedral 171
    and the tender-hearted community 57, 60
  1 Corinthians
    community organizing 84, 86, 92, 94, 95, 96
    Eucharist 39
    and the Garden Church 214
    pilgrims and the cathedral 173
    and rural ministry 219
  2 Corinthians, community organizing 84, 86
  Deuteronomy, and rural ministry 218
  Ephesians
    and disciples 17
    pilgrimage into the unknown 207
    and the tender-hearted community 57
  Exodus
    and disciples 11

pilgrimage into the unknown
199
Ezekiel, and the tender-hearted community 51
Galatians, pilgrims and the cathedral 178
Genesis, and disciples 11
Hebrews
  and disciples 11
  and rural ministry 220
Hosea, and the Garden Church 214
Isaiah
  and community organizing 85
  and pilgrimage into the unknown 196
  and rural ministry 220
James, community organizing 85
John
  edges 100
  and empire 190
  Eucharist 40, 42, 43, 44
  and the Southampton community 131
  and the tender-hearted community 56, 57, 58
1 Kings, pilgrims and the cathedral 172
Luke
  community organizing 85
  edges 101, 103
  and Eucharist 42
  and the Garden Church 211
  pilgrimage and the cathedral 169–70
  pilgrimage into the unknown 199
Mark
  edges 99–100
  pilgrims and the cathedral 171
Matthew
  community organizing 85
  and disciples 10, 20
  and empire 193
  rural ministry 221
  and the Southampton community 132
Micah, and rural ministry 218
Numbers, and pilgrimage into the unknown 198
2 Peter, and the Garden Church 212
Philippians
  community organizing 85
  and English parish churches 116
  pilgrimage into the unknown 202
Psalms
  community organizing 85
  and ecological conversion 136
  and Eucharist 47
  and rural ministry 217
Revelation
  and discipleship 17
  and empire 191
Romans, and the tender-hearted community 56
1 Thessalonians
  community organizing 85
  pilgrims and the cathedral 173
Blau, Johannes 12
blessing 11–12, 18, 242
Body of Christ 92–3, 94, 151
Bonhoeffer, Dietrich 52–3
Book of Common Prayer 41
Bosch, D. J. 13, 18, 65–6, 162n7
Bosch, David 116
both-and vision 154–6, 169, 234

INDEX OF NAMES AND SUBJECTS

Braaten, Carl 57
brain hemispheres 121–2
bread, and the Eucharist 47–8
bridging social capital 167
British Empire *see* empire
British Pilgrimage Trust 168
Brown, Paul, *Invisible Divides* 108
Brueggemann, Walter 199
Brunner, Emil 129
buffered self 118

Canterbury Cathedral 167–9, 173–5
Carey, William 10, 16
Cathedral Fabric Commission for England 175
cathedrals 166–9, 177–9, 234, 235
 and adults 173–7
 theology of pilgrimage 169–71
 and younger people 171–2
Celtic Christianity 19
Centre for Christianity and Culture (University of York) 177
Centre for Theology and Community (CTC) 84
Chan, Francis 212
change, culture 115–16
Chapman, Robert 38
Cheltenham Network Church 72–4
Chesterton, G. K. 43, 133
chit-chat 190
Chittester, Joan 201
Chrysostom, John 44
Church Intensive 212
Church Mission Society 113
Citizens UK 84, 88

class divides 108
climate emergency 134–5
Coles, Romand 31, 33–4
Colls, Robert 161
Common Table movement 47
Common Worship 41, 156
commoning 31
Communion by Extension 38
Community of Missionary Disciples (Bevans) 99
community organizing 84–5, 96
 and power 86–8
 and relationships 92–4
 and resurrection faith 94–5
 St Barnabas' Church case study 93–4
 St Martin's Church case study 88–92
complexity 77–9
Connectors 29
contemplative practices 201–2
contextualization 107, 131
Corinth 83–4
Cray, Graham 131, 133
 'On Mission With Jesus' 99
creativity 206–7
culture
 and Iranian Christians 227–8
 and relevance 153–6
culture change 115–16
Cycle of Prayer and Organising 85

Davison, Andrew 117
De la Taille, Maurice 42
De Lubac, Henri 40
death, of churches 70–4, 204
Declaration of Assent 75
decline 113–15, 141, 235
 and cathedrals 166

church attendance 65, 67
defamiliarization, of the secular 46
disciple-making 9
  mission and worship 11–14
  and Monty's Community Hub 130–1
  in a Post-Christendom world 10–11
  principles from Matthew (28.18–20) 15–20
  see also cathedrals
dissipation 118
diversity 27, 75, 143
  and the cathedral 169
  and empire 181, 183, 185–7, 191, 192
  and parish 153, 155
  and tender-hearted communities 53–6, 58, 61
Do Less (D.L.E.S.S.) 214, 242

earth amnesia 134–6
Easter Eve/Holy Saturday, Hodge Hill 30–1
ecological conversion 134
  earth amnesia 134–6
  fifth mark of mission 136–7
  Hazelnut Community 137–8
ecosystems 76, 77–9
edges 142, 234, 235
  and empire 187–91
  and the Gospels 98–9
  and Jesus 99–106
  in practice 106–10
  witnessing 187–91
  see also rural ministry
Edgy Learning Project 188–90
embodiment 79–80
Emmaus 235

journey of disciples to 169–70
empire 234
  British Empire 181–3
  a pilgrim church 192–3
  and public witness 187–91
  temptations of 183–7
English parish churches 112–23, 149–61
  enjoyment of God 150–2, 159–60
envisioning 60, 122
Eucharist 38–9, 77
  as gift 41–2
  as justice 44–5
  missional suggestions 45–9
  participation in 42–3
  and the Spirit 43–4
Everybody Welcome (Jackson and Fisher) 157
Ewell, Samuel 138
ex-offenders 190–1
exclusion
  and the Eucharist 47
  see also inclusion
expectations, institutional 54, 60, 79

faith, and pilgrim parishes 157–8
  resurrection 94–5
faithful disruptive missional practices 115–16
Fernando, Ajith 19
Fisher, G., *Everybody Welcome* 157
Fitzgerald, Tanya 182–3
Five Marks of Mission 12, 136, 143–4
Flett, John 14
flow, divine 207
Ford, David 83, 86

INDEX OF NAMES AND SUBJECTS

Foulger, Will 115
Found Theology 206
Four Stage Process of discipleship 19
Fowler, Corinne 182
France-Williams, A. D. A. 186
Francis, Pope 92, 134, 138, 187, 192
  The Joy of the Gospel 9
Fresh Expressions movement 99, 153, 187, 190
fringes *see* edges
'From Lament to Action' (Church of England) 186, 187
funding 184–5

Garden Church (Norfolk) 207, 210–15, 236–7
gathering 28–9, 30
gifts, Eucharist as 41–2, 43, 47
global dread 24
globalization 16–17
'God question' 154, 159
Gordon, Mary 83
Gospels 98–9
  John 77
    edges 100
    and empire 190
    Eucharist 40, 42, 43, 44
    and the Southampton community 131
    and the tender-hearted community 56, 57, 58
  Luke
    community organizing 85
    edges 101, 103
    and Eucharist 42
    and the Garden Church 211
    pilgrimage and the cathedral 169–70

    pilgrimage into the unknown 199
  Mark 99–100
    pilgrims and the cathedral 171
  Matthew
    community organizing 85
    and disciples 10, 20
    and empire 193
    Great Commission 10–11, 15–20, 77
    and rural ministry 221
    and the Southampton community 132
    and worship 77
  see also Bible
gratitude, and the Eucharist 43
Great Commission (Matt. 28.18–20) 10–11, 15–20, 77
Green, Michael 16
grieving, and making a new start 198–9
Guder, Darrell L. 17
Gurnell Grove4 109

Hardy, Daniel 237
Harper, Brad 18
Hauerwas, Stanley 44, 49
Haughey, John C. 92–3
Hazelnut Community 137–8, 141
Healy, Nicholas 234
heart language 62
hearts *see* tender-hearted communities
Hebrews, journey from Egypt to the wilderness 198–202
Heifetz, Ron 114
Hiestand, G. 155
Higton, Mike 183
Hippolytus 19
Hirsch, Alan 19, 211–12

Hodge Hill (Birmingham) 26, 27–8, 31–5
Holistic Mission (report) 45
Holy Spirit, and the early Church 205, 207
Hong, Angie 51, 62
Hooker, Richard 40
host to guest posture 141–3
Howson, Chris 59
Hull, John 239–40
Hunter, George G. III 19

identity
  ecclesial 15–16, 64–5
  and tender-hearted communities 58, 62
imagination 118
improvisation 83, 155
inclusion 51–62, 169
inculturation 107
Industrial Areas Foundation (IAF) 84
innovation 220–1
interconnectedness 56–8
interdependence 42–62, 43, 68, 78, 79
Invisible Divides (Williams and Brown) 108
Iranian Christians 223–30, 237
Islam in Persia 224–5
Islamic Revolution 225–7

Jackson, B., *Everybody Welcome* 157
Jenkins, Philip 16
Jenkins, Simon 168
Jennings, Willie James 185–6, 197, 205, 207
  After Whiteness: An Education in Belonging 183

Jesus Christ
  fringe dwelling (edges) 99–110
  and incarnation 202–4
Jews and Gentiles, uniting 17–18
Joining God in the Great Unravelling (Roxburgh) 211
Joy of the Gospel, The (Pope Francis) 9

Kauffmann, Stuart 205–6
Keifert, Patrick 113
Kwiyani, Harvey 21, 191

Laing, Olivia 182
Langton, Stephen 175
language 75–6, 78, 108
leavers, church 213
Leech, Fr Kenneth 86, 93
Leicester Cathedral 172, 176
Lings, George 132
listening 52–3, 107, 142
logic of empire 181–3, 185, 186, 187, 234
Lopes, Fr Marco 88–9, 90
Lotto, Beau 206
Luciani, Rafael 192

McGavran, D. A. 153
McGilchrist, Iain 121–2
Mann, Rachel 179
marginalization
  and empire 183–7
  and English parish churches 114
  in a neighbourhood ecology 26
  in urban communities 88, 95, 108
  see also inclusion
Martin, Jessica 40–1
Martin-Achard, Robert 13
Maxwell, Revd Marcus 229–30

INDEX OF NAMES AND SUBJECTS

Metzger, Paul Louis 18
migration/migrants 54–5, 93
  see also Iranian Christians
Mika, Carl 233
missio Dei 13–14, 78, 254
  and the five marks of
    mission 143–4
  and Monty's Community Hub
    (Southampton) 129
  and postmodernity 116–17,
    118, 141
Mission-Shaped Church
  (report) 38, 112, 239–40
missional economy 26
missionary disciples 9
mixed ecology 9, 66, 68, 75, 76,
  77–8
Modernity, and English parish
  churches 112–23
Moltmann, Jürgen 14, 66, 128,
  135
Monty's Community Hub
  (Southampton) 125–33, 142
Mountstephen, Philip, 'A Cornish
  Call to Pioneer' 206–7
moving ecclesiology 237

narratives 153
National Trust 182
neighbourhood ecology 22
  confessing and decomposing
    29–31
  defined 23–4
  gathering and attending 27–8
  lexicon 22–4
  neighbourhood as parish 24–6
  sending and witnessing 32–3
  slug analogy 22, 34–6
  tabling and communing 31–3
  village of God 33–4

  and worship 26–7
Net Zero 136
New Atheism 41
Newbigin, Lesslie 13, 14, 15, 16,
  64–5, 143
Newman, David 155
nostalgia 24–5, 33, 34

Odili, Jones Ugochukwu 203
offertory 48–9
Okesson, Gregg 187
Open System 120
organizing *see* community
  organizing
osmosis 119–20

parish churches 112–23, 149–61
Parish and People Movement 39,
  48
parishes 33, 64–9
  as pilgrim communities 150–8
parochial system 35
participation 117, 130
particularity 11–12, 15–16
Partnership for Missional Church
  (PMC) 113–22, 141
Paschal Mystery 116
passive dominion 136
patience 221, 236
Paul
  on the Eucharist 39
  how God chooses 219
  letters to the Corinthians 83–4,
    85–6, 91–2, 94–5, 96
  mutual empathy 56
  speaking truth in love 57
  uniting of Jew and Gentile 17
Percy, Martyn 150, 155
Persia, Church of 224
Peterson, Eugene H. 153, 155

251

pilgrim
  being 233–7
  see also cathedrals; empire; Garden Church; Iranian Christians; parish churches; rural ministry; unknown
pilgrim churches 159–61, 192–3
pilgrim communities 150–8
pilgrimage 167–9
  and adults 173–7
  theology of 169–71
  and younger people 171–2
Pioneering Parishes 197, 204
pioneers 190, 197
place-formation 24–6, 34
planting
  church 66–8, 70–4, 115, 203, 214
  and class divides 108
  see also Garden Church
play 206, 234, 235, 242
Post Office scandal 183–4
post-Christendom 141, 167, 213, 234
post-church 65
postmodernity 141, 112–23
posture 234–5, 243
power, and community organizing 86–8
power analysis 87–8
provisionality 201
public Christian witness 118–19, 122–3

Quash, Ben 206

racism 56, 186
reconciling 57–8
Reddie, Anthony 186
repentance 104–5

resonance 151, 153, 158, 162, 236
Richard III 176
risk-taking 160
Root, Andrew 151, 152–3, 154, 162, 235–6
Roxburgh, Alan, *Joining God in the Great Unravelling* 211
Ruddick, Anna 108–9
Rumsey, Andrew 24–6
rural ministry 217–22
Russell, Nick 109
Russian emissaries 45–6

St Aphrahat Church (Manchester) 229–30
St Barnabas' Church (Walthamstow, London) 93–4
St Martin's Church (Plaistow, London) 88–92
Samaria 100–3
Sanghera, Sathnam 182
Sarah, and mission 11
secular world, disciples in 18–20
Seedbeds (Winson Green) 108
sexual abuse scandals 184
Shaw, Martin 25
Sheehan, M. L. 202
silence, and Elijah 172
Simon the Pharisee 103–6, 108
Simpson, Ray 33
slave trade 174–5, 182, 186
slug analogy 22, 34–6
Snyder, Howard 214–15
social justice 60
social media 161
solastalgia 24, 31
Southampton, Monty's Community Hub 125–33, 142
Spellers, S. 55

INDEX OF NAMES AND SUBJECTS

Spirit, and the Eucharist 43–4
'Spiritual Capital' (Grub Institute) 166
Stillingfleet, Edward 35
Stone, Selina, *Tarry Awhile* 96
Strachan, O. 155
strangers 118
Strategic Development Fund (SDF) 185
symptoms, of the secular age 150

tabling 31
Tarry Awhile (Stone) 96
Taylor, Charles 118, 153
Taylor, John 16, 106–7, 184, 185, 187
Team Pilgrim 197
tender-hearted communities 51–3, 56–8
  drawing near 58–9
  and identity 58
  intentional relationships and embracing the unfamiliar 59–62
  interconnectedness 56–8
  vision/strategy/hope 63–6
Tennent, Timothy 10, 17
The East London Communities Organisation (TELCO) 88, 93–4
thinking environments 30
Thomas, St 224
Tilby, Angela 240
Together Towards Life (TTL) 187–8
Toppo, Telesphore 40
tradition 200, 220–1, 236
Trocmé, Etienne 40
Turner, Carlton 109

unity of mission 78, 79
universality 11–12, 15–16
unknowns 196–7, 208
  early Church 205–8
  incarnation of Jesus Christ 202–4
  journey from Egypt to the wilderness 198–202

Van Opstal, Sandra Maria 61–2
Vanhoozer, K. 155
Vaquerano, Nuvia 89, 90, 95
verb, Church as 233–4
'village of God' 33–4
Vision–Strategy–Culture 115, 159–60

walking 28–9
walking Church 237
Walls, Andrew 200
Ward, Graham 240
Webber, Robert
  Ancient Future Evangelism 19
welcoming 156–7
Wells, Sam 49
Whyte, David 199
Williams, Natalie, *Invisible Divides* 108
Williams, Rowan 43, 161, 187, 239
Willis, Robert 137
Wilson, T. 155
Wirzba, Norman 31, 135, 136–7
witnessing 140–5, 243
  see also community organizing; ecological conversion; edges; English parish churches; Southampton
women, portrayed in Canterbury cathedral 174

word the world 233–4
worship
  being 75–80
  see also disciple-making;
    Eucharist; neighbourhood
    ecology; planting; tender-
    hearted communities

Wright, N. T. 155

Xi'an Stele 224

Young, Frances 83, 86

www.ingramcontent.com/pod-product-compliance
Lightning Source LLC
Chambersburg PA
CBHW022044290426
44109CB00014B/970